The Pleasure of Punishment

Based on a reading of contemporary philosophical arguments, this book accounts for how punishment has provided audiences with pleasure in different historical contexts. Watching tragedies, contemplating hell, attending executions, or imagining prisons have generated pleasure, according to contemporary observers, in ancient Greece, in medieval Catholic Europe, in the early-modern absolutist states, and in the post-1968 Western world.

The pleasure was often judged morally problematic, and raised questions about which desires were satisfied, and what the enjoyment was like. This book offers a research synthesis that ties together existing work on the pleasure of punishment. It considers how the shared joys of punishment gradually disappeared from the public view at a precise historic conjuncture, and explores whether arguments about the carnivalesque character of cruelty can provide support for the continued existence of penal pleasure. Towards the end of this book, the reader will discover, if willing to go along and follow desire to places which are full of pain and suffering, that deeply entwined with the desire for punishment, there is also the desire for social justice.

An accessible and compelling read, this book will appeal to students and scholars of criminology, sociology, philosophy and all those interested in the pleasures of punishment.

Magnus Hörnqvist is Professor of Criminology at Stockholm University. In a series of research projects, he has investigated the productivity power in state-organised arenas and shown how normality and inequality are being created through interventions directed toward challenges of a conceived order. Publications in English include *Risk, Power and the State* (Routledge 2010) and articles in journals such as *Regulation & Governance, Philosophy & Social Criticism* and *Punishment & Society*. Publications in Swedish include a monograph on the Foucauldian analysis of power (Carlsson 2012) and an introductory book on social class (Liber 2016). It is essential reading for those engaged with penology, criminological and social theory and the sociology of punishment.

Routledge Advances in Criminology

Young Men and Domestic Abuse
David Gadd, Claire L. Fox, Mary-Louise Corr, Steph Alger and Ian Butler

Frank Tannenbaum: The Making of a Convict Criminologist
Matthew G. Yeager

Reinforcement Sensitivity Theory
A Metatheory for Biosocial Criminology
Anthony Walsh

Mafia Violence
Political, Symbolic, and Economic Forms of Violence in Camorra Clans
Edited by Monica Massari and Vittorio Martone

Analytical Criminology
Integrating Explanations of Crime and Deviant Behavior
Karl-Dieter Opp

Uniting Green Criminology and Earth Jurisprudence
Jack Lampkin

Social Bridges and Contexts in Criminology and Sociology
Reflections on the Intellectual Legacy of James F. Short, Jr.
Edited by Lorine A. Hughes and Lisa M. Broidy

Criminology and Democratic Politics
Edited by Tom Daems and Stefaan Pleysier

The Pleasure of Punishment
Magnus Hörnqvist

For more information about this series, please visit: www.routledge.com/ Routledge-Advances-in-Criminology/book-series/RAC

The Pleasure of Punishment

Magnus Hörnqvist

Routledge
Taylor & Francis Group
LONDON AND NEW YORK

First published 2021
by Routledge
2 Park Square, Milton Park, Abingdon, Oxon OX14 4RN

and by Routledge
605 Third Avenue, New York, NY 10158

Routledge is an imprint of the Taylor & Francis Group, an informa business

© 2021 Magnus Hörnqvist

British Library Cataloguing-in-Publication Data
A catalogue record for this book is available from the British Library

Library of Congress Cataloging-in-Publication Data
Names: Hörnqvist, Magnus, author.
Title: The pleasure of punishment / Magnus Hörnqvist.
Description: 1 Edition. | New York City : Routledge, 2021. |
Includes bibliographical references and index. |
Identifiers: LCCN 2020049489 | ISBN 9780367185329 (hardback) |
ISBN 9780429196744 (ebook)
Subjects: LCSH: Punishment–Moral and ethical aspects. |
Social justice. | Social control. | Power (Social sciences)
Classification: LCC HV8693 .H67 2021 | DDC 174/.93646–dc23
LC record available at https://lccn.loc.gov/2020049489

ISBN: 978-0-367-18532-9 (hbk)
ISBN: 978-0-367-76223-0 (pbk)
ISBN: 978-0-429-19674-4 (ebk)

Typeset in Times New Roman
by Newgen Publishing UK

Contents

Acknowledgements

This book has a long prehistory and I am grateful to all people who have offered input along the way, starting with David Scott, who, as the editor of the anthology "Why Prison?", encouraged me to think further on the Foucauldian idea of the productivity of power, and thus initially set me on this track. It became a chapter on the pleasure of punishment, specifically focused on the prison and the middle class. When Tom Sutton at Routledge asked me to write a book on the theme a few years ago at a criminology conference, the task first struck me as too daunting. I also needed much more time, more material and a wider scope. My colleagues at the department of criminology at Stockholm university have been a great support; especially thanks to Henrik Tham, Anders Nilsson and Janne Flyghed for useful comments on early drafts. Intelligibility has been the key challenge throughout, and they have reminded me of that. Being granted the RJ Sabbatical 2018, by *Riksbankens Jubileumsfond* (SAB18-0161:1), to write a research synthesis on the pleasure of punishment, entirely relieved me of teaching obligations for a full year, which I spent re-reading works in the philosophical tradition and making notes. The grant also allowed me to spend the autumn of 2019 as a visiting professor at the Mannheim Centre for Criminology in the London School of Economics, generously invited by Tim Newburn, sharing office space and thoughts with Janet Foster and Alice Sampson. Thanks also to Johann Koehler and Mats Deland for enthusiasm and feedback on the historical. I am especially grateful to Vanessa Barker for innumerable coffee chats at all stages of the project, and for challenging me on the issue why it mattered. Mellika Melouani Melani, my life companion, presented me to the worlds of art and opera, and inspired me to think of desire as unrestrained and as something to be pursued at all costs.

Introduction

Articulating the problematic of desire

The main aim of this book is to generate a better understanding of how punishment has provided audiences with pleasure in different historical contexts. The question – how punishment produces pleasure – is understood against the background of the problematic of desire. It is a problematic defined by the inescapable tension between desire and enjoyment. The problematic of desire was brought to the world's attention by Sigmund Freud. In a footnote, later added to the first of the *Three Essays on Sexuality*, he said that 'the only appropriate word' in German – *Lust* – was inevitably ambiguous, and designated 'the experience both of a need and of a gratification' (Freud 1953: 135 fn 2). The very word was ambiguous, and so was the corresponding conception. Freud's conception of pleasure covered both desire and satisfaction; on the one hand 'wishing, wanting and desiring' and on the other hand 'enjoyment and satisfaction' (Schuster 2016: 101). In itself, the distinction was not new. It was central to the classic Platonic approach to pleasure. In *Gorgias*, Plato treated desire as distress and satisfaction as the relief of distress, thereby posing the problem of transformation: how could experiences, ranging from acute pain to a mere sense of unease, transform into the very opposite, the experience of being at ease? Plato's conception of pleasure was modelled after the satisfaction of bodily needs: hunger, thirst and sex. There is a perpetual movement back and forth: desire turns into satisfaction, which recedes into desire, a desire that may turn into renewed satisfaction, or not, and so forth. Freud discovered the tension, or the radical disjunction between desire and enjoyment. Desire and enjoyment were essentially irreconcilable. There can be no simple match, no carefree immersion in everyday life. It has been explicated as forces pulling in different directions; 'desire goes one way, and satisfaction another' (Schuster 2016: 122). I prefer the metaphor of a gap to describe the relationship. Throughout the book, I will talk about the gap between desire and enjoyment. The word 'gap' emphasizes their essential irreconcilability, as well as the necessity to bridge the gap, by actions or interventions, to transform desire into enjoyment.

The pleasure of punishment may strike readers as an odd topic. Starting talking about 'the pleasure of punishment', I have noticed in the process of writing this book, often makes people associate it with sadism, or misogyny, and with cruelty and pain as the primary cause of pleasure. While that may not be altogether off the mark, the pleasure of punishment is far more ordinary than extraordinary, and closer to the everyday concerns of most of us. The topic deals with a central dimension of human experience: our lives as far as they involve notions of morality, of order and social esteem. The consumption of punishment is embedded in the socio-moral world simultaneously being enacted, and the perceived place of the audience in that world. It can have a soothing effect on desire, or produce intense excitation; yet only temporarily, as the tension between desire and enjoyment is inescapable. The underlying problematic can be approached from each side of the gap. Desire for recognition is located on one side. It pushes forward, driven by unease and guided by basic coordinates of status derived from social morality. The desire is volatile, transgressive, socially conditioned, and oriented toward others, striving to be fully part of the community while at the same time aspiring for distinction. On the other side of the gap, there is enjoyment. It is no less complex. Enjoyment can be conducive to individual well-being, and may be experienced as satisfactory, or even as the highest form of pleasure, as Nietzsche would argue, whereas psychoanalysis stressed that enjoyment is potentially harmful, necessarily partial, always precarious, and fundamentally dependent on others.

The key question is how punishment produces pleasure, and how it does so in relation to an audience, as opposed to those who are immediately affected by an offence. Given the problematic of desire, the question can be seen to be composed of a series of more specific questions, concerning the character of desire, the experience of enjoyment and the dynamic involved. Which desire is activated by punishment? How does shared consumption bridge the gap in particular social settings? What kind of enjoyment is produced? What is the dynamic like? The questions are simultaneously historical and conceptual, and will be pursued in four different settings. Implicit in the problematic of desire is moreover the political question. Can punishment be replaced? Can the desires of the audience be satisfied just as well in other ways? The political question has to wait until the end. Only by understanding what kind of desire goes into punishment, the precarious dynamic between desire and enjoyment and how punishment operates, will we be in a position to discuss what else – which other kind of collective action, beliefs or practices – might fill the gap and provide audiences with a similar satisfaction. It takes a certain willingness to pursue the topic, to go along, also with some of the most opaque and reactionary thinkers, to follow desire to places – in this case punishment – which are ugly, full of pain, suffering and misery. Yet like the owl which flies at dusk, or the treasure at the end of the rainbow, only at the very end of the journey will the reader discover that, deeply embedded and entwined with the desire for punishment, there is also the desire for social justice.

The study has been informed by a few basic considerations. I would like to briefly state them, for reasons of transparency. They include some notes on methods, on the state of the art, on the claims of this study, and the stakes involved.

CENTRALITY OF PHILOSOPHY: The audience experience was approached through the contemporary philosophical discussion. I worked my way back in history to find out what philosophers had said about the passions of punishment. Plato, Aristotle, Aquinas, Hobbes, Kant, Bentham and Hegel discussed the passions of punishment, mostly focusing on anger and vengefulness, as the most morally ambiguous, yet always considering pleasure at the margins. These discussions, as they were pursued in some of the most central works in the Western tradition of thought, such as the *Republic*, the *Nicomachean Ethics*, *Summa Theologica*, *Leviathan*, and the *Philosophy of Right*, or the *Genealogy of Morals* were read against the background of available knowledge on the social practices of punishment at the time, including the composition of the audience and the specific conditions at the scene of consumption. Besides the contemporary philosophers, I was able to draw on the works of classicists on ancient Greek tragedies, research on medieval representations of the afterlife, historians of public executions, psychoanalytic approaches to law, and criminological studies of recent developments in criminal justice, each of which represented a research field with its particular state of the art. All these sources were used to reconstruct the audience experience in four historical periods: ancient Greece (the fifth and the fourth century BCE), medieval Europe (the thirteenth and the fourteenth century), early-modern Europe (mainly the eighteenth century), and in the post-1968 Western world. Different arguments can be made for choosing to start with philosophy. With respect to antiquity and the middle ages, the central role of philosophy is partly derived from the fact that it is one of the few preserved sources on desire and enjoyment of the contemporary audiences. Philosophers may also be credited with acute observations on the sentiment of later audiences; Kierkegaard (1962) diagnosed *ressentiment* as a social condition in the mid-nineteenth century. Yet what above all makes philosophy useful are the concepts and the arguments. Starting with Plato's arguments on a third element of the soul, positioned in between reason and passion, philosophy has produced the categories to discuss desire and enjoyment: categories which in some cases are fundamentally reinvented with the transitions between historical époques, and in other cases retain their validity despite historical change.

CONCEPTS: The categories emerge from the historical analysis. The conceptual categories used to analyse the audience experience are not present from the start but emerge out of the analysis of the philosophical discussion. The problems which the philosophers sought to address could be explicitly concerned with the audience experience, such as the paradox of tragic pleasure, or how pleasure could be derived from the pain of others. The problems could also be organized around ethical concerns, for instance when striving to distinguish punishment from vengeance, how to avoid afterworldly punishment, or how to prevent punishment from being subverted by passion. In their attempts to solve these problems, philosophers in each period articulated specific understandings of the pleasure of the audience. Some of the categories are context-specific, such as the early-modern concept of the sublime (Burke) or the modern concept of *ressentiment* (Nietzsche). Other categories recur in all four periods – with respect to the basic categories of desire and of enjoyment. The objects of desire have shifted, along with the worlds inhabited by the audiences and the changing content of social morality. Yet the category of desire stayed the same. In the philosophical discussion, the desire for social esteem has in each period been treated as a volatile force of human motivation, always entwined with punishment. The desire has been celebrated as thumos in Ancient Greece (Plato 2013a; 2013b), condemned as pride in medieval Europe (Aquinas 1941), described as the desire for recognition on the brink of modernity (Hegel 2018), and more recently pinned down as essentially the desire to be fully part of society (Fraser 2000): hence, the absolute centrality of the desire for social esteem. On the other side of the gap, there are the Platonian and the Aristotelian paradigms. There does not seem to be any third alternative beyond these two paradigms (van Riel 2000). Enjoyment must be understood as either relief of distress or as absorption in activity. The more specific features of the experience differ according to the historical period, to the position in which members of the audience find themselves, or due to other circumstances. But the need to distinguish between Platonian and Aristotelian pleasure is persistent in all four historical periods. The implication is clear: the analysis should, in each period, focus on the desire for social esteem, as understood by contemporaries, and let the basic distinction between Platonian and Aristotelian structure the presentation.

SELECTIONS: Choosing the most influential. All three aspects of the selection – the choice of time periods, the choice of philosophers and the choice of punishment – are guided by the criteria of influence. In ancient Greece, the idea of rational punishment was discussed for the first known time by Plato, and the paradoxical pleasure of watching tragedies, which portrayed the dominant form of punishment at the time, was theorized by Aristotle. Together, they moreover present the two available paradigms of pleasure. In medieval Europe, Aquinas and Dante represented the culmination of theological arguments and of a literary genre, respectively, on punishments in the afterlife, and Aquinas explicitly addressed the problems attached to the pleasure of its consumption. The excitement of early-modern execution crowds stands out as the paradigmatic example of the pleasure of punishment, and should be included for that reason. Hegel was a natural choice due to his influence, his theorization of the emergence of criminal justice, and above all because of his account of the dynamics of desire. Kant and Bentham were likewise influential and discussed the passions of punishment from contrary perspectives, and Burke was included as the key theoretician of the early-modern sublime. The current period from the 1960s is noteworthy due to the unparalleled politicization of the desire for punishment, mainly channelled through the criminal justice system. Nietzsche was the first to articulate the disruptive character of pleasure in relation to punishment, and was together with Scheler the most influential philosopher on *ressentiment*, whereas psychoanalytic authors, above all Freud, Lacan and Žižek, discussed the obscene enjoyment of transgressive punishment in a modern context. This selection can be questioned on several grounds: the criteria of cultural intelligibility with respect to punishment, the lack of continuity between time periods and the exclusive reliance on philosophers in the mainstream of the Western tradition. On a more technical note, the referencing system of social science is far from ideal when applied to works with multiple editions and English translations. Instead, I follow the customary way to reference the works of Plato, Aristotle, Aeschylus, Aquinas and Dante which is used by scholars, who may prefer the old Greek or Latin original.

SHORT ANSWER: Concise formula of pleasure production. How does punishment operate to transform distress related to social esteem – as an acutely experienced loss of status, a vaguely experienced sense of unease, or as unfulfilled ambition to distinguish oneself over against others – into a radically different experience, either soothing or exhilarating? The basic pleasure formula can be stated in the following manner: punishment across different ages operates in the gap between desire and enjoyment, by promising to satisfy the incessant and never fully satisfied desire for status recognition, at the same time as it provides enjoyment, by recognizing spectators as part of the community or, alternatively, through the excitement of taking part in collective self-assertion. The elemental pleasure formula plays out differently depending on the historical and social setting. The categories allow for much variety. Punishment will be seen to generate different experiences to widely divergent audiences: male citizens in ancient Greece, the whole Christian community in the middle ages, the common people at the early-modern executions, and then, following the passage to modernity, to embittered yet relatively privileged spectators from afar, and to audiences of transgressions perpetrated in the name of the group to which they belong.

PRE-MODERN PLEASURE: Recognition mediated through the enacted world. Pleasure is understood in relation to the entire social world as it presented itself to the audience. The world-making character of punishment and its relationship to existential dilemmas of the contemporary audience are taken to be analytically central: more central than cruelty and pain, which may be the first that comes to mind when thinking about the pleasures of punishment. Each world has to be understood on its own terms. The compositions of the worlds were markedly different from one another in ancient Greece, medieval Europe, and in the early-modern period. The dilemmas facing the audiences nevertheless appear to have shared certain traits. In each period, punishment forged a community of spectators who shared the same predicament, and confirmed their place in the bigger scheme of things, caught between forces beyond their control and the necessity to gain recognition from their own community. The spectators struggled with the impossible requirements of the enacted world. They strived to satisfy the desire for social esteem, derived from the prevailing social morality, while the satisfaction was elusive due to the institution of punishment, powerful agents of justice and other forces beyond their control. At the same time, they were recognized by other people in the audience as one of them, precisely because their predicament was the same as everybody else's. This was the Platonic pleasure of punishment, as experienced by pre-modern audiences: a temporary satisfaction of the desire to be fully part of the community, mediated by existential dilemmas and the enacted world. Evidence of the Aristotelian pleasure of punishment, on the other hand, is inconclusive with respect to ancient Greece and medieval Europe. Concerning the early-modern period, the available documentation of early-modern execution crowds is consistent with two kinds of absorbed arousal: the carnivalesque and the sublime. On one analysis, the executions presented a crucial venue for the carnivalesque. Precisely because they were occasions for articulate display of official rank and social prestige, when undermined by ordinary people who were drinking and laughing, or mocking the authorities, this produced intense excitement within the crowd around the scaffold (Bakhtin 1968). Alternatively, the absorbed arousal at the execution site was sublime, in the sense suggested by Edmund Burke (1997). On this analysis, the audience were absorbed in the unfolding scenes, experiencing an almost irresistible attraction to violence, death or degradation, while experiencing a paradoxical elevation: awe, reverence, and respect.

PASSAGE TO MODERNITY: Pleasure became problematic. At the end of the nineteenth century, there was a sense that the pleasure of watching punishment had become problematic, as formulated by Friedrich Nietzsche in the *Genealogy of Morals*. While sharing the awareness, repeatedly formulated ever since antiquity, that punishment derived its ordering mission from the passions which also pushed it beyond all set boundaries, the disruptive power was attributed to pleasure rather than to anger. To discuss pleasure, in this way, was novel. Pleasure had become problematic, as a result of a series of transformations during the nineteenth century. Shared excitement and immediate absorption were rendered increasingly difficult at the scenes of punishment, due to the element of prohibition in social morality and changes in the penal practices, associated with the birth of the modern prison. At the same time, the tension between the desire for social esteem and its satisfaction was reinforced by eroded status hierarchies and the new contradictions of capitalism, making recognition increasingly precarious (Hegel 2018; Scheler 2017). Then, there was the new idea of punishment as somehow representing the audience. Before the nineteenth century, punishment, as opposed to private revenge, was mainly the domain of gods and worldly rulers. Yet with the evolution of state criminal justice and the gradual spread of democratic ideas, it became possible to imagine a state that could step in and act on behalf of groups of ordinary citizens. Consequently, the passage to modernity affected the experience of enjoyment, both as relief of distress and as absorption in excess. Recognition mediated through the enacted world and through the eyes of other spectators gave way to direct recognition. For large sections in the audience, a state-administered revenge exacted on groups identified as responsible for violating basic principles of order and morality sustained a collective self-revaluation, which involved immediate yet temporary relief of distress. The carnivalesque excitement and the sublime abandon, on the other hand, evolved into obscene enjoyment. The shared awareness of prohibition meant that excitation was reinforced at the same time as it was repressed. Modern punishment seemed to be safely enjoyed in the company of others only on condition of its public disavowal.

STATE OF THE ART: The silence on pleasure. Thirteen years after Nietzsche's observation that pleasure had become problematic in the context of punishment, Emile Durkheim published an essay, *Two laws of penal evolution*, where he, likewise deeply aware of the ambiguous role of passion, adopted the more conventional stance, and attributed the disruptive role to anger (Durkheim 1984). Pleasure was not mentioned. It was not considered, at a particular moment in time, after the passage to modernity, when Nietzsche and other writers, above all Sigmund Freud and Max Scheler, had discovered the fundamentally disruptive character of pleasure. Durkheim, who pioneered the sociology of punishment, who stressed the centrality of passion, and identified the audience as the key figure in punishment, all of which were decisive advances, incidentally initiated the long silence on pleasure within social science. The pleasure of the audience who witnessed punishment – the topic brought up by Nietzsche – would be mentioned at the margins but never reached the analysis of modern punishment. After Durkheim, the influential accounts of Elias and Foucault elaborated on the silence, by locating pleasure in a distant past, when the pleasure of punishment was assumed to be prolific and shamelessly expressed at the scaffold. The supposedly widespread enjoyment of public displays of cruelty dramatized the difference between a previous stage and the modern condition, whether conceptualized as self-control and refined manners (Elias 2012), as institutionally channelled moral outrage (Durkheim 1997) or as subtle techniques of power to increase productivity (Foucault 1979). Nothing was ever said about the pleasure of modern audiences. There was a deadening silence on pleasure in social science. At the same time, most people tend to believe that it is still there, and few would dare to argue that pleasure in fact disappeared with the passage to modernity. Instead, it seemed to become a well-kept secret in the hands of theoreticians who were often obscure and reactionary, such as Jacques Lacan or Peter Sloterdijk. Yet the topic is far too central to be allowed to stay obscure and reactionary.

COMPETING PARADIGMS: *The redundancy of pleasure.* The prolonged interest in the subject (*sujet*) in Foucauldian accounts – and to some extent also in Neo-Durkheimian accounts – during recent decades has shed light on its historical and social constitution, through the amalgams of power and discourse, yet incidentally pushed pleasure further to the side, as it appeared to be redundant. The paradigm of subject formation can be traced to Nietzsche, who originally advanced the idea – ironically likewise in the *Genalogy of Morals* – that punishment makes us who we are. It would come to involve a thorough appreciation of the productivity of punishment. But it was hard to find a role for pleasure that went beyond automatic satisfaction of a desire that was already fundamentally marked by power and privilege. Once constituted, people were essentially hard-wired to existing relationships of power through their desire. The pleasure of the audience was consequently erased, and only appeared in psychoanalysis, which picked up bits and pieces of what had been sidelined in social science, while keeping to their domain of the repressed and never seeming to discuss the same kind of punishments as historians or criminologists had in mind. At the same time, there is no way back from the analysis of power as productive, as opposed to strictly repressive. I intend to discuss the productivity of punishment from another angle, bracketing origins. What needs to be understood, according to the underlying problematic, is not what punishment 'does to us', but rather how punishment bridges the gap between desire and enjoyment, in different historical contexts. The problematic of desire goes beyond the constitution of subjectivities, and asks what happens with already constituted desire, in everyday life, as people navigate existing power imbalances and institutional encounters. It means addressing historic articulations of power and desire, without necessarily considering issues of identities, self-images or subjectivities. The answers provided may be related to issues of identity. What satisfies the desire can be tied to self-images, in a treacherous and ambiguous way. As Freud (1961) remarked, ordinary people tend to be much more moral and much more immoral than they like to believe, at one and the same time.

DEALING WITH THE REACTIONARY: How to be critical. In philosophy, the use of thought experiments is standard. The Western history of philosophy is littered with allegories, literary references and thought experiments. I have chosen to reproduce some of the examples – the plight of Agamemnon, why must there be a clear line of sight to hell, why choose a certain death in return one night of sexual pleasure – to reconstruct the world and the dilemmas as they may have presented themselves to the contemporary audience. Some of the examples are inherently problematic, and unavoidably raise questions such as 'whose desire?' and 'whose pleasure?' and 'at whose expense?'. The white male subject position being presupposed in several examples can be seen to silence the manifold of voices and experiences of people who did not fit into this narrow frame and had to bear the consequences. To simply reproduce the Homeric lightness with which female servants are executed for sex-related violations can be seen to naturalize views of women as a disposable property of men; the allegory including the white and the black winged horses in *Phaedrus* can be seen to reproduce racist stereotypes of a black body weighed down by physical need and a white body linked to spiritual values. Kant's example, as elaborated by Lacan, on the man who might embrace a certain death in return for one night of sexual pleasure, may primarily speak to heterosexual male phantasies. Given all the power imbalances that are incorporated in Western history, its history of philosophy being no exemption (Lloyd 1984), it is necessary to also take a critical look at the examples being recycled, but not necessarily in the form of normative rejection, or to once more expose them as male-centred and Eurocentric options that can only present themselves in an unchallenged world of privilege. Instead, what happens if one goes along all the way, to face the ugliness of desire? The suggested critical stance is demanding. It takes accepting that desire is shaped through systems of domination and that anyone in the audience – regardless of social position – can find satisfaction in killings, or participate in cheering execution crowds. Desire is ambiguous to the core, and enjoyment is always of the other, inherently linked to transgression, shaped by the experiences of patriarchy, heteronormativity, slavery, colonialism, capitalism, feudalism, or Christianity. Punishment tends to take spectators, whether privileged or oppressed, to places where guilt and enjoyment are inseparable. Yet by going along, by pursuing desire all the way, we may also find the desire for something radically different. If the desire for social justice is immanent in the most racist, or in the most horrifying acts, disentangling that aspect would be true to the original intention of critical theory, 'to liberate human beings from all circumstances that enslave them' (Horkheimer 1982: 244). The desire for punishment in the audience could be an ally of social justice, rather than working against it, on condition that it is addressed as such, as a desire for social justice.

CLAIMS: *Narrowed down.* This book offers a series of interpretations of how practices, understood by contemporary audiences as punishment, bridged the gap between desire and enjoyment in four different époques. More specifically, the claims concern how the classic tragedies in ancient Greece, how afterworldly punishment in medieval Europe, how public executions in Early-modern Europe, and how the prison, the death penalty and torture in the post-1968 Western world activated the desire for social esteem and provided enjoyment by recognizing spectators as fully part of the community or, alternatively, through the excitement of taking part in collective self-assertion. Given the nature of the undertaking, the conclusions reached must be tentative. The available evidence allows for several interpretations. Mine may serve to initiate a discussion that I hope will be questioned by others. I can only begin to imagine all the objections which can be raised. The relative sparsity of evidence from the thirteenth century – compared to the other time periods – means that interpretation can be seen to be insufficiently grounded. The current situation presents in a sense the opposite problem. The wealth of current research on topics related to the consumption of punishment means that much evidence can be mustered for the interpretation made here, yet also, at the same time, much more evidence that can be used to question it.

DYNAMICS: *Progressive or regressive recognition?* At the heart of the problematic of desire, conceived of as the inevitable mismatch between desire and enjoyment, lies the question of dynamic. The Hegelian master-and-slave dialectic captured the dynamics of desire, its precarious nature and dependence on the other, and, also, its ambiguity. In the very first version, the struggle for recognition was driven by the desire to restore social esteem (Hegel 1998), and marked by the inherent duality of that desire, torn between the wish to be fully accepted as part of the collective and the wish to assert oneself over against others. Hegel's fundamental intuition concerned the progressive side of recognition; individual claims for recognition would transcend existing institutional forms, successively pushing them to acknowledge and enable more freedom. Within the Hegelian tradition, recognition is seen to presuppose mutuality and be conducive to personal growth and societal well-being (Honneth 1992; Taylor 1975; Kojève 1969). However, the desire for recognition can just as well unfold in a different direction; toward intolerance, revenge and unrestrained self-assertion (Sloterdijk 2010; Fukuyama 2012). Punishment operates right in the middle of this dynamic with the capacity to provide recognition. Inserted in between desire and enjoyment, punishment can offer relief of the status concerns of an audience, or through the absorbed excitation of taking part in collective assertion. The direction of transcendence is not inherent in the dynamics of desire. Whether the progressive side or the regressive side of recognition takes precedence is a matter of struggle, influenced by external conditions, actions and interventions. There is no overall logic; desire for social esteem is inherently ambiguous and changes direction due to the everyday workings of power, and resistance.

RAISING THE STAKES: The indeterminacy of desire. To better understand how punishment operates in the gap between desire and enjoyment may shed light on the deep-seated popular support that drives punishment against better knowledge and at high social costs, as well as disclosing new points of intervention. The desire to be fully included, or to distinguish oneself over against others, does not necessarily translate into a yearning for punishment. There are less harmful ways of satisfying the desire. And there can be much more productive and creative ways of doing it. Thinking about it as a gap between desire and enjoyment that can be filled with more or less any collective action, or intervention within the dimensions of order and morality, means that the political options multiply far beyond criminal justice. It might undo the claustrophobic sense of being caught between, on the one hand, decades of political utilization of the dynamics of desire for strictly punitive ends, and, on the other hand, the critical analysis of the formation of subjects that are hard-wired to systems of domination, which left no point of intervention other than experimenting with new norms and prohibitions. There is, precisely at the level of desire, an entirely open question, whether the desire will develop into punitivity, into individual achievement, or social justice. The basic ambiguity is at the same time a space for indeterminacy, and thus contention. The option of social justice is inherent in the dynamics of desire, just like increased punitivity, an emphasis on conventional goals, or whatever happened to confer social esteem on an individual: a well-kept home, public office, wealth, military service, marriage, or, specifically in modern societies,

Introduction 11

educational merits and labour market position. The desire to oppose and to rebel, to refuse compromise, or to die for a cause are also cut from the same cloth – driven by notions of morality and justice, albeit in a very different direction: toward extended rights, new standards of respect, and levelling of power asymmetries. In the final analysis, desire is a political question. The task is not one of tempering desire, since, if history teaches us anything, desire for punishment cannot be tempered, only be made to reappear as desire for social justice.

References

Aquinas, Thomas (1941) *Summa Theologica*. London: Burns Oates & Washbourne.

Bakhtin, Michail (1968) *Rabelais and his world*. Cambridge, MA: M.I.T. Press.

Burke, Edmund (1997) *The writings and speeches of Edmund Burke. Vol. 1, The early writings*. Oxford: Clarendon Press.

Durkheim, Émile (1984) The evolution of punishment. In S. Lukes and A. Scull (eds.), *Durkheim and the law*. Oxford: Blackwell. pp 102 -132.

Durkheim, Émile (1997) *The division of labor in society*. New York: Free press.

Elias, Norbert (2012) *On the process of civilisation: sociogenetic and psychogenetic investigations*. Dublin: University College Dublin Press.

Foucault, Michel (1979) *Discipline and punish: the birth of the prison*. New York: Vintage Books.

Fraser, Nancy (2000) Rethinking recognition: overcoming displacement and reification in cultural politics. *New Left Review* 3: 107–120.

Freud, Sigmund (1953) *A case of hysteria, Three essays on sexuality, and other works. The standard edition of the complete psychological works of Sigmund Freud. Vol. VII (1901–1905)*. London: Hogarth.

Freud, Sigmund (1961) *The Ego and the Id, and other works. The standard edition of the complete psychological works of Sigmund Freud. Vol. XIX (1923–1925)*. London: Hogarth.

Fukuyama, Francis (2012) *The end of history and the last man*. 20th anniversary edn. London: Penguin.

Hegel, Georg Wilhelm Friedrich (1998) System der Sittlichkeit. *Gesammelte Werke, Band 5. Schriften und Entwürfe (1799–1808)*. Hamburg: Meiner.

Hegel, Georg Wilhelm Friedrich (2018) *The phenomenology of spirit*. Cambridge: Cambridge University Press.

Honneth, Axel (1992) *Kampf um Anerkennung: zur moralischen Grammatik sozialer Konflikte*. Frankfurt am Main: Suhrkamp.

Horkheimer, Max (1982) *Critical theory*. New York: Seabury Press.

Kierkegaard, Søren (1962) *The present age*. New York: Harper & Row.

Kojève, Alexandre (1969) *Introduction to the reading of Hegel*. New York: Basic Books.

Lloyd, Genevieve (1984) *The man of reason: 'male' and 'female' in Western philosophy*. London: Methuen.

Nietzsche, Friedrich (1989) *On the genealogy of morals*. New York: Vintage Books.

Plato (1959) *Gorgias*. Trans. by E. R. Dodds. Oxford: Clarendon press.

Plato (2013a) *Republic Books 1–5*. Trans. by C. Emlyn-Jones and W. Preddy. Cambridge, MA: Harvard University Press.

Plato (2013b) *Republic Books 6–10*. Trans. by C. Emlyn-Jones and W. Preddy. Cambridge, MA: Harvard University Press.

Scheler, Max (2017) *Das Ressentiment im Aufbau der Moralen*. Frankfurt an Main: Klostermann.

Schuster, Aaron (2016) *The trouble with pleasure: Deleuze and psychoanalysis*. Cambridge, MA: MIT Press.

Sloterdijk, Peter (2010) *Rage and time: a psychopolitical investigation*. New York: Columbia University Press.

Taylor, Charles (1975) *Hegel*. Cambridge: Cambridge University Press.

van Riel, Gerd (2000) *Pleasure and the good life: Plato, Aristotle, and the Neoplatonists*. Leiden: Brill.

1 The disappearance of pleasure?

The pleasure of punishment seems to have changed character with the passage to modernity. The first thing to note is the gradual disappearance of pleasure from public sight. Available historical research suggests that observable signs of pleasure at executions sites – laughter, cheers, drinking, merriness – became more infrequent in the nineteenth century, compared to the preceding two centuries. Any account of the transformation needs to consider the eyewitness accounts, which document the mood of the audience. The partial disappearance of pleasure from public sight should not be taken to indicate that pleasure as such disappeared, but rather that the experience of the audience changed character. Another indicator of change was that pleasure lost its former innocence in moral philosophy. The passions of punishment had been a recurrent theme in the philosophical discussion ever since ancient Greece. Yet the treatment underwent a noticeable shift during the nineteenth century. A comparison between Bentham and Kant on the one hand, and Nietzsche and Freud on the other hand, suggests that pleasure replaced anger as the most disruptive passion in the context of punishment, and became suspicious and socially inappropriate. Both kinds of evidence, the eyewitness accounts and the philosophical arguments, point toward a transformed experience of pleasure on the part of the audience. The nature of that transformation remains to be determined. Existing approaches in social science shed little light on the transformation, or tend to think of it in terms of disappearance. While the audience's pleasure may have persisted with an undiminished degree of satisfaction, despite new penal practices and the dislocations in social morality, ironically, some of the most influential accounts of the passage to modernity worked to efface pleasure, conceptually. The pleasure of punishment was first of all historicized. In the influential accounts given by Durkheim, Elias and Foucault, it was seen to be strictly confined to the early-modern period, when the enjoyment was shamelessly expressed at the scaffold. In the efforts, moreover, to understand how deeply punishment affected people in the audience, the enjoyment produced was tacitly assumed to be ephemeral. Given the prevailing problematic of subject formation, pleasure was redundant. In this chapter, I will discuss some key indicators, as well as available interpretations of the transformation during the nineteenth century.

In the order of appearance, they include the performance of early-modern execution crowds, the discussion on the passions of punishment by contemporary philosophers, followed by a critique of the historicization of pleasure in current social theory on punishment.

The disappearance of pleasure from public view

Early modern executions regularly presented 'theatres of cruelty' that were meticulously scripted and protracted in time (Evans 1996). The people had to watch – according to the principles of sovereign power. An audience of common people was required as part of the ritual, to enact and to confirm power of worldly and religious authorities (Foucault 1979). However, they also *wanted* to witness executions. Public executions were highly popular in the seventeenth and eighteenth centuries. The prospects of a hanging attracted spectators from all walks of life. In colonial America, 'all kinds of people came to watch – old and young, rich and poor, white and black, male and female—in numbers that were enormous for the era' (Banner 2002: 31). The popularity of public executions is undisputed, also in the context of pre-industrial Europe. In the larger cities, thousands of people were present, or even tens of thousands. To catch a glimpse of the events at the scaffold, spectators may have had to arrive hours in advance. Sometimes they had walked long distances. Most people, including those living on the countryside, had first-hand experience of executions. It has been estimated that an average person would witness at least one execution during their lifetime (Spierenburg 1984). Religious authorities and government officials generally encouraged attendance. Yet presence was voluntary. How come that public executions were so tremendously popular?

Most historians highlight their festive character. There is a wealth of eye-witness reports from different countries which described a shared festive mood at the execution site. The visible signs of amusement were striking to contemporary observers. A young French diplomat testified to having been driven by curiosity to attend a Stockholm execution in 1635, and was slightly abhorred by the sacrilegious behaviour of the crowd. Two men convicted for theft were mercilessly dragged to the gallows by the executioner, all the while

> a large crowd was gathering, and while no one expressed any sign of compassion /.../ On the contrary, our servants told us, who followed this sad spectacle closely, that the bystanders burst out laughing when one of the condemned struggled and made attempts to resist the ropes, as if it was a comical farce they were watching.
>
> (quoted in Sandén 2016 50).

Spectators started laughing as the hanging was imminent, and the French diplomat came to think of a comical farce. Similar observations were made in London. The British novelist Samuel Richardson noted 'a kind of mirth' among the onlookers at a Tyburn execution in the mid-eighteenth century. It was 'as if the spectacle they had beheld had afforded pleasure' (quoted in Gatrell 1994: 68). At the same site, Francis Grose, another British writer, described how 'one of the most solemn and dreadful scenes imaginable' were given 'the appearance of a fair of merry-making' (quoted in Gatrell 1994: 59).

The carnivalesque mix of humour and irreverence seems to have been to some extent culturally accepted at the scaffold. It was even ingrained in the use of language. The labouring class casually referred to executions as fairs – 'a hanging fair' (Linebaugh 1975: 66). The 'gallows humour' – an expression which is still in use in several European languages – thrived. On an execution day, some people took time off and looked forward to having a good time: eating, partying, and socializing. Some were dressed up, others were drunk. Contemporary analysis of the execution crowds often stressed the welcome escape from daily routine, blending everyday social needs with religious functions, chatting with friends and collecting relics from the dead (Gatrell 1994). Pickpockets and street vendors were busy. Expectation was in the air. To some extent, the outcome was uncertain. The prospects of last-minute pardons and other reversals made the event even more exciting. The condemned sometimes survived due to inept hangmen or technical malfunction, and stories were circulated about people who had fled the scene, after botched executions (Sarat 2014; Sandén 2016). The spectators were held in suspense, and their sympathies were unreliable. As has often been pointed out, the sympathies of the audience could go both ways. The priest's mandatory speech at the scaffoldprovided religious blessing but could also provoke indecent comments from parts of the audience. The same people who sat silently in the churches during the Sunday sermons could taunt the priests at the execution sites.

The eyewitnesses were not always conscientious observers with a primary interest in finding out the truth of the matter, or even in giving a correct account. The French diplomat in Stockholm was standing too far away to actually see what happened, and relied on observations made by his servants. Some eyewitnesses, such as Samuel Richardson, were morally alienated and made a point of not understanding the reactions of the audience. After noting the mirth among the execution crowd, he added that it was incomprehensible. The pleasure did not make sense to him. Many accounts of the sentiments at executions sites appear to have been biased by social class, or by contempt for the plebeian composition of the crowds (McGowen 2000; Spierenburg 1984). For this reason, the laughter, the cheering and other expressions of mundane pleasures may have been overemphasized. In addition, some of the eyewitnesses were outspoken opponents; they did not necessarily oppose capital punishment but were critical toward the practice of public executions. Charles Dickens was one of them. After attending a famous London hanging in 1840, with an estimated crowd of 30,000 people, he complained about seeing 'nothing but ribaldry, debauchery, levity, drunkenness, and flaunting vice in fifty other shapes' (quoted from Gatrell 1994: 60). To Dickens, this was a ground to end public gatherings around the gallows. On the other side of the Atlantic, when a Pennsylvanian parliamentary committee in 1824 proposed to abolish public executions, it stressed the expressions of enjoyment. The spectators – the committee explained – were immune to the moral education on display and returned from the execution 'evidently delighted', as they just wanted to 'be amused; to enjoy a day and season of mirth and indulgence' (quoted in Banner 2002: 151). It was ultimately about legitimacy. The blend of public pleasure and plebeian composition of the crowd operated as part of an argument for reformed penal practices. In the same vein, the British Quaker J. J. Gurney reported seeing large crowds of people, of all ages and 'chiefly of the lower orders', on their way to a hanging in 1816. While the execution was characterized as 'the most dreadful and melancholy'ceremony, the congregated audience displayed 'feelings of a pleasurable nature' (quoted in McGowen 1986: 319).

In any discussion of the pleasure of punishment, the behaviour of the early-modern execution crowd tends to present itself as a paradigmatic example. The images of cheerful mood, festivity, and debauchery are stark and provocative. The festive mood appears as one easily recognizable aspect of enjoyment. Execution crowds and their behaviour have been a matter of scholarly controversy ever since the 1970s. How much of a popular carnival was it? Were people insensitive to the suffering of others? Was power confirmed, or was it challenged? The available evidence seems open to several interpretations (Garland 2010; Spierenburg 1984; Laqueur 1989; Gatrell 1994; Burke 2009). The expressed relationship between the audience and the authorities was complex. The emotional reactions were to some extent orchestrated, and to some extent drawn from the repertoire of popular culture. The mood of the crowd – festive, rowdy and possibly insubordinate – appeared to contradict the setting, which was solemn, religious and gruesome. As often noted, the 'base and disorderly popular pleasures' threatened to rip the sacred aura from the ritual and turn it into its opposite – the profane (Smith 2008: 49). People could act irreverently in so many ways. Drunken and excited crowds turned capital punishment into the 'shabbiest of rituals', which 'lurched chaotically between death and laughter' (Laqueur 1989: 309). There was chanting, and obscenities were expressed straight into the air, and although these manners may have been frowned upon by middle-class observers, they were socially acceptable, or at least tolerated, in context. What started as a solemn ritual might end as a carnival of popular amusement – or it could stay a solemn ritual. The early-modern execution could be a space for defiance and for all sorts of enjoyment on the part of the audience. Above all, however, it was a venue for official power and politics (Gatrell 1994). The state controlled the judicial process. Whatever the crowd ended up doing, the entire event was staged by the authorities.

Taken together, the contemporary testimonies suggest that many executions were festive in some sense of the term. At the same time, they offer nothing more than a cue, and are included here to suggest that the early-modern public executions provided the people present with enjoyment. The testimonies provide little insights into the mechanisms involved, or the nature of the enjoyment. What gave rise to the enjoyment? It is difficult in retrospect, also given the evidence, to know the nature of the spectator's enjoyment, or the reasons why people turned out in such large numbers. Was it the anticipation of death by hanging, was it the prospect of having a day off, or was it the satisfaction of other social needs and obligations that their presence also might have implied? Popular culture seems to have embraced a wide spectrum of postures stretching from rebellious to deferential, from debauchery to curiosity. In *The Hanging Tree*, V. A. C. Gatrell summarised the available evidence on British execution crowds by saying that 'people steered a wavering course between tacitly ethical approval, sardonic and transgressive defiance, and mockery, sentimental anguish, or outright voyeurism' (Gatrell 1994: 196). Executions were a venue for ballads, broadsheets, jokes and drinking, which allowed for a variety of sentiments and responses on the part of the congregated audience, many of which were readily interpreted as signs of enjoyment. Yet far from all executions were festive. Many were the direct opposite: solemn official processions. In Germany, it has been argued, executions were tiresome, orderly and predictable until the beginning of the nineteenth century (Evans 1996).

During the nineteenth century, public expressions of penal excitement would become less common. The disappearance was a protracted process which extended well into the modern period. And it was always partial. There are many later examples of cheerfulness around the scaffold, from the mid-nineteenth century and onwards. For instance, in Owensboro, Kentucky, in 1936, a partying execution crowd of ten thousand people gathered during the night before the hanging (Laqueur 1989), and in 1999, the enthusiastic public response following the release of post-mortem photographs of an electrocuted man in Florida caused web servers to crash (Lynch 2000; see also Pratt 2000). Ten years earlier, in the same state, large crowds of people had chanted 'Burn, Bundy, Burn' on the eve of the execution of an infamous serial killer. For natural reasons, as one of the few countries which have retained the death penalty until this day, the examples mainly stem from the United States. If the concept of execution crowds is extended to cover extra-legal punishment, the range of examples multiplies. One can find reports of visible and audible signs of enthusiasm on the part of the audience from many political contexts such as Jim Crow lynchings in the American south or punitive mobs in Fascist Italy, especially during transition periods, when the ordinary workings of the state apparatus were distrusted by dominant social groups (Pfeifer 2004; Matteo 2017). Hence, festive execution crowds cannot be said to have disappeared. But they have become significantly less frequent in the modern period. It does not follow that people in general have become any less prone to embrace state violence, excessive or not. The twentieth century was full of large-scale atrocities carried out by state officials and supported by large sections of the domestic public. Some of the atrocities were understood as politically motivated whereas others were understood along the lines of punishments for acts of wrong-doing, by contemporaries. The mass executions of party officials, among many others, in the Stalinist Soviet Union of the 1930s tended to be understood as a mix of ideological necessity and punishment for ordinary offences, or treason (Sebag Montefiore 2004). The Nazi holocaust was driven by racially motivated goals to exterminate whole groups of people, enabled by the industrial organization of modern society, yet silenced in public contexts and mainly carried out in Poland, outside of Germany (Bauman 1989; Aly and Heim 2002). Diagnosing a general decrease in public expressions of enjoyment at the scenes of punishment must therefore come with certain qualifications. The frequency of public expressions of enjoyment cannot be used to support any Elian ideas of processes of civilization which go beyond the thin ice of public surface. Instead, what the decrease can be taken to indicate is that the experience of Western spectators may have changed, compared to those of early-modern execution crowds. The enjoyment was either privatized, as opposed to publicly shared with other people, or, if the enjoyment was shared, which it was at times, the awareness of prohibition would inevitably shape the experience.

The gradual disappearance of pleasure from public view was no doubt linked to the simultaneous disappearance of punishment from public view. Following the Enlightenment, public displays of cruelty were gradually abandoned (Spierenburg 1984; Garland 2010; Bessler 1997). Punishment moved indoors, and into the realm of cultural imaginary. An audience of eye-witnesses was no longer called for. While parents had regularly brought their children to watch hangings, as noted by a mid-eighteenth century visitor to London, to instil morality amongst other things, by the end of the century punishment increasingly relied on 'what remained unseen but imagined' (Wilf 1993: 51). The shift to the unseen was a consequence of the large-scale transition from corporeal punishment to imprisonment. The prison-building schemes across Western countries and the subsequent reliance on custodial forms of punishment meant that public venues disappeared, one after the other. By the end of the nineteenth century, there were few places to go, should you want to consume punishment in the company of others. In a short essay on the death penalty, Albert Camus described his father on one day shortly before the war in 1914. The father was enthusiastically looking forward to the first execution of his life. He walked away thinking that the guillotine was too mild a punishment, considering the crime, only to return home nauseated, lying down on the bed, suddenly starting to vomit. What actually happened that day, he kept for himself (Camus 1988). The experience must be typically modern. On the rare occasion of a public execution, spectators were unaccustomed. There was no longer any execution culture, with broadsheets and ballads.

The disappearance of public expressions of pleasure was certainly influenced by the changing penal practices. Yet that was not the whole story. The prison might well have turned into a venue for shared, on-site enjoyment. As it were, some of the most prominent penal reformers proposed that prisons should encourage, as well as be able to attract, spontaneous visitors. Jeremy Bentham, the British moral philosopher whose life coincided with the Enlightenment period, retained the idea that punishment should be open to the general public, and integrated it into the plans for the never realized model prison, Panopticon. The prison gates of Panopticon should be 'thrown wide open to the body of the curious at large' (Bentham 1843a: 46). Everybody would have access to the facilities, and curiosity and excitement were reasons to go. Bentham thought of the observation not only as the inspector's duty to discipline the inmates but also as a 'great and constant fund of entertainment' for the inspector, and for others. Looking through the blinders, it was suggested, could be attractive to the inspector's family members. While not always terribly exciting, the observation of inmates would combine utility with pastime, and was judged superior to window watching in a town-house (Bentham 1843a). It was thus perfectly conceivable to reconcile prison cells and public enjoyment. Jeremy Bentham's suggestion was further elaborated by Joshua Jebb, who designed Pentonville, one of the very first modern prisons. Jebb envisioned that the prison would attract well-dressed visitors, strolling and conversing in the prison halls, reminiscent of a contemporary shopping mall (Smith 2008). The plans for public prisons had been drawn. But this particular aspect was never to be realized. Panopticon-like prisons were built, such as Pentonville, but they would never provide a 'great and constant fund of entertainment' for families. The prison would not be opened to the public. Its doors have remained closed until today, and straightforward reactions from the audience were effectively prevented on the scenes of punishment.

Pleasure becomes problematic

With the birth of the prison, visible expressions of enjoyment were designed out of penal practice. But the gradual disappearance of pleasure from public view also indicated a more fundamental transformation of the audience's experiences. The pleasure of punishment did not go away, but was rendered problematic. It was problematic in the sense of being socially inappropriate. There was moreover a growing unease about its potential consequences. Pleasure had become suspicious, and might in the context of punishment even be inherently dangerous. In itself this was nothing altogether new; in a longer historical perspective, stretching back to ancient Greece, the pleasure of punishment had recurrently been treated as problematic. But it had always been considered less problematic than anger. What happened during the nineteenth century was that pleasure replaced anger as the most disruptive passion. The change was captured first by Nietzsche and then, more systematically, in Freudian psychoanalysis. The scale of change can be appreciated if the views of Nietzsche and Freud are compared to those of Kant and Bentham, one hundred years earlier.

Immanuel Kant and Jeremy Bentham represented different perspectives on punishment, with respect to the grounds of justification; one was strictly rule-based, and the other utilitarian. Yet they shared a common ambition to stifle excessive punishment and make penal practices at the time, at the end of the eighteenth century, more rational and more legitimate. In this context, in their endeavour to rationalize punishment, pleasure was seen as harmless, or innocent, whereas anger was considered volatile and potentially disruptive. I have chosen two excerpts, one from each of them, to illustrate their views on the passions of punishment. In Bentham's case, pleasure in the context of punishment was generally commendable. In *Principles of Penal Law*, a text that was published in 1830 but probably dated back to the mid-1770s (Bedau 2004), he argued that the pleasure of vengeance was a positive force, useful in social life and vital for law enforcement.

> Produced without expense, ... it is an enjoyment to be cultivated as well as any other; for the pleasure of vengeance, considered abstractly, is, like every other pleasure, only good in itself ... Useful to the individual, this motive is also useful to the public, or, to speak more correctly, necessary. ... Take away this spring, the machinery of the laws will no longer move.
>
> (Bentham 1843b: 383)

While anger and private vengeance had to be managed and phased out, the pleasure of vengeance was characterized in positive terms: as innocent ('an enjoyment to be cultivated as well as any other'), as inherently valuable ('only good in itself'), as generally beneficial ('useful to the public'), and as necessary for prosecution (without this pleasure, 'the machinery of the laws will no longer move'). Bentham was aware that the positive valuation could be controversial. He mentioned that other moral philosophers disagreed with his position, yet he did so only in a general manner, without engaging with their arguments in detail. He was confident; the pleasure of punishment was commendable on a number of accounts. There was only one qualification: it is commendable only if the executed punishment is legitimate. The pleasure is 'innocent so long as it is confined within the limits of the laws' (Bentham 1843b: 383). Should the punishment be contrary to the law, the corresponding pleasure became illegitimate. Although this was a significant reservation, penal pleasure was on the whole embraced.

In this respect, Bentham was a good representative of the 'new Epicureanism' in the eighteenth century. Pleasure was seen as legitimate, or innocent regardless of source, by many of his contemporaries. Whether stemming from eating, riches or punishment, pleasure was good (Kavanagh 2010). The eighteenth century meant that pleasure was freed from religious restrictions. Earlier conceptions had been embedded in a religious cosmology, often branded as 'worldly' and tangled up in Christian accounts of sin (Porter 1996). Christian dogmas could encourage excessive punishment, yet prohibited indulgence in the pain of others. Bentham's endorsement of the pleasure of punishment stood out compared to Medieval and Early-Modern philosophers, such as Aquinas (1941) and Hobbes (1996). In

Summa Theologica, the default stance was that the pleasure of punishment was wrong. It was sinful to take pleasure in the imposition of pain on others, also as a spectator. Centuries later, at the beginning of the early-modern period, Hobbes would reiterate the same prohibition in one of his arguments against vengeance. Vengeance was detrimental because it involved 'glorying in the hurt of another' (Hobbes 1996: 101). Vengeance was wrong partly due to the illicit character of the accompanying pleasure. Bentham, on the other hand, was less hesitant in his embrace of the pleasure. Influenced by utilitarian principles of good and evil rather than religious notions of sin, he valued pleasure irrespective of source. On the single condition that the punishment being exacted was not excessive, pleasure was legitimate. Bentham's positions on the pleasure of punishment stood out also with respect to later approaches, as pleasure was not tainted by transgression. There was no assumed connection to excess. The enjoyment was thought of as an innocent pastime, rather than as an insatiable lust.

The transgressive dynamics of punishment has been a constant concern within Western culture, and the eighteenth century was no exception. But if punishment was excessive, it was not because of pleasure. Excess was associated with anger, rather than with pleasure. In *Anthropology from a Pragmatic Point of View*, published in 1798, Kant continued the tradition of adopting a dual approach to vengeance, based on the close affiliation between anger and justice. Anger was partly legitimate, reflecting the ancient notion of righteous indignation, generated by experiences of injustice. In this capacity, the desire for vengeance was not only deeply rooted in human nature and social order but also closely affiliated to the desire for justice, which followed the dictates of reason. At the same time, Kant described the desire for vengeance in opposite terms – as highly and unambiguously disruptive.

> The desire for vengeance is one of the most violent and deeply rooted passions; even when it seems to have disappeared, a secret hatred, called rancor, is always left over, like a fire smoldering under the ashes /.../ It transforms the desire for justice against the offender into the passion for retaliation, which is often violent to the point of madness.
>
> (Kant 2006: 170f)

Vengeful anger was a kind of unlimited hatred, which corrupted the desire for justice, and threatened to thwart punishment in relation to the offence. The desire for justice was transformed and became excessively violent. Kant thus considered anger to be a highly disruptive passion, like so many others before him, while pleasure was innocent, and moreover of little consequence.

A century later, Friedrich Nietzsche treated pleasure as a naturally disruptive element, and paid less attention to anger. The destabilizing motion toward excess, which seems to be inherent in almost any account of punishment, was wholeheartedly attributed to pleasure. If punishment transgressed beyond the boundaries of reason and legality, it was not because of vengeful passions, such as uncontrolled anger, but because of unrestrained pleasure, and untempered desire. Nietzsche called attention to the presumed pleasures of cruelty. He started elaborating the notion of 'pleasure of cruelty' in the *Birth of Tragedy*, his very first work. It was also the book which inaugurated the modern study of Dionysus, the ancient Greek deity. Dionysus was the god of many things: wine, music, excess, loss of self, senseless violence, fertility, suffering and self-affirmation. Nietzsche foregrounded the internal dynamics involved. What had earlier been attributed to a transcendent deity – unbounded enjoyment and violence – was now transferred to the psychic interior of individuals (Heinrichs 1984). In the *Birth of Tragedy*, the Dionysic was an aspect of human experience; the 'horrible "witches' brew" of sensuality and cruelty' (Nietzsche 1967: 40). Similar remarks can be found scattered in other works. The pleasure of cruelty was a consistent theme in his oeuvre. In *Daybreak,* he described 'an unspeakable happiness at the *sight of torment*' (§113; emphasis in original). It was a collectively shared experience, associated with liberation and celebration.

> In the act of cruelty the community refreshes itself and for once throws off the gloom of constant fear and caution. Cruelty is one of the oldest festive joys of mankind.
>
> (Nietzsche 1997: § 18)

The recollections of ancient Bacchic cults, as they had been passed down, were one important point of reference. In that context, cruelty performed religious rather than punitive functions. There are plenty of reasons to doubt the idea of unrestrained pleasure in earlier times, and one should therefore stress that Dionysus was primarily an analytical principle to Nietzsche (Heinrichs 1984). In his later work, above all in the second essay of the *Genealogy of Morals*, the pleasure of cruelty was discussed in conjunction with punishment, and particularly with transgressive punishment. The shift of emphasis meant that the violence could not be wholly arbitrary, or imposed on transcendent grounds, but was tied to a specific action, which might have triggered the acts of cruelty. Punishment, for Nietzsche, was necessary to shape subjects who were reliable and acted in accordance with social norms. Yet the close link to celebration was maintained. There was no real party without cruelty, Nietzsche said, followed by the exclamation that 'there is so much *festive* in punishment' (Nietzsche 1989: II §6; emphasis in original). The aspect of excess was understood independently of the original violation. Instead, cruelty was driven by an internal dynamic. When punishment was transgressive, pleasure was generated in the process, for everybody who took part, and that pleasure was the driving force.

Nietzsche is generally seen to celebrate the pleasure of cruelty, and to some extent that may be true. But a closer reading of the scattered notes on the subject reveals that he articulated the contemporary sentiment that pleasure had become problematic. Nietzsche was commenting on a bygone world of unrestrained pleasure. He was not talking about his own times. In the *Genealogy of Morals*, the references dated back to the Middle Ages, or even further back, and writers such as Cervantes, Dante and Aquinas were invoked. It is a circumstance often overlooked. The époques of unrestrained pleasure were over – which explained the 'bitter taste' left upon reading Cervantes's novel *Don Quixote* (Nietzsche 1989: II §6). The reference to bitter taste was a far cry from pleasure. Although Nietzsche did not specify the exact passages in *Don Quixote*, there is a torture scene in the book where the duke and the duchess are not present but according to one interpretation 'derive all necessary pleasure from the account that is given them later' (Nabokov 1983: 71). Nietzsche suggested that contemporary readers found it be 'the funniest of books' and would 'nearly laugh themselves to death' whereas late nineteenth-century readers found torture scenes hard to digest (Nietzsche 1989: II §6). The argument was that people still enjoyed punishment while being unable to express it. Speaking about cruelty as 'one of the oldest festive joys of mankind', he sensed that something had changed – a certain cultural refinement was required – and hastened to add: 'Do you think all this has altered and that mankind must therefore have changed its character?' (Nietzsche 1997: §18). To his mind, the times had changed but not people.

Nietzsche may have been an astute observer of the modern condition; an excellent guide, if read as an observer of his own age, rather than as a commentary on earlier historical phases, or on an immutable human nature. He articulated what I take to be a more widely spread sentiment: that pleasure in the context of punishment had become problematic – more illicit, more disruptive and more shameful – in post-Enlightenment Germany. A cultural taboo unsettled the enjoyment. It was a matter of acknowledging the disruptive qualities of pleasure at a specific point in time. In earlier époques, 'when mankind felt no shame towards its cruelty', people could indulge in the intense excitement they experienced as spectators. It could be expressed in the company of others, in public and without shame. In the contemporary context, the pleasure of cruelty was not extinguished – it was still experienced by the audience. After all, he insisted, it was sincerely festive and mankind had not changed. But this pleasure required 'some kind of sublimation'; it had to be rendered harmless and inoffensive (Nietzsche 1989: II §7). The pleasure in cruelty was transformed into the imaginary and refashioned as compassion. Contemporary notions of tragic pity represented such an adaptation. Nietzsche did not explicitly discuss contemporary penal practices, and – since public executions were abolished in Germany in the mid-nineteenth century (Evans 1996) – he may have had little first-hand experience of the behaviour of execution crowds. Yet the same line of reasoning can be applied to public executions. The excitement over the suffering being witnessed at the scaffold came to be considered base or inappropriate and had to be turned into a refined indignation over suffering. The transformation was necessary. Within the perimeters of social morality, the enjoyment had to be sublimated. Unmediated enjoyment was inaccessible due the element of prohibition. And while compassion came across as the opposite of the pleasure in cruelty, in reality it was merely the socially commendable outlet of the same kind of excitement.

Sublimation involved the internalization of social prohibition. Nietzsche used the concept in the second essay of the *Genealogy* with respect to punishment and to the intense excitement designated as the 'pleasure in cruelty'. Several commentators have noted the similarities between Nietzsche's and Freud's views on sublimation, in particular with respect to its root causes in repression, effected by contemporary social norms (Gemes 2009; Phillips 2015). To Freud, sublimation was one of several responses to prohibition, or the fact that certain kinds of pleasure were illicit. In his interpretation, sublimation operated at the level of desire. It involved a displacement of the object of desire, when the original drive could not be expressed without encountering blame and censure. Forbidden desires were diverted, and given an alternative direction due to the internalized social morality (Freud 1931; Civitarese 2016). The prime example was the sublimation of sexual desire into artistic creativity. In an essay on the childhood memories of Leonardo da Vinci, Freud described how sexual desires could escape repression by being sublimated into scientific curiosity. Forbidden desires, such as the sexual attraction to his mother and, later in life, da Vinci's desire to have sex with men, were transformed into a powerful and socially commendable urge to know and to create exceptional works of art (Freud 1919). Just like in Nietzsche's approach to the pleasure of cruelty, the guiding idea was that the enjoyment was made consonant with the *fin de siècle* social morality, through a transformation effectuated by its prohibitions.

What was harmless became disruptive and dangerous over the course of the nineteenth century. Pleasure assumed formidable as well as shameful connotations that were foreign to eighteenth-century understanding (Kavanagh 2010). In the following century, anger stopped being the main concern in philosophical treatises on punishment. Nietzsche articulated pleasure as a problem in relationship to punishment. His treatment of the passions of punishment was in stark contrast to Jeremy Bentham, and other eighteenth-century writers such as Immanuel Kant and Edmund Burke, to whom pleasure was morally unproblematic in this context. For reasons that remain to be elucidated, Nietzsche might even be seen to represent a decisive turn in the Western discussion of passion and punishment. Since antiquity, passion was seen to undermine the legitimacy of punishment, as a pillar of social order, and in the long history of efforts to cleanse punishment from passion, to be discussed in the next chapter, excess was above all associated with unrestrained anger, or anger of the wrong kind. Pleasure had been present for the most part of this history, although rarely occupying a central spot. Instead, the problematic passion had been anger – anger, or emotions related to anger, such as hatred and righteous indignation. Anger was seen to be the most disruptive emotion, far more dangerous than pleasure. Pleasure presented all kinds of problems of ethical or theological nature, but anger threatened to undermine the institution from within. It was liable to escape the moderation of reason and instigate excessive punishment, which threatened existing political orders. During the nineteenth century, the focus shifted from anger to pleasure. The suspicion of subversion came to be directed towards pleasure.

Its complex and volatile features were later elaborated by Sigmund Freud beyond the specific context of punishment. With Freud, pleasure became a general problem (Schuster 2016). Psychoanalysis was born with the modern problem of pleasure: the combination of private enjoyment and public disavowal. It was originally articulated in terms of repression, a concept which Freud started elaborating in the 1890s (Brenner 1957). Repression meant that every individual felt compelled to curb drives that were associated with illicit pleasure, for instance in the domain of sexuality, or punishment. The experience of compulsion was rooted in social morality. Certain kinds of enjoyment were being suppressed to protect the well-being of all members of society, while at the same time generating inner tension, as the drives were unable to find satisfaction, and were instead manifested in guilt, shame and issues of mental health. The process of repression was never complete, and the drives would remain operative and continued to undermine the instituted order (Freud 1931; 1955). From this perspective, the pleasure of punishment was one kind of illicit pleasure, which was necessarily repressed. While gradually disappearing from public view, the excitement turned private and was accompanied by shame and public disavowal. Private shame replaced public display, and the constant suspicion of trouble, associated with passions generally speaking, as opposed to reason, was crystallized around a new object. Pleasure was no longer innocent, 'an enjoyment to be cultivated as well as any other', as Bentham had argued one hundred years earlier. It was suspicious, disruptive and repressed.

Making pleasure disappear: historicization and conceptual irrelevance

Just like pain seemed to disappear from punishment when the prison cell replaced the gallows, and the pain was no longer tangible, or readily observable – there were no limbs broken, no blood, no audible cries and no visible agony – so did pleasure appear to vanish from punishment with the gradual disappearance of public displays, since it was no longer immediately observable, in the form of laughter, chanting, cheering, or excited crowds. But as indicated by Nietzsche and Freud, pleasure did not disappear, no more than the pain of punishment went away. Instead, it changed character due to prohibition. Processes more encompassing than the increasingly secluded character of penal practices were in motion, which forced pleasure underground, or prevented it from being expressed in public. The nineteenth century saw wider changes in the social organization of emotional reactions, according to a widely shared assumption. Friedrich Nietzsche, Sigmund Freud, Èmile Durkheim, Norbert Elias and Michel Foucault – theoreticians that in many other aspects were miles apart – all converge in the view that something happened with the passage to modernity that fundamentally changed the conditions for the audience's experience of pleasure.

The transformation of punishment during the Enlightenment period has been extensively explored, as well as source of much controversy (Foucault 1979; Ignatieff 1978; Laqueur 1989; Melossi and Pavarini 1981; Rusche and Kirchheimer 1939; Spierenburg 1984; 1991). The transition from execution to imprisonment, the prevalence of riots, and the change away from public display have been central themes in a scholarly discussion, which at the time – the 1970s and the 1980s – involved much disagreement but, in retrospect, above all much historical evidence on punishment in practice. The protracted and partial disappearance of public excitement has been noticed in passing, taken for granted rather than studied in its own right. Embedded in some of the most influential accounts of the transformation was an idea of historical progress; or rather, to avoid the normative connotations of 'progress': a historicization of the pleasure of punishment, according to which it flourished in pre-modern times, only to gradually disappear from the public scene with the passage to modernity. Elias (2012), Durkheim (1997) and Foucault (1979) historicized pleasure in a particular way: *The pleasure of punishment was prolific throughout the early-modern period. Pleasure was shamelessly expressed at the scaffold. After that, it went away, or became much more infrequent.* Guided by very different concerns, Elias, Durkheim and Foucault can nevertheless be seen to subscribe to this common baseline story. They all used the early-modern period to describe a process in which the gradual disappearance of visible signs of enjoyment at the scenes of punishment indicated a diminishing role of passions at the level of individual experience. To Elias, the gradual disappearance of public enjoyment was a sign of increased self-control and changing sensibilities; to Durkheim, it signalled changes in social morality and the tempering role of the criminal justice system; and to Foucault, it indicated a sanitized and scientific deployment of power along with the corresponding, normalized subjectivities. As can be reconstructed from their main works, the three authors focused on different drivers, or aspects of the process. But the end result was the same with respect to the spectators' experience: there was less space for passion.

1. Norbert Elias argued that the enjoyment of cruelty used to be widespread and culturally accepted. Pre-modern societies were governed by unregulated consumption of cruelty and lack of empathy; 'the pleasure in killing and torturing others was great, and it was a socially permitted pleasure' (Elias 2012: 189). With the passage to modernity, on the other hand, such overt expressions were less frequent and no longer socially permitted. The approach foregrounded the social organization of emotions: how people were supposed to feel and behave when exposed to cruelty and pain. It was not altogether clear if pleasure, in addition, was taken to disappear as experience. In one single sentence, Elias could to talk about

the experience – 'the pleasure in killing and torturing others was great' – and about its social organization: 'it was a socially permitted pleasure'. The first part implied that the experience of pleasure had diminished at the level of individual experience: the audience ceased to draw satisfaction from cruelty, or acts of punishment. The second part suggested that the partial disappearance of overt expressions was a matter of changing social norms. In the second half of the nineteenth century, public displays of enjoyment were less socially accepted, or even tabooed, in relation to punishment, but also more generally. Elias thought of the disappearance as an integral part of the civilizing process. On this reading, all public displays of pleasure became more infrequent. 'Outbreaks of strong communal excitement' were less frequent (Elias and Dunning 2008: 44), as a result of stricter emotional control and changing cultural sensibilities. The shifting cultural sensibilities had a moderating effect on immediate expressions of enjoyment – in the consumption of punishment, or in other contexts.

2. 'Nowadays', Durkheim wrote at the turn to the twentieth century, 'it is said that punishment has changed', away from vengeful passions, to be firmly anchored in the state and in 'well premeditated foresight' (Durkheim 1997: 44f). But despite appearances to the contrary, passion was still the motor force of punishment. Interestingly, pleasure was not mentioned among the relevant passions. For Durkheim, punishment was above all an emotional reaction, which reinforced popular sentiments and a pool of shared values. He used the notion of collective consciousness (*conscience collective*) to refer to a bedrock of values, beliefs and sentiments, which permeated any given society: a social morality which remained tacit on a daily basis, but was expressed – and came to be known by the members of the society – through punishment (Durkheim 1997; Garland 1990). With the passage to modernity, vengeful passions remained the key driver, yet lost part of their earlier force. The 'lively emotion', the 'sudden explosion' and the 'outrage' had been replaced by emotions that were 'calmer and more reflective' (Durkheim 1984: 130). Apart from the moderation of anger, there was the emerging element of compassion for the punished offender and the growing concern for human dignity. Beyond changes in social morality, Durkheim stressed the importance of the development of a criminal justice system. While vengeful passions reigned more freely in pre-modern societies, modern societies had tempered the collective moral outrage in the institutions of criminal justice, by claiming monopoly on the legitimate exercise of violence, in a language of universal rights and impartiality. The vengeful emotions were transferred to the state, given a culturally approvable outlet, and helped, moreover, to socialize the audience, the 'honest people' for whose sake it was all done, not so much through deterrence, but by recreating a shared social world which provided guidance and emotional attachment for individual members of society (Durkheim 1997: 63; Garland 1990).

3. In the first part of *Discipline and Punish*, Foucault was attentive to public expressions of enjoyment, and described how early-modern executions could evolve into carnivalesque events 'in which rules were inverted, authority mocked and criminals transformed into heroes' (Foucault 1979: 61). All such popular expressions of excitement would disappear during the nineteenth century when public rituals of display were replaced by punitive techniques that were targeted at individuals in closed settings, far from public view. Foucault thus inscribed the disappearance of public passion in the general transformation of power. In the modern period, there was no such thing as collective expressions of pleasure. What happened was that penal practices went from being primarily repressive to primarily productive, which meant that mechanisms became technical, scientific and hidden in specialized institutions, where expectations and control singled out the individual from the collective (Hörnqvist 2010). Punishment was sanitized, hidden from public view, no longer relying on display and excess, but on social norms and science. The role of pleasure was acknowledged at the margins. In interviews from the same time period as *Discipline and Punish*, Foucault could state that power 'induces pleasure, forms knowledge, produces discourse' (Foucault 1980: 119). But in sharp contrast to the abundant focus on discourse and knowledge, as preeminent products of power, he never elaborated on the relationship between pleasure and power. Pleasure was a peculiar side-effect of power, and its role, if it had one, was reduced to rewarding individual compliance with the prescribed programmes, or with prevailing relationships of power.

Thus, along different lines of reasoning, Elias, Durkheim and Foucault all historicized pleasure and located it in a distant past. Public signs of excitement were projected into premodern Europe and worked to support the thesis of a radical break with the passage to modernity. The supposedly widespread enjoyment of public displays of cruelty dramatized the difference between a previous stage and the modern condition, whether conceptualized as self-control and refined manners (Elias), as institutionally channelled moral outrage (Durkheim) or as subtle techniques of power to increase productivity (Foucault). As a consequence, the pleasure of punishment was effectively historicized. It was tacitly associated with the public expressions of rowdy amusement and debauchery, or, alternatively – if the executions proceeded in an orderly fashion – with the sublime experience of terror, during a couple of centuries in European history. The silence on pleasure in modern contexts was conspicuous. There was little trace of Nietzsche's and Freud's sense that pleasure had become problematic and more disruptive with the passage to modernity. One might find points of commonalities with the positions of Nietzsche and Freud, above all with respect to the repression and the sublimation of modern pleasure. But none of them – Elias, Durkheim and Foucault – entertained the idea of its permanence, or its subterraneous effectiveness.

It was not simply a matter of unchallenged assumptions of historical progress. What ultimately decided whether pleasure was on, or off, the research agenda of social science was the particular set of concerns, according to which some things were worth investigating further. Given the problematic of desire, it is all about pleasure; how desire transforms into satisfaction, and back again into desire. Within a different and more influential paradigm in social science, however, pleasure is redundant. Given the problematic of subject formation, what needed to be understood was the complex relationship between punishment and subjection, not the everyday dialectics of desire. The problematic was tied up with the idea that punishment affects us in a more profound way than we like to believe. It was a question about what punishment does to us – to our identities or our subjectivities. The question goes back to Nietzsche, who originally advanced the idea that punishment makes us who we are. Through punishment, he argued, people were made reliable, equipped with a conscience and fit to enter into social agreements. Punishment was central for the ability to hold promises; 'to breed an animal with the prerogative to *promise*', (Nietzsche 1989: II § 1; emphasis in original). On Nietzsche's reading, pain was the effective mechanism. It had to hurt because only what hurts was remembered, and people easily forgot. 'The harshness of the penal law' indicated the trouble it took to conquer forgetfulness (II §3). People were subjugated into accountability, slowly moulded and made predictable through painful interventions. Punishment was not the only instrument, according to Nietzsche, as political tyranny and the morality of customs worked in the same direction, to constitute useful subjects.

Punishment was a clear-cut instantiation of power, as it relied on pain, approached individuals as an exterior force, which compelled them to do things against their will, and in addition symbolically manifested the futility of their attempts to resist. After 1970, Michel Foucault picked up the same theme of subject formation, while reframing the relationship in terms of productivity (Foucault 1998). The individual was not an independent entity, later subdued by exterior forces, in the process of manifesting their superiority. Instead, the individual was 'one of power's first effects' (Foucault 2003: 30). That was the deeper meaning of the famous reference in *Discipline and punish* to 'the soul' as the object of punishment. The productivity of punishment was epitomized by the birth of the prison, on the threshold to modernity. The prison embodied a discipline which subverted the level of conscious decision, evident in the precedence it gives to 'punishments that are exercise – intensified, multiplied forms of training' (Foucault 1979: 179). In this way, actions were made consonant with prevailing power structures, inside Western prisons, as well as in other social institutions. Individual behaviour was exposed to essentially the same kind of power across the social body, thereby dissolving the sharp distinction between prisoner and audience. On this analysis, power was exercised with rather than over against people, making them want what they wanted, and achieve what they wanted. The impact extended from behaviour to self-conceptions, stretching into the realm of desire: what we wish and who we think we are. In the decades following Foucault's death in 1984, subject-formation would become the mainstream approach to the productivity of power. The consequences at the level of subjectivity were central. The governmentality literature, which took its name from a re-discovered lecture held by Michel Foucault in 1979, paid attention to issues of personal identity; 'what forms of person, self and identity' were constructed (Dean 1999: 32; Rose and Miller 1992; O'Malley 2004). The idea of a socially constituted desire was defined in opposition to a natural desire. Judith Butler (1997), paradigmatically, said 'if, following Foucault, we understand power as forming the subject as well, as providing the very condition of its existence and the trajectory of its desire, then power is not simply what we oppose but also, in a strong sense, what we depend on for our existence and what we harbor and preserve in the beings that we are' (Butler 1997: 2). Analytically, the key concern was to find out how desire had been shaped historically, through discourses and struggles. Once constituted, however, people were essentially hard-wired to existing relationships of power through their desire. Consciously alluding to both meanings of the word 'subject' in French and English, they were referred to as 'subjects of desire' (Butler 1987).

In the late-modern prison, productivity equalled subject formation; interventions were seen to be 'a primary means of creating accountable and thus governable and obedient citizens' (Bosworth 2007: 68). Transformations of power, associated with neoliberal governance, came to expression in a condensed form within the prison. The research objective was to look behind the rhetoric of the law-abiding citizen and discover a manifold of attempts 'to breed an animal with the prerogative to promise'. There was a diagnosed shift from 'discipline' – the production of reliable subjects within institutions – to 'technologies of citizenship' through which individuals transformed themselves into better citizens, inside as well as outside of institutions (Foucault 1997; Cruikshank 1999). In an awkward way, the Foucauldian approach mirrored the stated ambition of the rehabilitation programmes employed in many if not most Western prisons. According to the official policy, the average prisoner had to be remodelled, according to ideas on social skills and anger management, which reflected labour market needs in the lower tiers of the service sector at the time (Hörnqvist 2010). To what extent subjects were in fact reconstituted was a matter of discussion. From one perspective, the prison appeared as a site for the production of wage labour, educating for the labour market opportunities awaiting inmates upon release. The productive techniques would compensate for the failure of previous attempts of subject formation within other institutions such as the family or the school. From a different perspective, the prison was a showroom intended for an outside audience: an ideological projection of an ordered microcosm of obedient wage labourers into the perceived chaos of unemployment and criminality (Hörnqvist 2008; 2013). Pleasure was analytically peripheral on both accounts. The problematic entailed a focus on how subjects were moulded through penal techniques, as opposed to how punishment operated in the gap between desire and satisfaction.

Although mostly associated with the Foucauldian tradition, the problematic of subject formation dictated research also beyond that tradition, as Durkheim's insight that the spectators were the central figure – punishment mainly exerts 'its effect upon honest people' (Durkheim 1997: 63) – came full circle, with the cultural turn, starting in the 1990s. Cultural representations, rather than organizational programmes and professional discourses, were considered to be the matter out of which subjects were moulded. If the impact on the audience was at best peripheral in Foucauldian approaches, in this context, it was crucial from the outset in a neo-Durkheimian context. The central assumption was that the vast majority come to know about punishment through consumption of popular culture. The audience was barred from the prison, except as visitors to friends and next of kin, and few people build their notions of contemporary punishments on first-hand experiences. Hence, the consumption of punishment migrated into popular culture. Punishment was no less present in everyday life. But it was enjoyed privately. Starting with Edgar Allen Poe and the Gothic literature (Smith 2009), enjoyment of punishment would predominantly take place in private. Punishment was consumed privately, comfortably on the sofa with a crime novel, by playing prison management games on the computer, watching documentaries on police brutality, or TV shows on prison gangs, or anyway vastly removed from the grim realities of punishment. Michelle Brown used the term 'penal spectator' to account for the audience's complicity, and raised the question what punishment does to us, at the level of emotions and self-conceptions. We must understand 'what kinds of subjectivities develop' as ordinary citizens consume punishment through popular culture (Brown 2009: 5). In a similar vein, Austin Sarat, picking up on Nietzsche's claims in the *Genealogy*, argued that cultural representations of capital punishment, for instance in popular films such as *Dead Man Walking*, not only shaped our conception of the death penalty but also contributed to the constitution of the modern, responsible subject (Sarat 1999; 2001). Embedded in both accounts was the concern that widespread cultural exposure to punishment produces a certain moral insensitivity on the part of the audience. Inadvertently, we learn to accept cruelty as part of the basic fabric of society. Punishment may thus affect our moral character, as well as other aspects of self-images or subjectivities. Once again, however, given the problematic of subject formation, there was little space for pleasure as an experience in everyday life, or how punishment operates in the gap between desire and satisfaction.

The consequences were wide-ranging in terms of scholarly lack of interest. There is a body of work in psychoanalysis (Freud 1955; Lacan 1992) and cultural theory (Žižek 1994; Eagleton 2005) which asserts that there is a persisting link between pleasure and the consumption of pain. The spectators' enjoyment, before as well as after the abolition of public executions, has been briefly touched upon at the periphery of the sociology of punishment

(Carrabine 2012; Hörnqvist 2013; Carvalho and Chamberlen 2018; Garland 1990). But the theme did not fit squarely into the shared historicization of pleasure, associated with Elias, Durkheim and Foucault, and has received limited attention in research on modern punishment. If it was not effectively historicized, it was treated as an obscure side-effect of power, associated with psychoanalytic insights into the irrational depths of the human psyche. While acutely attentive to pain, and meticulously tracking the transformation of pain within the modern institutions of punishment, from Sykes (1958) over Christie (1981) to Crewe (2011), social theory on modern punishment has not investigated pleasure, or the way in which punishment operates in the gap between desire and satisfaction.

The disappearance of pleasure in social theory may have been paradigmatic in the narrow sense: an effect of concerns and interests being located elsewhere, as opposed to the result of elaborate lines of reasoning, specifically to deny or to diminish the experience. At the same time, there is a long tradition of philosophical argumentation, starting in Ancient Greece, that was acutely aware of the passions associated with punishment and for this reason sought to erase them. The arguments of Kant and Bentham, briefly discussed in this chapter, as well as those of Aquinas, were part of that tradition. The passions were seen to be ever-present, threatening to undermine punishment from within: hence, the objective to purge punishment from passions, and make it rational. The distinction between punishment and vengeance was one central topic which drew on the more general opposition between reason and passion. Institutional developments, the slow monopolization of punishment by the state, the gradual evolution of an apparatus of criminal justice, and, in the nineteenth century, the invention of modern police forces and penitentiary systems staffed by officials incorporating the ethos of legality, further served to erase passions from punishment. The attempts culminated in the establishment of a concept of punishment in the mid-twentieth century, which focused strictly on the rule-based imposition of pain and avoided any mention of passions. Rational punishment finally seemed to be separated from impassionate vengeance. Yet it was a futile endeavour. The next chapter traces the impossible flight from passion which led to the modern understanding of punishment while retrieving what was left behind: the dimension of passion, excess, and social morality.

References

Aly, Götz, and Heim, Susanne (2002) *Architects of annihilation: Auschwitz and the logic of destruction*. Princeton: Princeton University press.
Aquinas, Thomas (1941) *Summa Theologica*. London: Burns Oates & Washbourne.
Banner, Stuart (2002) *The death penalty: an American history*. Cambridge: Harvard University Press.
Bauman, Zygmunt (1989) *Modernity and the holocaust*. Cambridge: Polity.
Bedau, Hugo (2004) Bentham's Theory of Punishment: Origin and Content. *Journal of Bentham Studies* 7(1): 1–15.

Bentham, Jeremy (1843a) Panopticon; or, The Inspection-House. *The Works of Jeremy Bentham* Vol IV. London: Simpkin, Marshall & Co. pp 39–66.

Bentham, Jeremy (1843b) Principles of Penal Law. *The Works of Jeremy Bentham.* Vol. I. London: Simpkin, Marshall & Co. pp 365–580.

Bessler, John (1997) *Death in the dark: midnight executions in America.* Boston, MA: Northeastern University Press.

Bosworth, Mary (2007) Creating the responsible prisoner: Federal admission and orientation packs. *Punishment and Society* 9(1): 67–85.

Brenner, Charles (1957) The nature and development of the concept of repression in Freud's writings. *The Psychoanalytic Study of the Child* 12(1): 19–46.

Brown, Michelle (2009) *The culture of punishment: prison, society, and spectacle.* New York: New York University Press.

Burke, Peter (2009) *Popular culture in early modern Europe.* Farnham: Ashgate.

Butler, Judith (1987) *Subjects of desire: Hegelian reflections in twentieth-century France.* New York: Columbia University Press.

Butler, Judith (1997) *The psychic life of power: theories in subjection.* Stanford, CA: Stanford Univ. Press.

Camus, Albert (1988) Reflections on the guillotine. *Resistance, rebellion, and death.* New York: Vintage International. pp 173–234.

Carrabine, E. (2012) Telling prison stories: the spectacle of punishment and the criminological imagination. In L. Cheliotis (ed.), *The arts of imprisonment: control, resistance and empowerment.* Farnham: Ashgate.

Carvalho, Henrique, and Chamberlen, Anastasia (2018) Why punishment pleases: punitive feelings in a world of hostile solidarity. *Punishment & Society* 20(2): 217–234.

Christie, Nils (1981) *Limits to pain: the role of punishment in penal policy.* Eugene, OR: Wipf and Stock.

Civitarese, Guiseppe (2016) On sublimation. *International Journal of Psychoanalysis,* 97: 1369–1392.

Crewe, Ben (2011) Depth, weight, tightness: revisiting the pains of imprisonment. *Punishment and Society* 13(5): 509–529.

Cruikshank, Barbara (1999) *The will to empower: democratic citizens and other subjects.* Ithaca, NY: Cornell University Press.

Dean, Mitchell (1999) *Governmentality: power and rule in modern society.* London: Sage.

Durkheim, Émile (1984) The evolution of punishment. In S. Lukes and A. Scull (eds.), *Durkheim and the law.* Oxford: Blackwell. pp 102–132.

Durkheim, Émile (1997) *The division of labor in society.* New York: Free Press.

Eagleton, Terry (2005) *Holy terror.* Oxford: Oxford University Press.

Elias, Norbert (2012) *On the process of civilisation: sociogenetic and psychogenetic investigations.* Dublin: University College Dublin Press.

Elias, Norbert, and Dunning, Eric (2008) *Quest for excitement: sport and leisure in the civilizing process.* Dublin: University College Dublin Press.

Evans, Richard (1996) *Rituals of retribution: capital punishment in Germany 1600–1987.* Oxford: Oxford University Press.

Foucault, Michel (1979) *Discipline and punish: the birth of the prison.* New York: Vintage Books.

Foucault, M. (1980) *Power/knowledge: selected interviews and other writings 1972–1977.* C. Gordon (ed.). New York: Pantheon Books.

Foucault, Michel (1997) *Ethics: subjectivity and truth. Essential works of Foucault, Volume 1.* P. Rabinow (ed.). New York: The New Press.

Foucault, Michel (1998) *The will to knowledge. The History Of Sexuality, Volume 1.* Harmondsworth: Penguin.

Foucault, Michel (2003) *'Society must be defended'. Lectures at the Collège de France 1975–76.* M. Bertani and A. Fontana (eds.). New York: Picador.

Freud, Sigmund (1919) *Eine Kindheitserinnerung des Leonardo da Vinci.* Leipzig: Deuticke.

Freud, Sigmund (1931) *Das Unbehagen in der Kultur.* Wien: Internationaler psychoanalytischer Verlag.

Freud, Sigmund (1955) *Totem and taboo and other works. The standard edition of the complete psychological works of Sigmund Freud. Vol. 13 (1913–1914).* London: Hogarth.

Garland, David (1990) *Punishment and modern society: a study in social theory.* Oxford: Clarendon.

Garland, David (2010) *Peculiar institution: America's death penalty in an age of abolition.* Oxford: Oxford University Press.

Gatrell, V. A. C. (1994) *The hanging tree: execution and the English people 1770–1868.* Oxford: Oxford University Press.

Gemes, Ken (2009) Freud and Nietzsche on sublimation. *Journal of Nietzsche Studies* 38: 38–59.

Henrichs, Albert (1984) Loss of self, suffering, violence: the modern view of Dionysus from Nietzsche to Girard. *Harvard Studies in Classical Philology* 88: 205–240.

Hobbes, Thomas (1996) *Leviathan.* Oxford: Oxford University Press.

Hörnqvist, Magnus (2008) The imaginary constitution of wage labourers. In P. Carlen (ed.), *Imaginary penalities.* Willan: Cullompton. pp 172–192.

Hörnqvist, Magnus (2010) *Risk, power, and the state: after Foucault.* Abingdon: Routledge.

Hörnqvist, Magnus (2013) Pleasure, punishment and the professional middle class. In D. Scott (ed.), *Why prison?* Cambridge: Cambridge University Press. pp 89–107.

Ignatieff, Michael (1978) *A just measure of pain: the penitentiary in the industrial revolution, 1750–1850.* London: Macmillan.

Kant, Immanuel (2006) *Anthropology from a pragmatic point of view.* Cambridge: Cambridge University Press.

Kavanagh, Thomas (2010) *Enlightened pleasures: eighteenth-century France and the new Epicureanism.* New Haven: Yale University Press.

Lacan, J. (1992) *The seminar of Jacques Lacan. Book VII. The ethics of psychoanalysis: 1959–1960.* New York/London: W. W. Norton.

Laqueur, Thomas (1989) Crowds, carnival and the state in English executions, 1604 – 1868. In A. Beier, D. Cannadine and J. Rosenheim (eds.), *The first modern society: essays in English history in honour of Lawrence Stone.* Cambridge: Cambridge University Press. pp 305–356.

Linebaugh, Peter (1975) The Tyburn riot against the surgeons. In D. Hay et al. (eds.), *Albion's fatal tree: crime and society in eighteenth-century England.* London: Allen Lane. pp 65–117.

Lynch, Mona (2000) On-line executions: the symbolic use of the electric chair in cyberspace. *Political and Legal Anthropology Review* 23(2): 1–20.

Melossi, Dario, and Pavarini, Massimo (1981) *The prison and the factory: origins of the penitentiary system.* London: Macmillan.

Millan, Matteo (2017) Origins. In J. Arthurs, M. Ebner and K. Ferris (eds.), *The politics of everyday life in fascist Italy: outside the state?* New York: Palgrave Macmillan. pp 19–49.

McGowen, Randall (1986) A powerful sympathy: terror, the prison, and humanitarian reform in early nineteenth-century Britain. *Journal of British Studies* 25(3): 312–334.

McGowen, Randall (2000) Revisiting the hanging tree. *British Journal of Criminology* 40(1): 1–13.

Nabokov, Vladimir (1983) *Lectures on Don Quixote.* New York: Harcourt Brace Jovanovich.

Nietzsche, Friedrich (1967) *The birth of tragedy.* New York: Vintage Books.

Nietzsche, Friedrich (1989) *On the genealogy of morals.* New York: Vintage Books.

Nietzsche, Friedrich (1997) *Daybreak. Thoughts on the prejudices of morality.* Cambridge: Cambridge University Press.

O'Malley, Pat (2004) *Risk, uncertainty and government.* London: Glasshouse Press.

Pfeifer, Michael (2004) *Rough justice: lynching and American society, 1874–1947.* Urbana: University of Illinois Press.

Phillips, Luke (2015) Sublimation and the Übermensch. *Journal of Nietzsche Studies* 46: 349–366.

Porter, Roy (1996) Enlightenment and pleasure. In R. Porter and M. Roberts (eds.), *Pleasure in the eighteenth century.* Basingstoke: Macmillan.

Pratt, John (2000) Emotive and ostentatious punishment: its decline and resurgence in modern society. *Punishment & Society* 2(4): 417–439.

Rose, Nikolas, and Miller, Peter (1992) Political power beyond the state: problematics of government. *British Journal of Sociology* 43(2): 173–205.

Rusche, Georg, and Kirchheimer, Otto (1939) *Punishment and social structure.* New York: Columbia University Press.

Sandén, Annika (2016) *Bödlar: liv, död och skam i svenskt 1600-tal.* Stockholm: Atlantis.

Sarat, Austin (1999) The cultural life of capital punishment. In A. Sarat (ed.), *The killing state: capital punishment in law, politics, and culture.* New York: Oxford University Press. pp 226–256.

Sarat, Austin (2001) *When the state kills: capital punishment and the American condition.* Princeton: Princeton University Press.

Sarat, Austin (2014) *Gruesome spectacles: botched executions and America's death penalty.* Stanford University Press.

Schuster, Aaron (2016) *The trouble with pleasure: Deleuze and psychoanalysis.* Cambridge, MA: MIT Press.

Sebag Montefiore, Simon (2004) *Stalin: the court of the red tsar.* New York: Knopf.

Smith, Caleb (2009) *Prison and the American imagination.* Yale: Yale University Press.

Smith, Philip (2008) *Punishment and culture.* Chicago: University of Chicago Press.

Spierenburg, Pieter (1984) *The spectacle of suffering: executions and the evolution of repression: from a preindustrial metropolis to the European experience.* Cambridge: Cambridge University Press.

Spierenburg, Pieter (1991) *The prison experience: disciplinary institutions and their inmates in early modern Europe.* Amsterdam: Amsterdam University Press.

Sykes, Gresham (1958) *The society of captives: a study of a maximum security prison.* Princeton: Princeton University Press.

Wilf, Steven (1993) Imagining justice: aesthetics and public executions in late eighteenth-century England. *Yale Journal of Law and the Humanities* 5(1): 51–78.

Žižek, Slavoj (1994) *The metastases of enjoyment.* London: Verso.

2 The impossible flight from passion

The modern concept of punishment was captured by H. L. A. Hart in his presidential address before the Aristotelian Society in October 1959. In the speech, later published as 'Prolegomenon to the Principles of Punishment' in the *Proceedings* of the society, he offered a definition, drawing on discussions with fellow British legal philosophers. The standard case of punishment bore five characteristics:

(i)   It must involve pain or other consequences normally considered unpleasant.
(ii) It must be for an offence against legal rules.
(iii) It must be of an actual or supposed offender for [the] offence.
(iv) It must be intentionally administered by human beings other than the offender.
(v)   It must be imposed and administered by an authority constituted by a legal system against which the offence is committed. (Hart 1959: 4)

Punishment was equated with the rule-based imposition of pain by a legal system. It was principled, proportionate, state-administered and crime-centred. The definition satisfied the high demands on clarity articulated within the contemporary philosophical community. It was the perfect combination of conceptual rigour and common sense. But the definition was also noteworthy for what it omitted. It contained no reference to personal interest, or to principles other than legal rules. There were no references to passion, to social morality or to recognition of status – aspects that had been integral to punishment in other historical contexts. Since its publication, the presidential address has been the natural point of reference for a large body of works on punishment (Brooks 2012; Fassin 2018). Needless to say, the definition has attracted criticism for neglecting some aspects (Feinberg 1970; Packer 1968). But the suggested amendments often involved only marginal changes. Hart's conception has been highly influential and surprisingly uncontroversial.

Above all else, the understanding was specifically modern. In this chapter, I will discuss the modern understanding of punishment, and the long and winding path that led to punishment being seen as impersonal enforcement of legal violations, and what was forgotten along the way. If it seemed uncontroversial, in the context of mid-twentieth-century Britain, it was not only because the concept corresponded to the penal arrangements at the time, but also because of its prehistory: a history that can be dated back to the fourth century BCE. The modern conception of punishment was the tentative end point of countless intellectual interventions and institutional changes to efface passion. This chapter reconstructs some steps on the way to the modern concept of punishment, based on some of the many attempts to separate punishment and vengeance. The steps were taken in philosophical discourse, as well as in institutional practice. As will be the procedure in this chapter, and in the following three chapters, some of the most influential contemporary philosophers – Plato, Aristotle, Aquinas, Hobbes and Hegel – will be read against the background of available knowledge on the institutional conditions of punishment at the time: the classical democratic period in ancient Athens, the thirteenth-century Catholic Europe, and the early-modern absolutist states, respectively. Starting with ancient Greece and the first known attempts to distinguish between punishment and vengeance, I will follow the construction of the modern conception, while at the same time retrieving what was left behind – and thus uncovering what had been suppressed, although essential to understand the modern predicament: the dimension of passion, excess, social morality and recognition of status. All the philosophers discussed in this chapter were above all trying to find the best way to cope with intentional acts of wrong-doing. Their immediate concern was to establish what characterized legitimate punishment. However, beyond the delicate, normative question of justification, they all engaged with the complex role of passions, and were aware of the presence of strong emotions, including pleasure, hatred and indignation, and their potentially destabilizing impact. Rereading the philosophical arguments, against the background of available scholarship on the historical context, will reveal a space between rational punishment and impassioned revenge, which has been filled with righteous anger, and imperatives of status restoration, amongst other things.

Distinguishing punishment from vengeance

Throughout the Western tradition of thought, punishment has been haunted by the fear of passions. Conceptual and institutional barriers have been erected and re-erected to keep passion in check. By far the most important barrier was the distinction between punishment and vengeance. Plato is generally credited with the idea. In *Protagoras*, he contrasted rational punishment with mindless revenge. The wider topic concerned virtuous behaviour: could it be taught, or was it innate? Protagoras, after whom the dialogue was named, was giving a speech on the origins of morality. His position was that virtue and morality were acquired through learning. Many people no doubt had difficulties in complying with existing norms. Yet given the right kind of interventions, their behaviour might be changed. Punishment could be such an intervention to effect change. In another dialogue, Plato compared punishment with medication. The judge was like a doctor, who cured the perpetrator-patient through a bitter cure of flogging, fines or prison (*Gorgias* 480b–d). With the right dosage, punishment could be instrumental in bringing about behavioural change. Vengeance, on the other hand, was ill-suited to effect changes for the better. Punishment was differentiated from vengeance: to 'punish in a rational way' was the opposite of retaliating 'unthinkingly like an animal' (*Protagoras* 324b). Whereas punishment was forward-oriented and took the future behaviour of the perpetrator into consideration, vengeance was merely concerned with past injustices. Above all, however, punishment was rational, as it was issued from the principles of reason, and not from passion. That was the main principle of differentiation: to simply seek revenge was to act 'unthinkingly like an animal'. Aristotle would later make use of the same metaphor in his arguments for governance according to the law: 'for appetite is like a wild animal, and also passion warps the rule even of the best men' (*Politics* 1287a). Since it was guided by passion and fully preoccupied with a past injustice, which by definition could not be undone, vengeance was thus unlikely to change the behaviour of the perpetrator, and more likely to effect harm at the societal level.

It has been said, with respect to the passage in *Protagoras*, that the distinction between punishment and vengeance 'must be regarded as one of the most momentous discoveries ever made by humanity' (Vlastos 1991: 187; see also Pauley 1994). Given the sketchy character of Plato's comments, and against the background of the existing penal practices, this might have been to overstate the case. Plato advocated the idea of rational punishment against the background of Athenian judicial institutions that were characterized by private vengeance and elite rivalry. In everyday life and culture, it was difficult to establish any foothold for a distinction between punishment and vengeance, in the sense that these terms have come to be understood today. There were no public prosecutors and no professional police force (Allen 2000). The Athenian courts were the only institution which bore any semblance to a modern criminal justice system. The courts were central pillars of the young democracy. Contemporary Athenians, it has been argued, saw the court as a forum for the common people to adjudicate in matters of rivalry and conflict within the elite (Cohen 1995). To what extent they also corresponded to modern ideas of justice has been the subject of intense discussion. Some argue that the courts testified to an emerging commitment to the rule of law, while other scholars argue that the courts merely provided additional instruments to exact vengeance (Forsdyke 2018; Cohen 1995). The legal codes were vaguely formulated, and the many ordinary citizens in the jury were not legally trained. While some of the contemporary penal techniques, such as fines, capital punishment and even prisons, would also be employed in the modern era, the responsibility for implementing punishments, even when issued by a public court, was often left to private citizens. The city-state had few organizational resources to enforce guilty verdicts (Allen 2000; Lanni

2016). But the idea had been planted. Plato's intervention set the terms of the future discussion, by introducing the idea that punishment could be made rational. Simultaneously, another idea was advanced, which would prove to be just as significant: that this required the suppression of volatile passions.

Since Plato, the difference between punishment and vengeance has been a recurring theme in Western thought. The idea of rational punishment, first advanced in *Protagoras*, initiated a long tradition, according to which the problem is separating what is vengeance and what is punishment, or to cleanse all traces of vengeance from punishment, and in particular all forms of irrational desire and emotions. With rational punishment poised against passionate revenge, the terms of the debate were set. The currently most influential articulation of the distinction was produced by Robert Nozick in *Philosophical Explanations*. On his analysis, vengeance came forth as the very opposite of punishment. It constituted the inverted image of the modern conception of punishment. As can be taken from the list of five features, vengeance was passionate, personal, irrational, excessive, and not necessarily based on a legal violation. The first three features of revenge were:

   (i)   revenge may be done for a perceived harm or slight, as opposed to a
         legal violation;
  (ii)   revenge was inherently limitless, as opposed to being proportionate and
         limited;
 (iii)   revenge was personal, as opposed to impartial and unconcerned.
         (Nozick 1981: 367)

The fifth feature concerned the presumed lack of generality; revenge was particular and did not comply with universal principles. The most intriguing feature was the fourth one. It is worth quoting the fourth criteria *in extenso* as it deals with the element of passion and pleasure, which saturated revenge but was virtually absent from retributive punishment.

> Revenge involves a particular emotional tone, pleasure at the suffering
> of another, while retribution either need involve no emotional tone or
> involve another one, namely pleasure at justice being done.
>
> (Nozick 1981: 367)

Whereas revenge was deeply emotional, and derived pleasure from the pain of others, punishment was either entirely free from passions or confined to the 'pleasure at justice being done'. Nozick's formulation suggests a moral or intellectual satisfaction, reasonable and potentially highly justified but very bleak in comparison with the passions of vengeance. As a whole, the distinction echoed a number of binary oppositions that have been invoked ever since Plato: the opposition between good and bad, law and honour, reason and passion, personal and impersonal, proportionate and disproportionate. None of these oppositions has been subject to more discussion and more detailed scrutiny than the opposition between passion and reason. So, if vengeance was 'inherently limitless', illicit, personal and disproportionate at the same time, that was fundamentally because it would not heed the commands of reason and was led astray by passions.

Until the nineteenth century, the distinction between punishment and vengeance carried a substantial amount of unfulfilled promise. The modern notion of punishment presupposed the evolution of a corresponding notion of crime and a separate sphere of criminal justice organized by the state. And this evolution was slow and by no means unilineal. During long stretches of Western history, private vengeance was the dominant form of punishment. The entire Middle Ages 'lived under the sign of private vengeance', and it was imposed 'as the most sacred of duties' (Bloch 1965: 125). Revenge was mandatory and private for those who had been wronged. In early-medieval Europe, there were no legal institutions that were separate from other social institutions, in terms of personnel or procedure (Berman 1983). Society was a patchwork of jurisdictions – with different rules for lay commoners, for the nobility, for the clergy, often in competition. Private and public law were intertwined and not clearly distinguishable from one another (Møller and Skaaning 2014). The imposition of punishment was guided by personal, by religious as well as rank considerations. Official relationships of power retained a personal character. The bond was personal, and so was the breaking of the bond. To members of the medieval society, legal rules had no universal validity, as the protector of a common good. Instead, it has been argued, 'law was viewed as a tool of vendetta and revenge' (Hanawalt and Wallace 1999: x). Passions, anger above all, were seen to be inextricably part of punishment, and one major line of demarcation was drawn between just anger and vengeful anger. Medieval literature is full of descriptions of royalties who – guided by anger – incurred excessive revenge in ways that contrasted sharply to the official virtues of rulership, such as clemency, mercy and justice (Althoff 1998). Contemporaries would thus distinguish between righteous and illegitimate revenge, rather than between punishment and revenge. Against this background, Aquinas insisted on precisely this further distinction: between punishment and vengeance. In the heart of Catholic Europe of the late thirteenth century, he held the view that there was a difference. Yet it was difficult to discern the difference, based on the existing penal practices and institutions, for similar reasons as in Ancient Greece; punishment assumed private forms, in the absence of states and public bodies with the capacity to prosecute offenders and execute punishments.

Conceptually, this posed a challenge, which was taken up in *Summa Theologica*. Aquinas could not find the line of demarcation within existing penal practices. The means employed were the same in both cases. Revenge made use of the 'means of punishment customary among men', and thus operated by depriving individuals of what they loved the most, such as life or liberty, riches or reputation (ST II-II, Q 108 A 3). Vengeance and punishment consequently imposed the same kind of suffering with the same methods. To complicate things further, punishment was not necessarily more legitimate, or more rational – the two aspects stressed by Plato and Aristotle. Vengeance could follow the dictates of reason and be legitimate, just like punishment. An act of revenge was justified, provided that the intention was to achieve some greater good, such as to uphold justice or to honour God. Instead, Aquinas highlighted another opposition, which would become an important element in the modern conception of punishment: the opposition between public and private. The objective of punishment was the common good. It was executed in view of the peace and virtue of all members of society, whereas private vindication constituted the goal of revenge (ST I-II, Q 96, A 3; see also Koritansky 2005). Anybody could make use of 'the means of punishment customary among men' based on some notion of wrongful behaviour, but not necessarily with the common good in mind. The public-private opposition covered the manner in which the pain was imposed, how decisions were taken, and with what objective in mind. Vengeance was associated with vested interests and private initiatives. Punishment, on the other hand, had to be imposed by a public body authorized by law. Although such bodies may have been in short supply, at the time of writing, Aquinas argued that 'to punish pertains to none but the framer of the law, by whose authority the pain is inflicted' (ST I-II, Q 92, A 2, ad. 3).

At the beginning of the early-modern period, Thomas Hobbes would repeat the need for a public body. In *Leviathan*, the chapter on punishment commenced with a definition that stressed its non-private character. Punishment was 'an evil inflicted by public authority, on him that hath done, or omitted that which is judged by the same authority to be a transgression of the law' (Hobbes 1996: 205). At first sight, Thomas Hobbes came close to the modern understanding of punishment as the rule-based imposition of pain by a legal system, targeting individuals who had been found guilty of crime. In *Leviathan*, as well as in other works, Hobbes stressed the justified and the rational, the proportionate and the public character of punishment, as opposed to vengeance, which depended on the passions of individuals, such as anger, hatred or ambitiousness (Gutnick-Allen 2016). The passions made vengeance unreasonable and dangerous. The illegitimacy of vengeance was, however, not fundamentally grounded in lack of rationality. Unlike Aquinas, Hobbes held that there was no legitimate vengeance on the part of the individual members of society. It did not matter how reasonable or justified it appeared to be. Hobbes's hostility towards vengeance was a corollary of the proposed violence monopoly of the sovereign, which in turn reflected the ongoing institutional changes in late-medieval Europe. The emerging nation states were monopolizing punishment, in competition with the church, feudal institutions and local judicial practices (Merback 1999; Spierenburg 1984; Giddens 1985). The increases in administrative capacity to enforce legal violations, to collect taxes and to make war on other nations were all crucial elements of state formation, and the right to private vengeance was suppressed in the process. The ultimate rationale of punishment was the common good. According to the doctrine of sovereignty, punishment was entrusted to state institutions in return for everybody's protection. At the same time, it incorporated an element of personal revenge. While substituting the feudal practices, the early-modern public executions retained a number of the characteristics traditionally associated with vengeance (Spierenburg 1984; Foucault 1979). Even when directed at transgressions of the criminal law, punishment contained aspects of status restoration, over-compensating for the violation of the sovereign's standing. Hence, punishment was not fully compatible with modern understandings and continued to have a private and wilful character, long after national criminal codes were established.

The differences between punishment and vengeance were fleeting well into the nineteenth century. But in the *Philosophy of Right*, published in 1820, Hegel argued that vengeance had been fully overcome by punishment.

> When right is posited as law and is known, every accident of feeling vanishes together with the form of revenge, sympathy, and selfishness.
>
> (Hegel 1952, §211)

Organizational practice and philosophical ideal were, on this analysis, no longer in contradiction. Punishment was universal and adhered to binding rules, and there was no longer any place for revenge. To Hegel, like other political philosophers before him, vengeance encapsulated the very opposite to punishment. But whereas Plato and Aquinas advocated the idea of punishment against the background of penal practices characterized by private vengeance, and Hobbes and Kant presupposed a public court system and a common criminal code, along with the sporadic outburst of sovereign vengeance at the scaffold, at the time of Hegel's writing, there had in addition evolved a distinct criminal justice system: large state organizations for the investigation of crime and for the execution of punishment. In many European countries, the early to mid-nineteenth century witnessed the emergence of a criminal justice apparatus, built around professional police forces and large correctional services. The police, the prisons and the courts were professional bureaucracies: rule-governed organizations staffed with state officials, who came to develop a bureaucratic ethos. Legal training and formal merit were gaining precedence over personal ties and aristocratic virtues (Kocka 2004; Lacey 2016). The evolution of the modern state was decisive, as perceptibly captured in the *Philosophy of Right*. Early on in his career, in the aftermath of the French revolution, Hegel was convinced that the transformation of vengeance into punishment required social institutions with the ability to abstract from the personal. That was a key mission of the state (Hegel 1998; Schmidt 2007). The later Hegel, the author of the *Philosophy of Right*, elaborated what it meant – or should mean – that punishment was administered by a state with a sizeable criminal justice apparatus. The personal and everything particular were sidelined for the sake of universality. When judicial processes were run on an everyday basis by civil servants, 'every accident of feeling' disappeared: anger and vengeful desires, pity as well as spite and prejudice. State officials, such as police and correctional officers, or judges, took the necessary decisions but left no personal mark. 'Those who administer justice are persons, but their will is the universal will of the law' (Hegel 1952: §102). Governance was strictly rational, devoid of emotions and unaffected by passions.

In the 1830s, the notion of *Rechtsstaat* was coined to capture the new principles of government. The notion developed out of Germany and later spread throughout the continent, and analogous expressions can be found in many European languages: in French, Italian and Swedish. The best English approximation is the 'rule of law' (Costa 2007; Zolo 2007). It was initially conceived as a critique of sovereignty; the idea gained strength in the nineteenth century, after centuries of autocratic rule of hereditary monarchs. As opposed to the unbounded power, envisioned by theorists of sovereignty, and its wilful deployment in practice, Rudolf von Jhering and Georg Jellinek, who were the legal engineers of the *Rechtsstaat*, stressed the necessary restraint of power, the self-limitation of the state. All citizens were attributed with a legal sphere which offered protection from undue administrative intrusions (Costa 2007). Punishment and any other coercive state interventions had to be foreseeable, and they should be applied impartially and universally, in a manner which respected the rights of individuals, in their capacity as citizens in a state rather than as subjects of a sovereign. In many respects, the rule of law had a long prehistory. The idea that all government of men must comply with impartial rules – one principal element of the *Rechtsstaat* – can be traced back to antiquity (Sellers 2014; Forsdyke 2018), as well as to medieval times (Tierney 1982: Møller and Skaaning 2014). In the modern sense, however, the rule of law presupposed a fully fledged state monopoly of violence, along with the build-up of professional bureaucracies. The successful concentration of punishment in the criminal justice apparatus not only phased out early-modern penal practices and pushed competitors to the side. It also meant the state could constrain its representatives from excessive outbursts of power. Passion, particularity and personal interest were counterposed by rule-based regulation and further constrained by legal rights entrusted to individual citizens. Punishment, it appeared, had finally been purged from passion.

It has been said about punishment in the nineteenth century that it needed 'to be dispassionate in order to be just' (McBride 2007: 8). In principle all strong emotions should disappear from the public surface of penal practice. And by the end of the century, punishment did seem to be dispassionate, and successfully cut off from vengeful desires. The cleansing of passion, the long campaign starting with Plato, to eradicate passion from punishment, seemed to have been settled with the establishment of a state-administered criminal justice system, governed by principles of impartiality and universality. From this perspective, the rapid decrease of visible signs of enjoyment at the scenes of punishment was not only a function of changes in social morality, but also actively pursued in political theory, as well as firmly rooted in administrative reforms. All vestiges of private passion were confidently brushed to the side in Hegel's *Philosophy of Right*, as well as in the legal notion of *Rechtsstaat*. The resolution may ultimately have been philosophical, but it was under-pinned by institutional change. In the following century, the process of sep-aration from vengeance would continue. Official discourse on punishment was further stripped of emotions, as punishment came to rely on the dis-passionate search for scientific truth (Pratt 2002). The bureaucratic ethos of state officials would be reinforced by the powerful sanitizing force of psych-ology and medical science. As a consequence, in 1959, the notion of pun-ishment as state-administered imposition of pain for legal violations could appear uncontroversial. Hart saw no need to mention passions. The modern concept of punishment rested on its successful separation from passion and revenge, and while many of the processes involved, above all the evolution of a criminal justice apparatus under state auspices, unfolded largely unper-turbed by philosophical argumentation, the separation was also the result of a protracted and very explicit discussion of the role of passions.

The dual role of anger

When some of the most influential philosophers in the Western tradition drew the boundary to vengeance, in the context of different historical situ-ations and penal practices, the most immediate concern was to establish what characterized legitimate punishment. They were moral philosophers, trying to find the right way to cope with intentional acts of wrong-doing. However, beyond the delicate, normative question of justification, they were all acutely aware of the ineradicable presence of strong emotions, including pleasure, hatred and indignation, and their potentially destabilizing impact. The modern concept of punishment can be seen to be born precisely out of this awareness. It incorporated a vision of an institution built on laws, rationality and universality, as opposed to social status, passion and personal interest. The volatile passions that went into and came out of punishment were not to be allowed to run the show. The fear that punishment would be undermined from within by the very passions it sought to address has been a constant con-cern, ever since Plato's days. Francis Bacon (1955) spoke of revenge as 'wild justice'; Cesare Beccaria warned that punishment must not be 'the instrument of furious fanaticism' (Beccaria 1778: 52), Immanuel Kant described the vengeful passions as 'often violent to the point of madness' (Kant 2006: 171) and Emile Durkheim called passion 'the soul of punishment', which 'ceases only when exhausted' (Durkheim 1997: 86), just to mention a few, well-known examples from different time periods. The formulations can be taken to convey the same basic insight, or moral concern. The element of trans-gression was endemic. Punishment for transgression may at any moment turn into a punishable transgression. There was a thin line between the making of justice and a new and avengeable injustice. While punishment stabilized authority, violent passions and notions of justice, it could at the same time be destabilized from within by the very passions and notions which punishment strove to satisfy, constantly driving it beyond the legally instituted boundaries. It was a dilemma, which has been acknowledged beyond the confines of particular scholarly traditions (Durkheim 1997; Shklar 1990; Eagleton 2005; Smith 2008; Adut 2018). Punishment tended to undermine itself. The basic justification was derived from the ordering mission, to recreate an endangered order, while constantly, in its ambition to do so, overstepping the principles derived from that order, and thus threatening to lose its basic justification.

The distinction between punishment and vengeance represented one approach to the dilemma. The two horns of the dilemma were attributed to punishment and vengeance, conceived of as separate and distinct activities. The distinction homogenized punishment, precisely by focusing so consistently on vengeance. Just as punishment was thought of as one thing, vengeance was *the* alternative, and hence everything that punishment was not. Punishment was by definition freed from emotional expressions of vengefulness, enjoyment or other powerful emotions, from private initiative and from excessive violence. The aura of aloofness, impartiality, legal security, foreseeability and legitimacy that came with the modern notion should make punishment into a powerful stabilizing force in the recreation of social order: that, and that only. By assigning passions and all forms of illegitimate action to vengeance, punishment was unburdened from its troubled history and the constant concern for passion-driven excess. Partly as a response to this easy way out of the dilemma, critiques have argued that the two practices are in many cases indistinguishable from one another, and that vengeance has been misrepresented. Historically, it was maintained, vengeance has been consistently associated with barbarity, whereas punishment was tied to civilization; one practice was chaotic and the other ordered (Zaibert 2006; Shoemaker 2005; Miller 1998). Now, while the dichotomy between civilization and barbarity may adequately represent the position taken by Hegel, or modern analytical philosophers such as Nozick, such sweeping remarks also tended to obscure a very different side of the Western tradition of thought, located in the space between reason and passion. Some of the most influential European philosophers did not think of vengeance as necessarily illegitimate, or barbaric. Notions of righteous revenge survived until the Enlightenment period, among philosophers, such as Thomas Aquinas (1941) and Immanuel Kant (2006). The desire for revenge was thought to be deeply grounded in both human inclination and social order, and not necessarily unjustified.

Plato may have been the central point of reference for the distinction between rational punishment and impassioned revenge. He was the rationalist philosopher with little sympathy for passion and public opinion in politics. He was the aristocratic critique of Athenian democracy and court practices, who looked down on 'sophists' like Isocrates, who sold their skills much like lawyers do today (Klosko 2006; Allen 2000). That being said, the simple opposition between reason and passion was foreign even to Plato. Although passions were generally considered as an inferior guide to human action, not all passions were bad. Certain passions that animated punishment were good, or good under certain circumstances. Plato discussed the topic, referring to the third element of the soul in the *Republic*. Somewhere in between reason and irrational passion, there was a whole dimension of human experience, which was activated in the process of punishment and which was partially embraced, up until the eighteenth century. Latter-day dichotomies carry the risk of misrepresenting the long and complex discussion of the role of passions in punishment, as well as, more specifically, foreclosing any discussion of pleasure and punishment that is not easily reducible to obscene enjoyment.

Anger was without any doubt the central passion in philosophical discussions on punishment before modernity. It was also the most problematic passion, and subject to conflicting valuations. In Ancient Greece, the dual role of anger in everyday life and culture came to expression in the classic tragedies (McHardy 2008). The tragedies enacted the free range of vengeful passions on stage. They showed how punitive anger could be destructive – fuelling never-ending cycles of mandatory vengeance, within families and between generations. For the leading characters, the consequences were disastrous no matter what they did, destroying whole families and initiating wars between city-states. In the *Oresteia*, written by Aeschylus, the entire city of Troy was sacked in response to a supposed abduction; a daughter was sacrificially killed by her vengeful father, who was then ambushed and killed by his wife, who went on to be murdered by her son. One injustice led to another, and the response was not contained by any legal institution. Only in the very end was a court summoned to settle the dispute. At the same time, anger was considered socially useful. There was 'an anger proper to a judge' (Macleod 1982: 129). In this capacity, as an instrument of justice, anger was valued positively. In *The Wasps*, a comedy by Aristophanes, the anger manifested in the courtroom was indispensable for the city-state's independence, in the wars against the Persians, and moreover helped the individuals guarding their honour (Allen 2000). Anger derived from social honour was commendable, if given direction by reason. Reason and passion were not opposed in a wholesale fashion. Instead, it was a matter of finding the right relationship between passion and reason. Anger regulated by reason was indispensable, whereas unreasonable anger was destructive. Nothing demonstrated the fundamental duality of anger better than the Furies, the Greek deities of vengeance. Although often presented as the arch-symbol of unreasonable fury, the Furies were at the same time, in the context of their most famous appearance, ultimate preservers of social order. For the most part of the *Oresteia*, the Furies help stage the intrafamilial killings and circles of revenge, and in the third part they continue to demand the death of Orestes, as punishment for murdering his mother. But the role of the Furies changes, as they take part in the resolution of the conflict. They participated in the trial against Orestes, and finally accepted the divine verdict that freed Orestes from punishment. In the very end, they assumed a new position on Acropolis as the city-state's protectors (Podlecki 1966; Goldhill 2004; for a contrary interpretation, see Schroeder 2004). The Furies appeared both as protectors and as destroyers of order. In both capacities, they were powered by anger, which stemmed from a shared pool of social morality and notions of honour.

Thomas Aquinas continued the discussion of the complex role of passions. In the context of Catholic Europe in the thirteenth century, anger was seen, also by essentially rationalist philosophers such as Aquinas, to have an indispensable role in the process of punishment. In *Summa Theologica*, in deliberating whether anger was a sin or not, Aquinas stressed that 'if one desire revenge to be taken in accordance with the order of reason, the desire of anger is praiseworthy' (ST II-II, Q 158, A 2, co.). Anger had to be tempered and given direction by reason, only then was it a useful vehicle for justice. It was, however, difficult to distinguish between virtuous and sinful anger, even at the level of theory. Like all passions, anger was subject to double standards: Aristotelian notions of virtue and Christian notions of sin. Anger was double-edged; both necessary and catastrophic; on the one hand a useful passion, and on the other hand a cardinal sin. At heart, it was not a sin. Aquinas saw anger as a passion triggered by experienced injustice, which motivated individuals to seek vindication (Miner 2009). Anger was positively connected to justice and human happiness. It was a basic emotional response, in the encounter with obstacles, injustice or pain, which frustrated the attainment of legitimate goals. In this sense, vengeful passions were conducive to human happiness (Knuutila 2004). At the same time, anger was a sin. The passion could lead astray, and give rise to punishment that was not at all deserved, in which case it was a cardinal sin. There was a fine line between anger as a vehicle for justice and anger as a cardinal sin. For an external observer it was difficult to determine which anger was justified. Instead, Aquinas directed attention to the intention of the actor; 'in the matter of vengeance, we must consider the mind of the avenger' (ST II-II, Q 108, A 1, co.). It was sinful, if the intention was to impose pain and suffering on the perpetrator. It was legitimate, if the intention was to achieve a greater good beyond the act of punishment. One might still wish to impose pain, yet the underlying objective had to be derived from reason and involve a greater good. It was a fine line – and a fine line with potentially huge implications for the one who was angry, since wrongful punishment might in turn be punished; in fact, punished in the harshest conceivable way, eternally in afterlife.

Aquinas proceeded from the assumption that 'punishment is referred to God as its first author' (ST I, Q 114, A 1, ad. 1). Human passions and penal practices were understood within the context of the Last Judgement. Divine justice in the afterlife, either in purgatory or in hell, added a further dimension to the institution of punishment. It was the aspect of a higher justice, which operated on sins, rather than on the violations of worldly laws. The afterworldly aspect duplicated the problem of vengeance, and put punishment administered by humans at severe risk. In the worst case, punishment would entail eternal damnation, as exemplified by the fate of archbishop Ruggieri in the *Divine Comedy*. In Dante's vision, the author was led by the Roman poet Virgil through hell. As they descended, the gravity of the sins increases and the punishments became ever more formidable. In a stony landscape, on one of the lower regions, the visiting couple find thieves, pimps, fraudsters and corrupt leaders mercilessly exposed to 'horned demons armed with heavy scourges', who were incessantly beating the naked backs of the crowd (*Inf.* Canto XVIII: 35). They continued wandering, and at the bottom of hell, among the punishments for the very worst transgressions, such as fratricide and treason, one of the most famous encounters in the entire *Inferno* took place. Submerged in ice, two souls had frozen together in a single hole and only their heads protruded from the ice. One head was constantly gnawing on the other. As the couple came within hearing distance, it turned out that the upper head belonged to count Ugolino della Gherardesca, who supposedly betrayed the city-state of Pisa in 1288. According to Dante, the count was a traitor, and hence could expect eternal damnation of the worst kind. What was perhaps more surprising was that the other head belonged to archbishop Ruggieri Rubaldino, who meted out della Gherardesca's worldly punishment after he was found guilty of treason. In hell, the archbishop is constantly being exposed to the count, who sinks 'his teeth into the other just where the brain's stem leaves the spinal cord' (*Inf.* Canto XXXII: 128–9). There was obviously a higher justice in operation that overruled existing legislations. The judge, who punished treason, ended up in a far worse situation in the afterlife than the one he originally punished, because he was judged by another judge, according to a law above the law. As it were, the archbishop's punishment in the afterlife was brought upon him by the punishment that he authorized in this life. He had imprisoned count della Gherardesca, together with his two sons and two grandchildren, in a tower in Pisa, where they would all die of starvation. Dante related the suffering of the children, locked up in the tower without food (*Inf.* Canto XXXIII). Their horrific fate was interpreted through the dual lens of Christian theology and public opinion at the time. To Dante, the punishment was more corrupt than the original crime of treason (Oreglia 1991). Count della Gherardesca may have betrayed the city, which he was set to protect, but archbishop Rubaldino went too far in the punishment of treason, as it included the innocent children. The archbishop should have restricted himself to punishing the count and spared his children, in which case he might have avoided Dante's inferno.

During the middle ages, the two-tier system of punishment was explicit, and one could find comfort or, alternatively, cause for concern in the idea of a divine justice, which put all kinds of injustices on trial, including the excess that was endemic in punishment. The punishment of the archbishop and the count in the *Divine Comedy* illustrated the double recourse to a higher law. The archbishop was punished for his excessive punishment of the count. The second punishment (of the archbishop) was excessive as well, by most standards, but according to the principles of divine justice it was entirely justified. The idea of a higher justice, which under certain conditions justified excess, was not confined to the medieval world. Following the middle ages, ideas of the Last judgement gradually lost influence. But the empty space left by divine justice was filled by principles which were rooted in other historical contexts. The idea of a higher justice was incorporated in political theories of sovereignty during the early-modern period, and in notions of *raison d'état*, reasons of state which overruled the existing legislation (Foucault 2007). Principles above the law would continue to operate in modern contexts, to warrant officially prohibited and cruel acts of punishment. In modern contexts, these principles were often rooted in social morality, rather than derived from theories of the state or from religious notions of divine order. In contemporary contexts, transgressive punishments typically defy the criminal code but follow a higher law, which has been seen as a condensate of the way of life of the community (Žižek 1994). Emile Durkheim (1997) used the notion of collective consciousness (*conscience collective*) to account for the temperance of passions as well as for the persistence of the sacred in punishment. It captured the mundane aspects of moral condemnation while at the same time incorporating the transcendent qualities of punishment: the impression that the imposed justice relied on something more fundamental than the individuals involved. As sacred, it could operate as a higher principle sustaining excess (Smith 2008). To justify transgression is not normally the most prominent function of social morality; on the contrary, it is more often associated with moderation and convention. It tends to be implicit, or sedimented in actual practices, as emphasized by Hegel (1952), who foregrounded the lived morality (*Sittlichkeit*) as opposed to the abstract morality of Kant – universal principles, which were valid regardless of context. Yet under certain conditions, social morality may be hypostatized as justice and dictate punitive anger toward acts that deviate from its shared habits, normative expectations, and notions of the world (Paskewich 2014). In this capacity, social morality may sustain passion and excess, operating alongside the law, without being officially acknowledged as punishment.

Punishment as status restoration

Hart's famous definition epitomized the modern state-centred conception. Punishment was essentially impartial enforcement of the existing legislation – or, simply: law enforcement. Punishment was bound to one specific model: legal rules were the only conceivable ground for punishment and violations were thought of as crime. The definition did not allow for the invocation for other principles, which – if violated – may constitute ground for punishment. In the process of its establishment, the modern concept not only pushed passion and vengeance to the margins but also consigned competing principles of rule violation to oblivion. Historically, violations of the principles underlying the distribution of social esteem have frequently been punished. Perpetrators have been punished with the chief objective to restore status to the injured party. To use the word punishment in this context is to presume that punishment may be more than law enforcement. I believe that punishment can be many things, within certain perimeters. To my mind, the main criterion is cultural intelligibility: for something to be an act of punishment it must be recognizable as such by contemporaries. The pain imposed on the perpetrator should be felt to be deserved by contemporary audiences, on the grounds of a violation of some basic principle. People need not necessarily endorse the principle in question, the penal practices, or the specific punishment being meted out. Quite to the contrary, they may radically disagree. But they will perceive the traction of the principle being violated, and comprehend the intervention as punishment, and not as arbitrary cruelty, show of force or odd fancies. The intelligibility was cultural since it depended on shared notions of the world and shared social meanings. The staunch refusal to let Antigone bury her dead brother may for instance strike modern theatre audiences, watching Sophocles' famous play, as an odd fancy of the god Creon. The heroism of Antigone's defiance might even derive some of its force from the incomprehensibility of the divine dictate. Yet it was perfectly in accordance with the contemporary penal practices, and must have been understood as such, as punishment rather than as whimsical cruelty, by audiences at the Great Dionysia. Being executed without burial, placing the dead body in the open, for everybody to see, was the ultimate punishment in ancient Greece, because of its particularly dishonourable effect (Allen 2000). Antigone's insistence on burying her brother may have demonstrated a tension between the Homeric morality and the emerging civic ideology (Fowley 1995), but it was above all an attempt to rescue him from the worst infamy of contemporary penal practices.

In ancient Greece, the object of punishment was above all acts of disrespect. The acts themselves were not necessarily different. The Areopagus court made famous in the *Oresteia* specifically processed murders. Other Athenian courts processed transgressions that courts have attended to in many other societies as well: adultery, violence, theft, defamation, or fraud. While some of the actions being punished were crimes, on current understandings, what had been violated was not primarily the law but the social esteem of the injured party. The concern with social esteem was ingrained in the very notion of punishment. The most frequent Greek word for punishment was *timoria* and the verb 'to punish', *timoreisthai*, also meant 'to assess and to distribute honour' (Allen 2000: 61). To punish was to restore status and efface the mark of dishonour in relation to the community, or in the eyes of other people. One way to understand the function of punishment was along the transaction model: through the infliction of pain, punishment removed social esteem from the punished and returned it to the party who had suffered the violation. When someone had been subjected to acts of wrong-doing, the social esteem had to be restored, either by seeking justice through the courts, or by taking revenge at any cost, since it was imperative to requalify as a full member of the community (Herman 1993). The two alternatives represented different ways of accessing and restoring social esteem. Revenge relied on private resources and transferred it straight away, whereas court litigations relied on the ability to convince the jury. To win the case, one needed to appeal to notions of honour and appropriateness, as well as to anger and other passions of the jury members. The existing legislation seems to have been secondary for the outcome. Not even the litigant necessarily referred to the law during the hearing (Allen 2000).

The courts were a venue for punishment and for conflict resolution. While adhering to the logic of private vengeance, the courts negotiated the restoration of social esteem, for ordinary people who presented their cases. In this capacity, the proceedings were a public concern to an extent that is almost inconceivable today, or for any other society for that matter, because of the central place of the court in daily politics, and because of the scale of public participation. Each year six thousand men were selected to serve as jurors (Harris 2013). The average male citizen spent a significant amount of time in court. A typical court hearing was presided over by a jury, composed of anything ranging from a few hundred to several thousand citizens, who were chosen by lot (Lanni 2016). The litigants, in other words, stood before a large crowd of people, which they needed to win over. Verdicts were based on majority votes passed by the assembled citizenship. Although all citizens were equal before the law, in principle, the courts reflected the prevailing distribution of rank and privilege. Individuals from families who could mobilize a wealth of resources were much more likely to vindicate their rights in court, as they were well trained to speak in public, or could afford to hire a professional speech-writer. Poor citizens were dependent on the support of more influential individuals to assert their claims. The courts were also circumscribed in other ways, which reflected the existing, socially stratified notions of status. Female citizens only possessed a portion of the amount of social esteem attributed to their male counterparts, and needed in addition to be represented by a male citizen. Slaves had almost no social esteem at all, and were generally excluded from the courts. The many alien residents, also known as *metics*, were likewise excluded from presenting their cases in court, as a rule, although there were exceptions (Lanni 2016; Harris 2013; Griffith 1995). The courts in fourth-century BCE Athens were thus a space thoroughly organized around social esteem rather than law. They reflected the logic of private vengeance and rested on private power. However, although anger and individual status were the basis for the claims made, the proceedings included the public interest in ways that private vengeance did not, as the litigants had to present their cases in public and appeal to a shared language of desert (Allen 2000; McHardy 2008).

Litigants attempted to reclaim their lost social esteem by persuading members of the jury – or their fellow male citizens – in ways that resonated with existing notions of anger, honour and social status, as shown by Danielle Allen (2000), using as evidence texts written to be given as speeches before the court. Isocrates, who started his career as a professional speech-writer, wrote in one of the preserved texts:

It is not on behalf of any injury from blows that I come to court trying to get justice from him but because I suffered indignity *[aikia]* and dishonour.

Isocrates instructed the litigant to continue by saying that because of this, 'it is fitting for free men to be the most angry', and urged the court to 'inflict the greatest penalty' on the one who was standing charges (quoted in Allen 2000: 50). In this way, members of the jury would be led to understand the magnitude of the insult to his standing, and the need to undertake action to restore social esteem. The gravity of the assault was not measured by the degree of physical harm, or the 'injury from blows' received. The assault was conceived from the perspective of social esteem. The litigant had suffered indignity and dishonour, because of the blows; and because of the indignity and the dishonour generated by the blows, he was angry. The invoked standard was the experienced anger. Isocrates gave the instruction to emphasize the anger, and the jurors were expected to fully understand that passion, which stemmed from the perceived violation of status and propelled the judicial process, all the time being double-edged: sometimes perpetuating cycles of vengeance and sometimes resolving the conflict in court.

Isocrates was of the same generation as Plato, and went on to become a well-known orator in Athens. Isocrates and Plato represented opposing views on truth and public opinion, philosophy and rhetoric, as commonly discussed under the topic of 'sophism'. Yet the two intellectuals also represented different approaches to punishment. Whereas Plato contrasted rational punishment with unreasonable revenge, thereby sowing the seeds of a modern conception of punishment organized around legality and reason, Isocrates, on the other hand, stood for an approach which was organized around social status and passion. The approach was moreover embedded in the contemporary court practice, as opposed to Plato's rationalism. On this model, anger played a central role in the process of punishment. It was an instrument to reach justice: a verdict that would restore the social status of the injured party. The loss of esteem in relation to the community triggered vengeful passions. The more severe the violation, the angrier one was expected to be. Punishment thus relied on non-legal principles of desert and conceptions of transgression. It emphasized rather than suppressed passion, as well as highlighting the crucial role of recognition of social status within the community. Instead of an institution built on crime and dispassionate law enforcement, punishment unfolded along the axis disrespect, rational passion and social status. In all these respects, punishment as status restoration differed from modern understandings of punishment as law enforcement.

The concept of punishment as status restoration guided by passion would survive far beyond ancient Greece. It was also embedded in medieval accounts of righteous revenge, and the decisive role of anger in that context. In *Summa Theologica*, Aquinas maintained that revenge was grounded in the natural inclinations of human beings, above all in anger. It was a passion provoked by a perceived violation of one's status in the eyes of the community. 'All causes of anger', he argued, can be 'reduced to slight' (ST I-II, Q 47, A 2, co.). Slight was always relative to social standing, on this essentially Aristotelian account. Someone was not being given due respect, or was treated disrespectfully, given determinate expectations of esteem. Slight was a very broad concept, in Aquinas's treatment. It covered situations when people acted carelessly, or intervened in the lives of others for no good reason. 'Forgetfulness', for instance, was 'a clear sign of slight esteem', as were ungrounded attempts to stop friends from doing what they had set out to do (ST I-II, Q 47, A 2, ad. 3). Anger was a passion rooted in a fine-grained understanding of status violation. It called for restoration of honour in the face of subtle slight, or more severe forms of wrongdoing, involving force or fraud. Only through punishment could the passion be quelled and the loss of social esteem be reclaimed. Anger could thus animate the quest for justice, in a perfectly rational manner. But it was never an entirely reliable guide. Under certain conditions, anger was a cardinal sin punishable in the afterlife; for instance, if one merely wanted to satisfy personal ambition for social status. Anger was thus incorporated in very different ways in the institution of punishment; as legitimate passion to restore social status, and as the motor force behind renewed violations, this time of the principles of divine justice.

For Thomas Aquinas, as for many people in thirteenth-century Europe, punishment in the afterlife was in a sense the real punishment. All worldly punishments were executed under divine oversight and were moreover bleak in comparison to what the afterlife held in prospect. Graphic illustrations of the sufferings imposed on wrongdoers were commonplace. Hell was communicated to the largely illiterate population through sermons and visual art. Church visitors could watch the damned being tortured on mosaics and paintings all over the continent. In this sense, everyone had to consider the Last Judgement and the horrific punishments in hell (Fudgè 2016; Morgan 1990). Given that cultural intelligibility is the hallmark of punishment, divine justice must qualify, even if never carried out in the material world. Dante's *Divine Comedy* may be the most well-known text on late-medieval conceptions of punishment (Shoemaker 2009). Yet it was by no means unique, but represented the high point of an entire literature genre on the afterlife. In the preceding centuries, heaven and hell had been captured with increasing level of detail, and from this perspective the *Divine Comedy* represents the literary culmination (Morgan 1990). The divine justice was depicted in systematic and detailed fashion. What strikes the modern reader is precisely the level of detail. As has been noted with respect to contemporary visual representations in the churches, there was 'an abiding interest in order and authority at all levels, and in hell no less so' (Fudgè 2016: 145). Sin was the major ground for punishment, and the concern for systematicity was in particular devoted to the punishment of sin. When thinking about the relationship between transgression and punishment in the *Divine Comedy*, Dante was not guided by existing legislation regulating human affairs. Instead, he employed standards which were a mix of Aristotelian distinctions on vice and Christian notions of sin (Morgan 1990). Upon leaving hell, Dante and Virgil ascended up the Mount Purgatory, where the purpose of punishment was to purify the souls on their passage to paradise. In this part of the poem, the punishments mirrored the sins committed during their lifetime. The pain was imposed based on their performance in this world. Yet Dante was not concerned with transgression in relation to other people; actions involving anger, gluttony or envy might harm fellow members of society but were above all transgressions of the underlying moral-ontological order. The inner meaning was the same in all cases. To sin was to turn away from God, in particular to turn away from the love of God, toward self-love and worldly interests. Ultimately, every sin was 'a denial of the divinely ordained order' (Ellrich 1984: 62). As a mix of theological tenets and Aristotelian morality, the divine order constituted the ground on the basis of which punishments were issued in relation to specific rule violations. For Dante, like Aquinas, the divine order was the principle for punishment in the afterlife, operating parallel to the imperatives of status restoration in this life.

The concept of punishment as status restoration would remain operative, also as new punitive principles emerged, such as sovereignty, or the criminal law. Throughout the early-modern period, the expansion of state punishment was caught in the field of tension between 'the king's two bodies' (Kantorowicz 1997), one aspect corresponding to the deeply personal and another aspect to the ultimate ground for political power. Sovereignty was an articulation of the supremacy of worldly power over against the church (Brown 2010), along with the theorem of the monarch as the unique representative of the Christian god. The idea that violations concerned the status of the regent rather than universally applicable laws was salient in theories of sovereignty. The idea was activated in relation to political opposition as well as in the context of mundane wrong-doing. On the one hand, the sovereign stood above the law, and could invoke the necessity to punish political enemies at will (Schmitt 2009). The exercise of power was not necessarily rule-based, not necessarily tied to a predefined crime, and not necessarily uniform but also depended on solipsistic *raison d'état* which overrode the stated law (Loick 2012; Foucault 2007; Foisneau 2013). On the other hand, ordinary transgressions also contained an element of violation of the king's standing; 'in every offense there was a *crimen majestatis*' (Foucault 1979: 53). While enforcing the criminal code, punishment restored the source of royal recognition. The elaborate display would ritually affirm the sacred status of the regent. And just as every offence was an affront to the king's standing, the early-modern executions contained an element of personal revenge. The common use of mercy, granted by the monarch, who could overturn death sentences pronounced by courts of law, further reinforced the personal character of power (Hay 1975). Early-modern punishment consequently incorporated the personal aspects of status restoration while at the same time capturing the transcendent qualities of divine justice. The public executions were simultaneously of this world, a restoration of royal status in the eyes of the congregated audience, and a delegated divine justice, putting the audience in touch with the basic order underlying the world. Of course, punishment in the early-modern period also contained a range of elements – national criminal codes, state administration, law schools – that pointed towards the law as the principle for punishment: the principle that would become hegemonic in modernity. Yet passion and status recognition, principles from preceding époques, were by no means discarded as grounds for punishment.

Eventually, the longstanding philosophical discussion on the differences with respect to vengeance, in combination with the far from unilineal evolution of the institutional framework of criminal justice, led to the modern concept of punishment as law enforcement. Alternative conceptions of punishment, rooted in other historical contexts, were pushed to the side by focusing strictly on crime and legality – but also by presenting vengeance as the sole alternative, and passion as dangerous and avoidable. Yet a rereading of the philosophical arguments, against the background of available scholarship on the historical context, revealed a dimension of punishment located in between rational punishment and impassioned revenge. Three features appear to have been consistent from ancient Greece until the early-modern period. First of all, the dual role of passion; anger, in particular, was often approached in a nuanced manner, rather than condemned as irrational. Anger was on the one hand necessary in the search for justice, and on the other hand anger was dangerous and needed to be suppressed. Secondly, there was a persisting awareness of the paradox of transgression. Punishment derived its basic justification from the ordering mission but was inherently transgressive and constantly undermined, by passion and by competing principles. Finally, the conception of punishment as status restoration remained influential until the nineteenth century. Violations of social esteem were the object of punishment, and punishment derived its function from the necessity of injured parties to reclaim their status in the eyes of other members of the group. The modern concept of punishment can be traced all the way back to Plato, who likened the passions of punishment to the mindless fury of an animal, which was in opposition to what reason called for, in *Protagoras*. Yet the wider spectra of experiences, which were firmly tied to social esteem but located somewhere between rational punishment and impassioned revenge, can also be traced back to Plato, who rejected the simple opposition between passion and reason, in favour of a third element of the soul, which was elaborated in *Phaedrus* and in the *Republic*. This whole dimension was referred to as *thumos*, and will be the topic of the next chapter.

References

Adut, Ari (2018) *Reign of appearances: the misery and splendor of the public sphere.* New York: Cambridge University Press.

Allen, Danielle (2000) *The world of Prometheus: the politics of punishing in democratic Athens.* Princeton: Princeton University Press.

Althoff, Gerd (1998) Ira regis: prolegomena to a history of royal anger. In B. Rosenwein (ed.), *Anger's past: the social uses of an emotion in the Middle Ages*. Ithaca, NY: Cornell University Press. pp 59–74.

Aquinas, Thomas (1941) *Summa Theologica*. London: Burns Oates & Washbourne.

Aristotle (1944) *Politics*. Trans. by H. Rackham. Cambridge, MA: Harvard University Press.

Bacon, Francis (1955) Of revenge. In *Selected writings*. New York: Modern Library.

Beccaria, Cesare (1778) *An essay on crimes and punishments. With a commentary attributed to Monsieur de Voltaire*. Philadelphia: R. Bell.

Berman, Harold (1983) *Law and revolution: the formation of the Western legal tradition*. Cambridge, MA: Harvard University Press.

Bloch, Marc (1965) *Feudal society. Volume 1*. London: Routledge & Kegan Paul.

Brooks, Thom (2012) *Punishment*. Abingdon: Routledge.

Brown, Wendy (2010) *Walled states, waning sovereignty*. New York: Zone.

Cohen, David (1995) *Law, violence, and community in classical Athens*. Cambridge: Cambridge University Press.

Costa, Pietro (2007) The rule of law: a historical introduction. In P. Costa and D. Zolo (eds.), *The rule of law: history, theory and criticism*. Dordrecht: Springer. pp 73–149.

Dante Alighieri (2002) *The Inferno*. Trans. by R. Hollander and J. Hollander. New York: Doubleday.

Durkheim, Émile (1997) *The division of labor in society*. New York: Free Press.

Eagleton, Terry (2005) *Holy terror*. Oxford: Oxford University Press.

Ellrich, Robert (1984) Envy, identity, and creativity: Inferno XXIV-XXV. *Dante Studies, with the Annual Report of the Dante Society* 102: 61–80.

Fassin, Didier (2018) *The will to punish*. Oxford: Oxford University Press.

Feinberg, Joel (1970) *Doing & deserving. Essays in the theory of responsibility*. Princeton: Princeton University Press.

Foisneau, Luc (2013) Sovereignty and reason of state: Bodin, Botero, Richelieu and Hobbes. In H. A. Lloyd (ed.), *The reception of Bodin*. Leiden: Brill. pp 323–342.

Forsdyke, Sara (2018) Ancient and modern conceptions of the rule of law. In J. Ober (ed.) *Ancient Greek history and contemporary social science*. Edinburgh: Edinburgh University Press. pp 184–212.

Foucault, Michel (1979) *Discipline and punish: the birth of the prison*. New York: Vintage Books.

Foucault Michel (2007) *Security, territory, population. Lectures at the Collège de France 1977–78*. Houndmills, Basingstoke: Palgrave MacMillan.

Fowley, Helene (1995) Tragedy and democratic ideology: the case of Sophocles' Antigone. In B. Goff (ed.), *History, tragedy, theory: dialogues on Athenian drama*. Austin: University of Texas. pp 131–150.

Fudgé, Thomas (2016) *Medieval religion and its anxieties: history and mystery in the other Middle Ages*. New York: Palgrave Macmillan.

Giddens, Anthony (1985) *A contemporary critique of historical materialism. Vol. 2, The nation-state and violence*. Cambridge: Polity.

Goldhill, Simon (2004) *Aeschylus, the Oresteia*. Cambridge: Cambridge University Press.

Griffith, Mark (1995) Brilliant dynasts: power and politics in the 'Oresteia'. *Classical Antiquity* 14(1): 62–129.

Gutnick-Allen, Signy (2016) *Thomas Hobbes's theory of crime and punishment*. Diss. School of History, Queen Mary University of London.

Hanawalt, Barbara, and Wallace, David (1999) Introduction. In B. Hanawalt and D. Wallace (eds.), *Medieval crime and social control*. Minneapolis: University of Minnesota Press, pp ix–xvi.

Harris, Edward (2013) Introduction. In E. Harris, D. Leão and P. J. Rhodes (eds.), *Law and drama in ancient Greece*. London: Bloomsbury Academic. pp 1–24.

Hart, H. L. A. (1959) Prolegomenon to the Principles of Punishment. *Proceedings of the Aristotelian Society* 60: 1–26.

Hay, Douglas (1975) Property, authority and the criminal law. In D Hay et al. (eds.), *Albion's fatal tree: crime and society in eighteenth-century England*. London: Allen Lane. pp 17–63.

Hegel, Georg Wilhelm Friedrich (1952) *The philosophy of right*. Oxford: Oxford University Press.

Hegel, Georg Wilhelm Friedrich (1998) System der Sittlichkeit. *Gesammelte Werke, Band 5. Schriften und Entwürfe (1799–1808)*. Hamburg: Meiner.

Herman, Gabriel (1993) Tribal and civic codes of behaviour in Lysias I. *The Classical Quarterly* 43(2): 406–419.

Hobbes, Thomas (1996) *Leviathan*. Oxford: Oxford University Press.

Kant, Immanuel (2006) *Anthropology from a pragmatic point of view*. Cambridge: Cambridge University Press.

Kantorowicz, Ernst (1997) *The king's two bodies: a study in mediaeval political theology*. Princeton: Princeton University Press.

Klosko, George (2006) *The development of Plato's political theory*. Oxford: Oxford University Press.

Knuuttila, Simo (2004) *Emotions in ancient and medieval philosophy*. Oxford: Oxford University Press.

Kocka, Jürgen (2004) The middle classes in Europe. In H. Kaelble (ed.), *The European way: European societies in the 19th and 20th centuries*. Oxford: Berghahn. pp 15–43.

Koritansky, Peter (2005) Two theories of retributive punishment: Immanuel Kant and Thomas Aquinas. *History of Philosophy Quarterly* 22(4): 319–338.

Lacey, Nicola (2016) *In search of criminal responsibility: ideas, interests, and institutions*. Oxford: Oxford University Press.

Lanni, Adriaan (2016) *Law and order in ancient Athens*. New York: Cambridge University Press.

Loick, Daniel (2012) *Kritik der Souveränität*. Frankfurt a. M.: Campus Verlag.

Macleod, C. W. (1982) Politics and the Oresteia. *The Journal of Hellenic Studies* 102: 124–144.

McBride, Keally (2007) *Punishment and political order*. Ann Arbor: University of Michigan Press.

McHardy, Fiona (2008) *Revenge in Athenian culture*. London: Duckworth.

Merback, Mitchell (1999) *The thief, the cross and the wheel: pain and the spectacle of punishment in medieval and Renaissance Europe*. London: Reaktion Books.

Miller, William (1998) Clint Eastwood and Equity: the virtues of revenge and the shortcomings of law in popular culture. In A. Sarat and T. Kearns (eds.), *Law and the domains of culture*. Ann Arbor: University of Michigan Press. pp 161–202.

Miner, Robert (2009) *Thomas Aquinas on the Passions. A study of Summa Theologiae, 1a2ae 22–48*. Cambridge: Cambridge University Press.

Møller, Jørgen, and Skaaning, Svend-Erik (2014) *The rule of law; definitions, measures, patterns and causes*. Basingstoke: Palgrave Macmillan.

Morgan, Alison (1990) *Dante and the medieval other world*. Cambridge: Cambridge University Press.

Nozick, Robert (1981) *Philosophical explanations*. Cambridge, MA: Harvard University Press.

Oreglia, Giacomo (1991) *Dante. Liv, verk & samtid.* Stockholm: Carlssons.

Packer, Herbert (1968) *The limits of the criminal sanction*. Stanford: Stanford University Press.

Paskewich, Christopher (2014) The roots of political community: thumos and tradition in Ancient Greek thought. *Anamnesis*, http://anamnesisjournal.com/2014/09/roots-political-community-thumos-tradition-ancient-greek-thought, accessed 26 October 2019.

Pauley, Matthew (1994) The jurisprudence of crime and punishment from Plato to Hegel. *American Journal of Jurisprudence* 39: 97–152.

Plato (1959) *Gorgias*. Trans. by E. R. Dodds. Oxford: Clarendon Press.

Plato (1976) *Protagoras*. Trans. by C. C. W. Taylor. Oxford: Clarendon Press.

Plato (2013) *Republic Books 1–5*. Trans. by C. Emlyn-Jones and W. Preddy. Cambridge, MA: Harvard University Press.

Podlecki, Anthony (1966) *The political background of Aeschylean tragedy*. Ann Arbor: University of Michigan.

Pratt, John (2002) *Punishment and civilization: penal tolerance and intolerance in modern society*. London: Sage.

Schmidt, Steffen (2007) *Hegels System der Sittlichkeit*. Berlin: Akademie Verlag.

Schmitt, Carl (2009) *Politische Theologie: vier Kapitel zur Lehre von der Souveränität*. Berlin: Duncker & Humblot.

Schroeder, Jeanne (2004) *The triumph of Venus: the erotics of the market*. Berkeley: University of California Press.

Sellers, Mortimer (2014) What is the rule of law and why is it so important? In J. Silkenat (ed.), *The legal doctrines of the rule of law and the legal state (Rechtsstaat)*. Cham: Springer International Publishing.

Shklar, Judith (1990) *The faces of injustice*. New Haven: Yale University Press.

Shoemaker, Karl (2005) Revenge as a "medium good" in the twelfth century. *Law, Culture and the Humanities* 1(3): 333–358.

Shoemaker, Karl (2009) The problem of pain in punishment: historical perspectives. In A Sarat (ed.), *Law, meaning, and violence: pain, death, and the law*. Ann Arbor: University of Michigan Press. pp 15–41.

Smith, Philip (2008) *Punishment and culture*. Chicago: University of Chicago Press.

Spierenburg, Pieter (1984) *The spectacle of suffering: executions and the evolution of repression: from a preindustrial metropolis to the European experience*. Cambridge: Cambridge University Press.

Tierney, Brian (1982) *Religion, law and the growth of constitutional thought, 1150–1650*. Cambridge: Cambridge University Press.

Vlastos, Gregory (1991) *Socrates: ironist and moral philosopher*. Ithaca, NY: Cornell University Press.

Zaibert, Leo (2006) *Punishment and retribution*. Aldershot: Ashgate.

Žižek, Slavoj (1994) *The metastases of enjoyment*. London: Verso.

Zolo, Danilo (2007) The rule of law: a critical reappraisal. In P. Costa and D. Zolo (eds.), *The rule of law: history, theory and criticism*. Dordrecht: Springer. pp 3–71.

3 The ambiguous desire for recognition

What kind of desire is the desire for punishment? The question, as far as it concerns the audience, turns on whether there exists a more or less permanent desire specifically to punish. Is there, as Nietzsche indicated on many occasions, a latent lust for cruelty and revenge in the population, which can be satisfied by acts of punishment? It would be a reservoir of punitivity, which would be difficult to satisfy in any other way, whether it was natural or socially constructed in the first place. The alternative is that the desire to punish would be part of a broader register of desire. Is there, in other words, a distinguishable desire that is tied specifically to punishment, or could the same desire just as well, under other circumstances, be satisfied in other ways? It is a complex question marred with pitfalls. One can distinguish a desire for wealth, a desire for sex, or a desire to win – and the 'kind of desire' will be defined in terms of what satisfies the desire. The desire for wealth would be satisfied by riches, the desire for sex by sex, and so on. In the same vein, one could assume a desire for punishment. However, to identify the desire in terms of a specific object would be to beg the question. While perfectly true, it would not be very informative to speak about a desire for punishment, which is satisfied by punishment. Here the question 'what kind of desire?' is posed against the backdrop of the problematic of desire. Desire is assumed to be desire for something – for something located on the other side of the gap between desire and enjoyment. What this something is must not be predetermined, or assumed to be satisfiable only by the object at hand.

I will argue for the position that the desire for punishment belongs to a broader register of desire. It is the desire to be fully part of society, or to distinguish oneself over against others. The argument will once again start with Plato and Aristotle. They referred to the desire as *thumos*. From the very outset, it was intimately connected with both punishment and social esteem. Later attempts reflected the same tension between retaliatory rage and the desire for recognition. Aquinas would discuss the persistence of *thumos*, its nuances and many ambiguities in a Catholic medieval context. During the Enlightenment, Hegel addressed the desire for recognition in terms of vengeance. The final section of the chapter analyses recent attempts to rehabilitate *thumos* undertaken in conscious opposition to Hegel's intuition that individual claims for recognition will necessarily transcend existing institutions and realize more freedom. It is shown that desire for recognition can turn toward intolerance, revenge and unrestrained self-assertion, and still find satisfaction.

Thumos: torn between vengeance and competition

Plato described *thumos* as the third element of the soul. The famous allegory of the chariot, as related in *Phaedrus*, may serve to introduce the multifaceted desire. It is a tale of two horses and one charioteer, and how they perform together. Talking about the sources of human motivation and the excessive nature of desire, Socrates described a chariot being pulled by two winged horses. One of the winged horses was white and the other was black. The black horse was mortal and incarnated the drive toward immediate satisfaction of bodily appetites, such as hunger, sex and thirst. The white horse represented *thumos*, which was likewise non-rational, but very different from the black horse. The white horse made a noble impression, had finer features and a better posture. Unlike the black horse, which was 'crooked in shape' and 'companion of excess and boastfulness', it needed no whip as it responded to 'spoken orders' of the charioteer (*Phaedrus* 253e). The two horses made the chariot move through their combined power. The charioteer, representing reason, did the steering. While unable to move the chariot, the charioteer alone could distinguish the real good and find the way forward. The allegory of the chariot might seem to convey yet another image of the familiar relationship between reason and passion. The extended campaign to cleanse punishment of passion, which started with the passage in *Protagoras* where Plato associated the desire for vengeance with the mindless fury of a beast, operated on the binary opposition reason and passion, which was central to the formation of the modern concept of punishment. Desire would on this analysis be uniformly non-rational and pleasure-seeking, suggesting all sorts of detours from what is suggested by reasoned principles and deferred gratification. The white horse in the allegory was, after all, just a horse, albeit with better posture; 'erect in form and clean-limbed, high-necked' (*Phaedrus* 253d). Like the black horse, it was non-rational, powerful and difficult to control. While necessary to set the chariot in motion, both horses contained the seeds of irrational excess. But that would be to miss the point, or the third element of the soul, which was likewise part of Plato's teachings.

The allegory is better read as presenting a way out of the simple opposition between reason and passion. The main observation to be made is that the two horses are different from one another. Socrates presented them as each other's opposites. The white *thumos*-horse was immortal and associated with transcendence. It was 'a lover of honour when joined with restraint and a sense of shame, and glory' (*Phaedrus* 253d). It was very different from the black and mortal horse, which pursued goals associated with satisfaction of bodily needs. As opposed to the black horse, which quickly tired when the bodily needs were satisfied, or if the object of desire was out of reach, the white horse might pull forever, as it was immortal and inspired by eternal and unchanging values, such as glory. The white horse was 'a companion of true glory', potentially transcending mortal restraints (*Phaedrus* 253d). The *thumos*-horse was still a beast, and as such unable to find its way without a charioteer. But while the black horse was insensitive to rational reasoning and followed bodily needs, which were imperative, excessive and boundless, the white horse was oriented toward social esteem and able to hear the voice of reason. Under circumstances it could be called back by reason, or take rational advice. The two horses pulled in different, at times even contrary directions. When falling in love, for instance, Socrates described how the black horse took the lead, forcing the carriage toward the beloved one, excited by the prospects of having sex. At the mere sight of the object of desire, the black horse rushed forward, oblivious of the charioteer's whip. Even the charioteer tottered. In this situation, the white horse showed restraint and high principles in a pursuit blinded by love, set in motion by bodily desire. The white horse struggled in the yoke, held back by reason but also by shame – it was said to drench 'the whole soul with sweat from shame and alarm' (*Phaedrus* 254c).

The relationship between the charioteer, the white horse and the black horse illustrated Plato's view of the tripartite nature of the soul – divided into reason, *thumos* and appetite, respectively. The claims concerned the nature of human motivation rather than the composition of the soul (Cooper 1999). On this reading, there were three kinds of desire: one propelling people toward the satisfaction of physical needs, another related to understanding and to deliberation, and then there was a third kind of desire, *thumos*. *Thumos* is translated variously by 'anger', 'spirit', 'passion', or 'temper' (Pearson 2012: 5). In the current literature, it is mostly left untranslated, to avoid choosing one meaning over another. I will do the same and refrain from translating the term, and instead highlight its foreign character by using italics. *Thumos* has rarely been discussed in the context of punishment, beyond a rather narrow circle of classicists. Yet it could be relevant for discussions on what kind of desire might have gone into punishment not only in ancient Greece but also in later historical periods. I believe that *thumos* is essential to understand what the audience sees in punishment. The concept referred to a register of desire, which is of central importance for the institution of punishment in any society, and for everyday lives of individuals as well, for that matter; a register stretching from the desire for retaliation to the desire for social status.

From the outset, *thumos* was tied to punishment, anger and social esteem. In Book IV in the *Republic* Plato argued that *thumos* was a distinct third element of the soul, which was neither rational nor necessarily irrational. He started the argument by referring to the anger of a man who had been treated unjustly; in such cases *thumos* will persevere through 'hunger and cold and all such things, and, by enduring, overcome them without ceasing from noble acts until it achieves its end, or dies' (440d). The condition was exemplified by Odysseus, who, upon his return after the long journey, found out about the licentious living of a large group of suitors, who had established themselves in the household during his absence. The suitors had made advances to marry his wife Penelope and had moreover been sleeping with the female servants referred to as maids. Odysseus was furious because of the gross insult this was seen to involve, and was anxious to vindicate his honour. When Odysseus, disguised as a beggar, caught sight of the maids, he was consumed by the idea of killing them all, on the spot. But he managed to restrain his anger, struck his breast and rebuked his heart as Homer put it, tempering 'the irrational passionate part' of the soul (*Republic* 441c). In that very moment, *thumos*'s call to action was controlled by reason. Odysseus was infuriated but managed to control himself with great restraint. But the desire for vengeance and the perceived need to restore social esteem continued to be felt. So, given some time to lay out plans, he killed the suitors and ordered the execution of the maids (*Odyssey* XX–XXII). In this respect, Odysseus constituted a good example of someone who was acting on a desire for status recognition. His course of action was not dictated by some primordial anger but above all by sensitivity to prevailing notions of social esteem. The severe punishment of what in essence constituted a violation of household rules was mediated by reason and dictated by the need to vindicate Odysseus's social status in the eyes of fellow members in the community.

If there was a core meaning of *thumos*, it referred to anger, and above all to anger triggered by violations which called for reparation (Cooper 1999; Pearson 2012). It was a specific kind of anger, rooted in the experience of injustice and perceptions of social esteem. The centrality of such anger was prominent in the Homeric poems, written well before the democratic period. In the *Iliad*, Achilles was absorbed by righteous indignation when Agamemnon, his commander in the Trojan War, deprived him of a treasured war prize, an action that was experienced as unbearable violation of social esteem. Achilles's anger contained elements of resolution, courage and even pleasure, famously characterized as 'far sweeter than honey' (*Iliad* 18.109). The concept of *thumos* remained marked by its origins in the Homeric world of mandatory vengeance. But *thumos* may not necessarily be equated with anger, or with archetypical images of vengefulness. In the parable of the chariot, the *thumos*-horse was characterized as a companion of true glory without any reference to vengeful passions. While anger may have been central, it was by no means the only emotion associated with *thumos*. In *Rhetoric*, Aristotle defined 12 different emotions, which would-be public speakers had to be familiar with if they were to persuade the audience. At least seven of them could be seen to be *thumos*-related: anger and hatred, of course, and, beyond that, fear, confidence in the face of danger, feeling disgraced, righteous indignation, envy, and eagerness to match the accomplishments of others (Cooper 1999). The recognition of status in the eyes of others was central in this context. As Gregory Klosko pointed out, *thumos* covered 'a range of emotions concerned with someone's image of himself and his desire that others share that image' (Klosko 2006: 74). The experience of disgrace, righteous indignation, envy, and the wish to match others were emotions associated with social assertiveness, and with how one was perceived by other people, measured by the prevailing standards of social esteem. All of the emotions were in one way or another bound up with the recognition of social status and one's experienced standing in the community. Yet strictly speaking, *thumos* was not an emotion. It was a desire. In the Aristotelian tradition, 'desire' is the generic term for what makes people act. Desire sets in motion; 'what is called desire is the sort of faculty in the soul which initiates movement'. Like all desires, *thumos* was first and foremost 'action-prompting' (*De Anima* iii 10, 433a31–b1). On an Aristotelian reading, *thumos* spurred people to act in particular ways – to take revenge, to be courageous, to seek public office, or to mind one's reputation.

On all accounts, *thumos* was the impassioned urge to take revenge, and thus linked to a specific event and certain emotions, above all anger. Beyond that, there is less agreement. The meaning of *thumos* is contested. There are different opinions as to the meaning of *thumos*, and its relationship to reason and to virtue. While some scholars limit *thumos* to retaliatory desire, other scholars include more than the urge to avenge injustice: above all the desire for social esteem. A narrow conception stands against a broader conception of *thumos*. On the first reading, primarily based on Aristotle's discussion of the term, *thumos* was the desire for retaliation in response to a perceived slight – full stop (Pearson 2012). Aristotle stressed that *thumos* was triggered by acts of disrespect, or slight. Slight, in turn, was subdivided into three species: 'contempt', 'spite' and 'insult' (Pearson 2012: 113). The common denominator was the violation of the norms of social esteem, which was the underlying framework to understand offences at the time. In this capacity, *thumos* was a powerful source of motivation – almost like a force of nature. It was thought of as a physical reaction. The blood circulating around the heart came to a boil; at the time, that was one prevalent metaphor used to describe anger induced by injustice (Oksenberg Rorty 1992). And even today, the boiling of the blood remains a metaphor for anger in everyday language. When something makes my blood boil, I am so angry that I can hardly control myself.

During the democratic period, *thumos* seems to have acquired a wider meaning, beyond anger and the desire for revenge. The connotations shifted toward 'spiritedness and a sense of honour' (Urmson 1990: 168). The broader conception of *thumos* has been advocated most persuasively by John Cooper and is supported by textual evidence from Plato's *Republic*, as well as by a different interpretation of Aristotle. On the second reading, *thumos* refers to assertiveness in social life more generally: competitiveness and the desire for social esteem. On this other reading, *thumos* is a more general desire. The retaliatory desire belongs to a family of 'spirited desires', which 'are competitive in character, they aim at self-assertion as an agent, as a person to be taken serious practical account of, in comparison and in competition with other agents' (Cooper 1999: 276). The desire was not necessarily triggered by a specific event, or an act of injustice. The object of *thumos*-desire was 'competitive success and the esteem from others that comes with it' (Cooper

1999: 135). Rather than being a desire for retaliation, it was a natural part of social interaction, in a competitive and socially stratified society such as ancient Athens. On this reading, thus, the urge for vengeance was part of a larger or more complex desire: the concern for social esteem, or the perceived need to restore, maintain, or gain social esteem, as defined in the community. The desire for punishment to avenge injustice would be of the same kind as career-mindedness, or the will to uphold an unstained reputation.

The wider desire extended far beyond punishment and into other areas of life. At heart, it was the desire to be accepted as a socially valuable member of the community. The desire may be more urgent, or more compelling, in the context of punishment, when someone had experienced a sudden loss of social esteem, following acts of disrespect, in the form of slight or more serious offences. A punitive intervention to restore social esteem was called for, if the person were to be seen as a respectable member of the community – by other people. But the desire for punishment was the same desire as manifested in other areas in life. *Thumos* was immediately bound up with issues of morality, community and social status (Koziak 2000). It was the desire to count as a full member of the group, on the conditions set by social morality. As such, it would not be tied to a specific intervention, such as punishment, but rather to the pursuit of conventional goals, or goals which may confer esteem upon the actor in the eyes of the community. *Thumos* would thus be oriented toward group conformity. But it was at the same time moving people beyond group conformity toward individual distinction. *Thumos* was transgressive, assertive and competitive, constantly pulling people in different directions, toward group conformity and toward individual distinction. While focused on the achievement of conventional goals, *thumos* was also the wish to assert oneself amongst fellow companions, seemingly stopping at nothing, persevering through hunger and cold and similar trials 'until it achieves its end, or dies', as Plato put it. As Francois Dubet (2009) has noted in a modern context, the desire for social status is inherently contradictory, oriented both toward conformity with the group and toward individual distinction. *Thumos*, taken as the wider desire for recognition, may, fundamentally, be the urge just to belong and to escape the anxiety of being dismissed, or being looked down upon, but it does not stop there and evolves into the wish to distinguish oneself, within the same group. People thus strive, at one and the same time, to be just like everybody else within the group and to stand out within the group, in competition with other members. This is a complexity, if not a contradiction, at the level of desire.

Instead of choosing sides in the scholarly discussion on whether the broad or the narrow conception best captured Aristotle's use of the term, one might conclude that *thumos* was complex and fundamentally ambiguous. In that case, the notion of *thumos* appears fraught with ambiguity, torn between emotional responses to acts of disrespect and the overarching striving for social esteem in the community. The corresponding desire would be inherently complex, stretching between two poles: the urge to avenge injustice and the striving for social esteem. The complexity of *thumos* – its ability to include opposites – is precisely what makes the concept useful to understand the desire that went into the audience's consumption of punishment in ancient Greece, as well as in other societies. The basic coordinates of desire can be assumed to differ in between historical periods, and along prevailing lines of social division (Butler 1997; 1990). In Athens, the audience were predominantly male citizens, and the examples of Odysseus's and Achilles's rage and subsequent vengeance may primarily have spoken to the male part of the population. But it does not follow that *thumos* was only for them. The options may not have been available to the overwhelming majority of female citizens, slaves and foreign residents. But they too must have felt the traction of *thumos*, which transcended given conditions. At the most basic level, the desire to belong as fully part of social interactions is not confined to a particular social group.

The persistence of *thumos*

Whether taken as a specific desire for punishment or as a more general desire for social esteem, *thumos* has been embedded in very different contexts, from Plato and onwards. In each period covered by this study, *thumos* has been acknowledged as a powerful source of motivation, and its moral implications have been discussed by some of the most influential philosophers. I will discuss the positions advanced by Plato and Aristotle in ancient Greece, by Aquinas and Dante in medieval France and Italy, by Hegel in early-modern Germany, and – in the next section – by Sloterdijk and Fukuyama in a current Western context. In each context, the desire to gain – or equally important: regain – social esteem was volatile, fundamentally ambiguous and balancing at the margins of legitimacy. *Thumos* has consistently received a dualistic treatment, in terms of legitimacy. In Western culture, generally speaking, envy and pride have been detested whereas competitiveness and status-seeking have been celebrated. Yet that is generally speaking: the emphasis placed on the various elements of *thumos* has shifted, and the dualisms which have framed the understanding have likewise changed, between the chosen periods. The desire has been celebrated at times and deprecated at other times, torn between religious notions of sin and worldly notions of social status, and linked to shifting goals, sometimes directed at compliance with rules of honour and at other times geared towards respect for equal rights.

The ancient celebration of *thumos* was never unqualified. Like appetite, or bodily needs, *thumos* was by definition non-rational, and as such deficient. Yet first Plato and then Aristotle considered *thumos* as a prerequisite to achieve some of the higher values in life (Cooper 1999; Pearson 2012). It was as an essential part of human motivation; the goals associated with reason, such as intellectual curiosity, or the ambition to rule wisely, were not for everybody, whereas indulgence in bodily pleasures was ephemeral and without lasting value. As the third element of the soul, *thumos* bore a complex relationship to reason. Aristotle argued that *thumos* was to some extent rational. It was very different from the bodily needs, which were entirely irrational. *Thumos* incorporated reasoning: deliberation and understanding were essential to achieve goals that conferred social esteem. It heard the voice of reason, Aristotle wrote, yet 'imperfectly' (*Nicomachean Ethics* 1149a). The desire could not be fully rational. In the normal course of events, it was reason's natural ally. Unless 'destroyed by a bad upbringing', Plato said, *thumos* would side with reason, against the appetites, as 'naturally auxiliary to the rational' (*Republic* 441a). In the parable of the chariot, the white *thumos*-horse figured as an indispensable ally of reason. In other contexts, *thumos* was more unreliable and could go against reason. As observed over and again, *thumos* might easily backfire, in eruptions such as the unrestrained rage of Achilles, who chose to die young in return for eternal glory, or in cycles of mandatory revenge stretching over generations. Social esteem and its derivates – glory, the noble, or honour – can be desired independent of what is conducive to individual well-being, reasoned political goals, or other rational interests. Thus, while *thumos* was generally considered consistent with reason, it was sometimes the very opposite, in the pursuit of social status.

The desire was inherently volatile and had to be tempered by reason. The case of Odysseus's homecoming was exemplary in this respect. His desire to kill the maids and the suitors was not a rational desire, in the Platonic sense. Odysseus was someone who had been subject to a violation of the rules of social esteem, which triggered a specific desire to punish the perpetrator. It was not the ambition to rule wisely, or to understand the true nature of vice. But the desire incorporated reason and measure. After all, Odysseus did not act on his initial impulse to seek revenge and paused to deliberate, taking relevant conditions into account. At the same time, the desire came across as non-rational and transgressive. Especially the premeditated execution of the maids has puzzled commentators, since it appeared to be excessive in relation to their offence, or the act of sleeping with the suitors, whether compelled to do so or not. *Thumos* in the broader sense, as the desire for social esteem, was embraced with the same reservation. The desire had to be properly checked by reason; if not, the result was the 'timocratic' character. In the *Republic*, Socrates, speaking for Plato, gave the following portrait of a 'timocratic' person whose qualities, to his mind, were a mix of good and bad. The character was wilful and educated. It was someone who was concerned with the pursuit of public esteem and valued military achievements higher than art and culture; smooth, arrogant and sometimes ruthless. 'While such a person would be harsh on slaves', Socrates remarked, 'he would be civil to free men and very respectful to those in authority, keen to hold office and ambitious' (*Republic* 549a). As a young adult, this person tended to despise money, but later in life there was a noticeable trace of avarice. In this case, *thumos* led astray as well, but not in the shape of holy rage or excessive revenge, but in the single-minded obsession with achieving conventional goals for oneself, such as holding a public office.

In medieval Europe, the ambivalence of *thumos* in both capacities – as retaliatory desire and as the desire for social esteem – was radicalized. There was a thin but sharp line between commendable assertiveness and cardinal sin. Aquinas and Dante lived in a world squeezed between religious notions of piety and worldly notions of social esteem. The retaliatory desire of the ancient Greece was embraced by both writers, as a ground for rational vengeance; at the same time, the revenge was constantly at risk of condemnation in the afterworld, precisely for being marked by the same assertive desire. *Thumos* was encouraged as an essential virtue to do justice and to restore social esteem, while being tempered by the imminent threat of divine justice. Most members of the medieval community were, on the dominant religious understanding, destined for punishment in the afterworld, either eternally or for some time. The punishments in hell were endless, whereas the punishments in purgatory were temporary, designed as penance, to purge the soul from sin, before its ascendance to heaven. Each sin was purged through a kind of penance that was adjusted to its particular features. Dante's account in the *Purgatorio* was entirely structured after the seven mortal sins, with libertines and revellers on the shelves at the top of Mount Purgatory. Further down, and punished more severely, were the souls whose earthly existence was marked by the *thumos*-related passions of hatred, envy or pride. Pride was the root of them all. Any desire to assert one's social esteem had to be balanced against a religious doctrine, according to which pride was the essence of all sins (ST I-II, Q 77, A 5; ST I-II, Q 84, A 2). Pride was the gravest of sins, since it represented the very opposite of the love of God, namely inordinate self-love. Hence, the punishment was designed to humble. The penance of the prideful, in Dante's poem, was to carry boulders, which bent down their heads and forced their gaze toward the ground. Those who had been obsessed with their own perception could no longer see themselves – or how they were perceived by others in the community. The prideful were forced to humility by the laws of nature; the weight of the stone reminded them of their place in the larger scheme of things.

Ascending up *Mount Purgatorio*, Dante encountered the wrathful; in a vision, he saw people, blinded by anger, slaying a young man with stones. In medieval Europe, anger was linked to reason and justice. But under certain circumstances, it was a cardinal sin (Miner 2009), and this was such a case. The wrathful were punished by being engulfed in a cloud of black smoke, which smelled of foul air and prevented them from seeing anything. The foul, black smoke reflected the anger that had clouded their judgements during life. The souls were doomed to spend their time in blindness until their sins of anger had been purged. Envy occupied the shelf positioned between pride and anger, as it was seen to include elements of both. The envious, like the prideful, were obsessed with their own share of esteem, competing with others, once again turning away from the love of God. They looked in the wrong direction, to compare their fortunes with those of their neighbours, anxiously competing for power, honour and status, in 'fear they may lose because another rises' (*Purg*. XVII: 119). The penance for envy was excruciatingly painful. The sinners were forced to sit like beggars in the sun with the eyelids sewn up with iron threads, with tears pouring out from 'the horrible seam' (*Purg*. XIII: 83). The punishment reflected Dante's view of envy as a sin of the eye. The notion of envy as deviant vision was commonplace in contemporary literary texts (Langum 2016). Hence the punishment, which was directed specifically at the eye. The proud and the angry were also punished in ways that impacted on their ability to see. But the vision of the envious was punished directly. They were blinded, facing the sun with stitched-up eyelids. In their blindness, the envious were supposed to train the inward eye to discover truths about human frailty, and learn to re-focus on God's wisdom, love and justice (Kirkpatrick 2004).

In a culture which cherished vengeance and social esteem, and recourse for injustice in the end was private, the worst deadly sins were *thumos*-related: pride, envy and anger. The three passions were interlinked in a sacrilegious dynamic, which cast an inescapable shadow over the desire for social esteem. Pride fuelled anger and envy, which taken together signalled excessive preoccupation with the self, involving a turning away from God along with a desire to transcend one's allotted position in the scheme of things (Ellrich 1984). It seems to have been an inevitable contradiction. *Thumos* was constantly encouraged in medieval Europe, by the organization of social life, while being tempered by Christian notions of sin and the corresponding threat of severe punishment in the afterworld.

In early-modern Europe, the combined influence of a landed aristocracy, the whims of sovereignty, and the remnants of feudal culture encouraged rather than checked *thumos*. Social honour and military glory were dominant values (Hirschman 1977; Kocka 2004). They exerted an influence not merely within a numerically small aristocracy. Social esteem saturated the entire social order. Its distribution was based on estates and birth-right, and status came to expression in the way of life of all different social strata, often underlined by exterior signs of belonging. It was heavily stratified, and circumscribed by perceptions of rigidity. Social esteem was had or lost, rather than achieved (Weber 1972). The desire for social esteem was relatively unchecked by competing systems of valuation, after the demise of the Christian cosmology, yet before capitalism. Medieval notions of divine justice had lost their grip over the population, while social esteem had not yet been partially pushed to the side by capitalism, or replaced by new principles for social stratification, oriented toward achievement and private gain. The young Hegel was much inspired by the French revolution, while writing within the context of *l'ancien regime*, in which social esteem was absolutely central. The centrality of social esteem in the contemporary German society can be read off from the very first version of the master-and-slave dialectic. The first version in *System der Sittlichkeit*, written a few years before the publication of the *Phenomenology* in 1807, articulated a specific conception of the dynamics of desire – conceptualized as the struggle for recognition. In my reading, it is an account of the desire that went into the struggle for recognition, and which may be integrated in a wider story with potentially rather disheartening consequences, as opposed to the hopes usually attached to it. Although Hegel never commented on the ancient Greek notion, the first version of the master-and-slave dialectic beautifully illustrated the two aspects of *thumos*. The desire for recognition was, at one and the same time, the urge to avenge injustice and the desire to be part of a community as a worthy member.

As opposed to the later version in the *Phenomenology*, the struggle for recognition was set in motion by a specific event; in this case, a crime. The struggle started with a theft. The theft above all involved a breach of the honour code (*die Ehre*), and was experienced as a personal offence by the victim (Hegel 1998). The injured party had been deprived of property, but had also, and more importantly, lost status in the eyes of other members in the community. The theft, interpreted as an act of disrespect, put the reputation at immediate risk. The perpetrator was known; it was 'the other' in the struggle for recognition. Victim and perpetrator were locked in conflict. There was, at this point in Hegel's presentation, no third party with the capacity to resolve the conflict. The initial offence therefore instigated a series of confrontations between the two parties. Each party was taking turns, exacting revenge. The struggle followed the logic of private vengeance. The initial breach of honour was followed by one-sided attempts to restore social esteem. At stake was the recognition of being a worthy member of the community (Honneth 1992). Both parties wanted to secure such recognition, but in the end, both were unsuccessful. As a consequence, they had to continue; there was no real alternative. Not being granted recognition was assumed to threaten the entire social being, and Hegel's master-and-slave dialectic illustrated the relentless nature of that desire. People will do anything to gain or regain social esteem, in the eyes of fellow members of the community. So, the struggle for recognition evolved into a life-and-death struggle, culminating in murder. But the conflict had not been settled; instead, it escalated beyond anybody's control. With one opponent dead, the right to revenge was passed on to the family of the fallen, which continued the struggle, eventually escalating to war (Hegel 1998). The parable, which captured the Hegelian version of the state of nature (Constãncio 2015), showed that it was not possible to gain recognition strictly in everyday interaction between individuals. Instead of being granted recognition as fully part of the community, the community was torn apart. To restore social esteem was thus ultimately impossible without state intervention.

In *System der Sittlichkeit*, the struggle for recognition was propelled by the desire to restore social esteem. From the very outset, the desire was ambivalent, as the struggle was set in motion by feelings of not being recognized and the need to vindicate oneself in the eyes of others. Both parties were torn between their immediate responses to acts of disrespect and their overarching striving for social esteem in the community. Hegel's early account of the master-and-slave dialectic thus incorporated the original ambiguity of the ancient Greek notion of *thumos*, between a narrow and broad conception.

What drove the struggle for recognition was *thumos* in the narrow sense – the desire for punishment as status restoration; starting with a theft and culminating in murder. The struggle unfolded within the context of a culture in which rank-specific social esteem was anxiously guarded. The desire was always more than a desire for punishment – and linked to the positive state of being recognized as a worthy member of the community. The desire for recognition was in other words a desire to gain status as full partner in social interaction. It was the basic desire to be acknowledged as part of the community. As Nancy Fraser has noted, to be recognized in terms of status is to be accepted 'as a full member of society' (Fraser 2000: 113); it is to be considered as 'one of us', a worthy participant in any kind of interaction. The desire for vengeance was a manifestation of that general desire, when suddenly being deprived of status following an offence.

Hegel treated *thumos*-like desire as a positive force in history, while being fully aware of its irrationality and volatility. Taken by itself, the desire for vengeance was unreservedly considered as a bad thing. As suggested in the *Philosophy of Right*, it should be eradicated, since vengeance was personal and particular, as opposed to rational and universal. But the eradication of vengeance happened because of and not despite vengeful desire. That point was conveyed by the first version of the master-and-slave dialectic. Experiences of *non*-recognition of social esteem triggered desire and sustained a struggle for recognition, which was eventually beneficial to all members of society. The bitter conflict between the two parties motivated by transgressive passion evolved – according to an immanent logic – into stable institutions through which goals associated with justice and rationality were attained. In *System der Sittlichkeit*, the resolution of the conflict between the two parties required the intervention of social institutions, which could act as representatives for the whole community (Hegel 1998). That was the historic mission of the state. The state resolved the struggle for recognition by providing the conditions for everybody's sense of social worth. Through the state, vengeance could be transformed into punishment (Schmidt 2007). The retrieval of social esteem was elevated from everyday interaction in the community to a higher authority, which responded according to universal rules and without passion. What had started as cycles of revenge ended in social institutions capable of offering recognition to everyone.

The dark side of recognition

Some recent attempts to rehabilitate *thumos* were undertaken in conscious opposition to what was perceived to be centuries of neglect. Modern scholars had come to forget about this powerful and non-material wellspring of social action, it was argued. Francis Fukuyama's *The End of History and the Last Man* and Peter Sloterdijk's *Rage and Time* emphasized its continued importance in the contemporary world. The two works were part of a limited set of literature that has discussed the ancient accounts of *thumos* within the context of a conservative political critique of the contemporary world (see also for instance Strauss 1989; Paskewich 2014). Interestingly, the two authors reflected the same tension between the narrow conception of *thumos* as retaliatory desire (Sloterdijk) and the broader notion of *thumos* as competitiveness and status-seeking (Fukuyama) as the ancient discussion.

Both attempts were set in a decidedly modern political context. *Rage and Time*, originally published in German in 2006, was concerned with the perceived eruption of rage in world politics, in the wake of the 'nine-eleven' terror attacks in 2001 (Couture 2016). The rage manifested in the terror attacks was a righteous anger, driven by pride and the wish to assert oneself on the world arena, yet essentially defensive – a response to status infractions associated with US involvement in Muslim countries. Western liberal democracies stood unprepared, according to Sloterdijk, or had gone soft due to their material affluence and insufficient outlet of 'thymotic energies' (Sloterdijk 2010: 13). Achilles's holy rage had been forgotten, which was regrettable, since it was tied to valiance and other virtues of the Homeric world. The forgetfulness extended from anger to all the virtues it once supported: the whole dimension of social life that comprised 'human pride, courage, stout-hearted-ness, craving for recognition, drive for justice, sense of dignity and honour, indignation, militant and vengeful energies' (Sloterdijk 2010: 14). The post 'nine-eleven' eruptions of rage in politics showed that *thumos* had not disappeared. It was only partially suppressed by civilization. Fukuyama likewise approached *thumos* as a central force in modern politics. The turnover of the real existing communist regimes in 1989 constituted the point of reference, and the book *The End of History and the Last Man*, published just a few years later, was widely read as a guide to the historical meaning of the events. Fukuyama argued that people rebelled for non-material reasons, and not due to economic factors, or the lack of consumer goods. While the political regime in Czechoslovakia, for instance, was able to deliver in terms of social security, it humiliated ordinary people on a daily basis, injuring their sense of dignity, which eventually drove them out on the streets to protest (Fukuyama 2012). To him, this was a testimony of the persisting strength of *thumos*. But it was not the disproportionate revenge of Achilles. *Thumos* was instead associated with the defence of moral values that were embedded in one's cultural context; 'when those values are not recognized by other people', he claimed, it 'gives rise to feelings of anger' (Fukuyama 2012: 172). *Thumos* was on this reading an incarnation of social morality. Anger was not primordial but steeped in a moral form, or mediated by basic notions of justice and esteem.

Fukuyama and Sloterdijk restated the ancient notion of *thumos* to capture the political force of anger, pride and shame in an age which to their mind was blind to higher, or immaterial, values. Fukuyama presented a broader approach, compared to Sloterdijk, by downplaying rage in favour of moral values, foregrounding violations of human dignity rather than preparedness to fight wars and channel rage. Taken together, they illustrated the classic ambiguity of *thumos*; the tension between status-seeking and retaliatory desire. In addition, and more surprisingly, they invoked Hegel's struggle for recognition to support their positions. Sloterdijk and Fukuyama considered *thumos* to be the essence of Hegel's concept of recognition, either without further qualification (Fukuyama 2012), or with the amendment that the Hegelian striving for recognition portrayed *thumos* as 'conditioned by civilization' (Sloterdijk 2010: 24). Their reference to Hegel may seem unorthodox, as it requires a reading that differs in a key respect from what is generally thought to characterize recognition. On most available accounts within the Hegelian tradition (Kojève 1969; Taylor 1975; Honneth 1992; O'Neill 1996), recognition is reciprocal and conducive to personal growth and societal well-being. The tradition also harbours a different approach to recognition, associated with Jean-Paul Sartre and Judith Butler, according to which domination is the ground for recognition. Satisfaction of desire involves sustaining subjection, as conformity to asymmetrical power structures is the precondition for recognition (Bertram and Celikates 2015; see also McNay 2008). Recognition is the final yet questionable reward for subject formation. Sloterdijk and Fukuyama, on the other hand, can be seen to question the majority approach from the point of view of desire rather than subject formation. Their accounts of *thumos* are the opposite of what is conventionally associated with the dynamics of recognition: one-sided rather than mutual, confined to social esteem, and defensive rather than progressive. A discussion of these three characteristics, and how they differ from influential approaches in the Hegelian tradition, as exemplified by Kojève (1969), Taylor (1975) and Honneth (1992), will reveal a new ambiguity of *thumos* – balancing between the bright side and the dark side of recognition – and, beyond that, a convergence in the shared emphasis on social morality, as providing the basic coordinates of desire.

1. *One-sided rather than mutual.* There are few traces of Hegelian dialectic. The logic is one of one-sided assertion rather than mutual struggle. Sloterdijk's rage is monologic. Achilles was acting on anger, consumed by the idea of restoring honour, without taking the responses of other people into account. He was not satisfied by the death of Hector, his main antagonist in battle. The rage drove Achilles to drag Hector's dead body behind his chariot around the walls of Troy; dragged by its heels, in a final act of disrespect. He went too far and did not care. Fukuyama reproduced the one-sidedness at the level of values, when he characterized the Hegelian desire for recognition as 'a form of self-assertion, a projection of one's own values on the outside world' (Fukuyama 2012: 172). The other can accept the projected values, or reject them; winning or losing. Recognition is conditional on the surrender of the other. From a more conventional Hegelian perspective, this appears as an odd kind of recognition, without mutuality, produced seemingly regardless of the other. Most interpretations of the master-and-slave dialectic tend to think of the other as the main character in the account. At the most basic level, it is a story about

how hard it is to satisfy desire, precisely because it depends on the other. The other is – and has to be – an autonomous agent, capable of granting as well as withholding recognition. Historically, by stressing the interactional dimension, Hegel took a significant step forward with respect to existing approaches to recognition. The idea of struggle was a radical invention compared to Fichte's rights-oriented model of recognition (Honneth 1992). Now, there may well be an element of recognition also in one-sided assertion. What appears as one-sided assertion between individuals may reveal the utmost dependence on the other – in the shape of the big Other. As I will argue, this is precisely the kind of recognition provided by punishment. Extreme disregard for specific others may involve extreme sensitivity to the expectations of social morality and be rewarded by the generalized other (Lacan 1992; Žižek 2006). The necessary mutuality need not involve specific individuals. For the later Hegel, recognition was embedded in institutionalized social practice (Honneth 2003). If so, what appears as monologic rage, or one-sided projection of values, may in fact involve far-reaching perceptiveness to existing status orders.

2. *The reduction to social esteem.* The recognition concerned social esteem, and only social esteem. In their attempts to revive the ancient conception of *thumos*, Sloterdijk and Fukuyama stressed the centrality of pride and honour, shame and revenge, dignity and ambition in social life. To speak of recognition in this way makes sense. There appear to be some widely acknowledged cross-references making up a cluster of family resemblances oriented around social esteem. The corresponding words – 'status', 'prestige', 'honour', 'dignity' and 'recognition' – are interwoven in everyday language (Sennett 2003). For a long time, moreover, it may have been the only conceivable recognition. Status recognition was the primordial form of recognition, historically (Taylor 1992; Honneth 2003; Welskopp 2013). But the emphasis on social esteem comes across as reductive, by modern standards. As discussed in the Hegelian tradition, new forms of recognition came forth during the nineteenth century, linked to the state, to education and the family. The family offered love and emotional support, and the state provided equal opportunity and respect for legal rights (Honneth 2011). Through the educational system, individuals earned merits, which could be realized in the emerging labour markets in return for higher income. Consequently, more things than social esteem came to be expected and desired in the interaction with other people and the wider community. Alongside the desire for social honour and competitiveness, the desire for recognition extended into political rights – to be seen as a citizen or as part of a specific group – and emotional support – to be seen with loving eyes in the private sphere. The desire for recognition came to include more than social status. In a modern context, the emphasis on social esteem may thus appear reductive.

3. *Backward-looking and defensive, rather than progressive.* Sloterdijk and Fukuyama stressed the defensive and potentially violent affirmation of social esteem. By doing so, they illuminated what might be referred to as the dark side of recognition. The conservative thrust to rehabilitate *thumos* tended to be backward-looking, yearning toward what had been lost, or was felt to be endangered: individual honour or collective values. Fully appreciating *thumos* would make people 'redeem what they possess' (Sloterdijk 2010: 16). What they possessed was above all status. Social status and capacity for retaliation took precedence over other values which, on a different analysis, were equally much a part of recognition, for instance mutual respect, equal rights, and emotional support. It was a world in which social esteem must be actively upheld and sometimes violently defended, much like in the early version of the master-and-slave dialectic, without recourse to institutional redress. The vision could not be any more different from the more typical Hegelian prospect of collective progress. In *System der Sittlichkeit*, the struggle was powered by individual desire to recover lost social esteem, at any cost. Yet while the struggle for recognition could be fierce and violent, it evolved into stable institutions and mutual respect, and a corresponding expansion of autonomy at the societal level. The entire process took place via negativity; that was the dialectical twist. Experiences of non-recognition sustained the desire for more recognition. Desire was transgressive, and evolved through negativity, but in one direction, and one direction only: toward more recognition and increased liberty.

In light of these differences, *thumos* as envisioned by Sloterdijk and Fukuyama had few and strenuous ties to recognition. It might appear to be the opposite rather than the essence of the Hegelian dynamics of desire. Within the tradition, one-sided assertion and dominance have generally been dismissed as inauthentic, or a skewed form of recognition. Oppression – and related experiences – had a place in the analysis, but only as moments along the way toward full recognition. In the recent German reception, associated with Critical Theory, it was axiomatic that recognition always represented 'the opposite of practices of domination or subjection' (Honneth 2007: 325). Hegel's fundamental intuition was one of historic progress; individual claims for recognition transcended existing institutional forms of recognition, successively pushing them to acknowledge and enable more freedom (Honneth 1992). Each stage of recognition led to more encompassing demands – for extended rights, increased status or emotional caring – being placed on the existing institutions. A similar vision recurred in other influential readings of Hegel, such as Charles Taylor's communitarian interpretation. The *Phenomenology* described a process toward full human self-realization, as a progressive externalization of inner strivings, and the corresponding evolution of social conditions. The recognition being provided in mutual interaction with significant others was vital for the growth of individuals, for their sense of who they were and developed into (Taylor 1975; 1992). In the French reception, starting with Alexandre Kojève, desire represented the motor force in history, constantly prompting actions that transcended the prevailing condition. As such, it could involve hunger, followed by the quest for food. But in this respect humans were no different from animals. The desire for recognition was the specifically human desire. Everyone wanted to be recognized by others in the community, representing a value which was desired by others. The struggle for recognition would eventually lead to the equal recognition of all individuals, although each desire was blind, defensive and insisting on unconditional satisfaction (Kojève 1969). In all these lines of reception, the struggle for recognition was unequivocally progressive, in terms of personal growth, self-knowledge, extended recognition or more freedom.

There are thus two very different accounts of the dynamic of the desire for social esteem. On the one hand, there is the conservative thrust to rehabilitate *thumos* (Fukuyama 2012; Sloterdijk 2010) and on the other hand, the dominant approaches to Hegelian recognition (Kojève 1969; Taylor 1975; Honneth 1992). The two sets of accounts are in some respects diametrically opposed to each other. Yet both of them are nonetheless firmly rooted in the basic characteristics of the desire, as well as in a common conception of the source of the desire. From my perspective, the strength of the two sets of accounts is that they capture each of the main directions of *thumos* – toward one-sided assertion, a strict focus on status, and defensiveness, or, alternatively, toward mutual respect, emotional support and equal rights. Taken together, they further highlight the central importance of social morality, which provides the basic coordinates of the desire for social esteem.

Same desire, contrary outcomes. In the writings of Plato and Aristotle, *thumos* was already highly ambiguous. The desire could find satisfaction in vengeance, or in the common good, in ways that could appear to be irrational or rational, narrow-minded or in accordance with higher values. The direction toward defensive assertion was always present, as one option. *Thumos* is blind in one important sense. Desire, by its very nature, transcends the given, as it insists on immediate satisfaction. But the direction of transcendence is not inherent in the dynamics of desire. Neither of the two main directions can be taken for granted. The direction should be approached as an outcome which is influenced by external conditions, and not in terms of immanent logics. In the mainstream Hegelian tradition, it was postulated that individual desire for recognition by necessity led to ever-increasing recognition – also at a societal level: more freedom, and social institutions conducive to more recognition, and individual growth. But the desire for recognition may also work counter to the evolution of social institutions and personal development. The desire for recognition can propel processes toward punishment of non-conformity, as well as toward enlarged tolerance and respect for legal rights. Once in motion, however, as desire is operating in one direction rather than the other, there seems to be an inherent logic at work, rooted in the basic characteristic of desire. Being provided with more rights and more status is transgressive, in that the desire cannot be durably satisfied and always incorporates a yearning for more: more of the same. In this respect, the desire to be recognized as a full member of the community, or the urge to avenge personal injustice is no different from less complex desires, such as hunger or thirst. The dark side is just as transgressive as the bright side of recognition, but in a very different direction: toward intolerance, violence, calls for justice, the discovery of new groups to persecute, new forms of deviance, and more punishment.

The underlying social morality. On both sets of accounts, social morality provided the basic coordinates for the desire for social esteem. Hegel foregrounded the lived morality (*Sittlichkeit*), which differed between communities, with respect to what conferred status, the principles of punishment, standards of expectations, and notions of what the world was like. Social morality was behind the shifting content of *thumos*-related virtues and vices in ancient Greece, medieval France, and early-modern Germany. The collective morality of the group was the source of desire – and that which, if violated, provoked anger and propelled collective action (Fukuyama 2012). On that common basis, *thumos* could find satisfaction in conventional goals, which conferred social status on the individual, such as higher education, a well-kept home, military service, gainful employment, a spotless reputation, conspicuous consumption, or whatever happened to confer social esteem on an individual. This shaped the basic coordinates of desire. Hence, strictly speaking, my desire is not my desire. To gain recognition, it is never about what I want, but what I take that others expect from me. As Slavoj Žižek put it bluntly; 'the original question of desire is not directly "What do I want?", but "What do others want from me?"' (Žižek 1997: 9). The key figure is the other, whose desire it is. It can be significant others, specific people in everyday life. But it can also be interpreted as a generalized other, the lived social morality and stratified notions of status, which are embedded in practices such as punishment. Generalized, but never undifferentiated, and always fine-tuned to the social positions of individual members. On this basis of expectations, *thumos* can be deflected from individual status concerns, toward higher values, associated with justice and morality. These were idealized abstractions derived from the way of life of the community, which contained the seeds of narrow-mindedness and violence, and could dictate punitive anger toward acts of nonconformity (Paskewich 2014), while allowing people to conceive of themselves as companions of true glory, like the white-winged horse in Plato's parable.

On this line of reasoning, there is no particular desire to punish which is shared by the population and which can only find satisfaction in punishment, and punishment alone. There is no need to posit a natural lust for cruelty – nor is there a need for a socially constructed one. Instead, there is a desire to be fully part of society, which is generic and which may be satisfied by punishment – and a range of other actions, achievements and institutions: the personal, irrational rush to action and the prudent achievement of conventional goals in life. The beauty of the *thumos* concept is that it deals with complexity and duality already at the stage of desire. In ancient Greece, *thumos* oscillated between a narrow meaning – the desire for revenge, uncontrollable anger in the face of a specific violation, immediate restoration of social honour – and a broader meaning: the desire for social esteem, conferred by achievement of conventional goals. The desire drew support from social morality and existing notions of order and justice, yet was inherently dualistic, predisposed to excess and to conformity, marked by uncontrollable anger and calculated concern, by personal affliction and general notions of justice. In the field of tension between reason and passion, *thumos* was treated as an elusive third element of human motivation, which has been persistently discussed and ambiguously valued in the Western tradition of thought. Vengeance and status-seeking have been balancing at the margins of legitimacy, as reflected in Aquinas's positions on vengefulness (it could be rational) and status-seeking (it could be a cardinal sin). The fundamental ambiguity was further reflected in Hegel's first version of the master-and-slave dialectic, and sharply exposed in recent attempts to rehabilitate the concept by Sloterdijk and Fukuyama, which suggests that there may be a dark as well as a bright side of the dynamic of the desire for recognition of status. In the next chapter, I will follow this desire to the other side of the gap to discuss its satisfaction in three premodern historical contexts: the tragedies in ancient Greece, the depictions of hell in medieval Europe and the early-modern public executions, as consumed by contemporary audiences.

References

Aquinas, Thomas (1941) *Summa theologica*. London: Burns Oates & Washbourne.

Aristotle (1926) *The 'art' of rhetoric*. Trans. by J. H. Freese. Cambridge, MA: Harvard University Press.

Aristotle (1968) *De anima. Books II and III*. Trans. by D. W. Hamlyn. Oxford: Clarendon Press.

Aristotle (1976) *Nicomachean ethics*. Trans. by J. Thomson. Harmondsworth: Penguin.

Bertram, Georg, and Celikates, Robin (2015) Towards a conflict theory of recognition: on the constitution of relations of recognition in conflict. *European Journal of Philosophy* 23(4): 838–861.

Butler, Judith (1990) *Gender trouble: feminism and the subversion of identity*. New York: Routledge.

Butler, Judith (1997) *The psychic life of power: theories in subjection*. Stanford, CA: Stanford Univ. Press.

Constâncio, João (2015) *Struggle for recognition and will to power. Probing an affinity between Hegel and Nietzsche*. In K. Hay & L. dos Santos (eds.), *Nietzsche, German Idealism and its critics*. Berlin: De Gruyter. pp 66–99.

Cooper, John (1999) *Reason and emotion*. Princeton: Princeton University Press.

Couture, Jean-Pierre (2016) *Sloterdijk*. Cambridge: Polity.

Dante Alighieri (1997) *Divine Comedy. Longfellow's translation*. Champaign, IL: Project Gutenberg.

Dubet, Francois (2009) *Injustice at work*. Boulder: Paradigm Publishers.

Ellrich, Robert (1984) Envy, identity, and creativity: Inferno XXIV-XXV. *Dante Studies, with the Annual Report of the Dante Society* 102: 61–80.

Fraser, Nancy (2000) Rethinking recognition: overcoming displacement and reification in cultural politics. *New Left Review* 3: 107–120.

Fukuyama, Francis (2012) *The end of history and the last man.* 20th anniversary edn. London: Penguin.

Hegel, Georg Wilhelm Friedrich (1998) System der Sittlichkeit. *Gesammelte Werke, Band 5. Schriften und Entwürfe (1799–1808).* Hamburg: Meiner.

Hirschman, Albert (1977) *The passions and the interests: political arguments for capitalism before its triumph.* Princeton: Princeton University Press.

Homer (2004) *Odyssey. Books 13–24.* Trans. by A. T. Murray. Cambridge, MA: Harvard University Press.

Homer (2015) *The Iliad.* Trans. by P. Green. Oakland: University of California Press.

Honneth, Axel (1992) *Kampf um Anerkennung: zur moralischen Grammatik sozialer Konflikte.* Frankfurt am Main: Suhrkamp.

Honneth, Axel (2003) Redistribution as recognition. A response to Nancy Fraser. In N. Fraser and A. Honneth (eds.), *Redistribution or recognition?: a political-philosophical exchange.* London: Verso. pp 110–197.

Honneth, Axel (2007) Recognition as ideology. In B. van den Brink and D. Owen (eds.), *Recognition and power: Axel Honneth and the tradition of critical social theory.* Cambridge: Cambridge University Press. pp 323–347.

Honneth, Axel (2011) *Das Recht der Freiheit: Grundriss einer demokratischen Sittlichkeit.* Berlin: Suhrkamp.

Kirkpatrick, Robin (2004) *Dante, the Divine comedy.* Cambridge: Cambridge University Press.

Klosko, George (2006) *The development of Plato's political theory.* Oxford: Oxford University Press.

Kocka, Jürgen (2004) The middle classes in Europe. In H. Kaelble (ed.), *The European way: European societies in the 19th and 20th centuries.* Oxford: Berghahn. pp 15–43.

Kojève, Alexandre (1969) *Introduction to the reading of Hegel.* New York: Basic Books.

Koziak, Barbara (2000) *Retrieving political emotion: thumos, Aristotle, and gender.* University Park: Pennsylvania State University Press.

Lacan, J. (1992) *The Seminar of Jacques Lacan. Book VII. The ethics of psychoanalysis: 1959–1960.* New York: W. W. Norton.

Langum, Virginia (2016) *Medicine and the seven deadly sins in late medieval literature and culture.* New York: Palgrave Macmillan.

McNay, Lois (2008) *Against recognition.* Cambridge: Polity.

Miner, Robert (2009) *Thomas Aquinas on the Passions. A study of Summa Theologiae, 1a2ae 22–48.* Cambridge: Cambridge University Press.

Oksenberg Rorty, Amélie (1992) *De Anima* and its recent interpreters. In M. Nussbaum and A. Oksenberg Rorty (eds.), *Essays on Aristotle's* De Anima. Oxford: Clarendon Press. pp 7–14.

O'Neill, John (1996) Introduction: a dialectical genealogy of self, society, and culture in and after Hegel. In J. O'Neill, (ed.) *Hegel's dialectic of desire and recognition: texts and commentary.* Albany: State University of New York Press. pp 1–25.

Paskewich, Christopher (2014) The roots of political community: thumos and tradition in Ancient Greek thought, http://anamnesisjournal.com/2014/09/roots-political-community-thumos-tradition-ancient-greek-thought/.

Pearson, Giles (2012) *Aristotle on desire.* Cambridge: Cambridge University Press.

Plato (2005) *Phaedrus*. Trans. by C. Rowe. Harmondsworth: Penguin.

Plato (2013a) *Republic Books 1–5*. Trans. by C. Emlyn-Jones and W. Preddy. Cambridge, MA: Harvard University Press.

Plato (2013b) *Republic Books 6–10*. Trans. by C. Emlyn-Jones and W. Preddy. Cambridge, MA: Harvard University Press.

Schmidt, Steffen (2007) *Hegels System der Sittlichkeit*. Berlin: Akademie Verlag.

Sennett, Richard (2003) *Respect in a world of inequality*. New York: W. W. Norton.

Sloterdijk, Peter (2010). *Rage and time: a psychopolitical investigation*. New York: Columbia University Press.

Strauss, Leo (1989) *The rebirth of classical political rationalism*. Chicago: University of Chicago Press.

Taylor, Charles (1975) *Hegel*. Cambridge: Cambridge University Press.

Taylor, Charles (1992) The politics of recognition. In A. Gutmann (ed.), *Multiculturalism and the politics of recognition*. Princeton: Princeton University Press. pp 25–74.

Urmson, James (1990) *The Greek philosophical vocabulary*. London: Duckworth.

Weber, Max (1972) *Wirtschaft und Gesellschaft*. Tübingen: J. C. B. Mohr.

Welskopp, Thomas (2013) Anerkennung – Verheissung und Zumutungen der Moderne. In A. Honneth, O. Lindemann and S. Voswinkel (eds.), *Strukturwandel der Anerkennung. Paradoxien sozialer Integration in der Gegenwart*. Frankfurt am Main: Campus. pp 41–73.

Žižek, S. (1997) *The plague of fantasies*. London: Verso.

Žižek, S. (2006) *How to read Lacan*. London: Granta.

4 The paradox of tragic pleasure

In *Poetics*, Aristotle approached the conundrum, how watching the pain of others can be pleasurable. The Attic tragedies of his time presented the audience with horrific acts of violence and intra-familial betrayal, seemingly without end. At the same time, they provided pleasure to an audience. That is the paradox of tragic pleasure: the satisfaction received by watching the pain and suffering of others. Many well-known philosophers have had something to say about the problem, as it continued to puzzle over the centuries. No one articulated the paradox better than David Hume in the short essay *Of Tragedy* published in 1757:

> It seems an unaccountable pleasure, which the spectators of a well-written tragedy receive from sorrow, terror, anxiety, and other passions, that are in themselves disagreeable and uneasy. The more they are touched and affected, the more are they delighted with the spectacle.
>
> (Hume 1987: 216)

This is an eloquent and oft-cited formulation of what appears counter-intuitive: the more 'sorrow, terror, anxiety', the more pleasure. Given that pain and pleasure are conflicting emotions, how can the consumption of pain generate pleasure? Accustomed lines of reasoning did not seem to apply. Watching pain should be painful. But as indicated by Hume, pain was pleasurable within the context of tragedy. Hence the paradox.

The problem of 'pleasure in watching pain' first surfaced in the analysis of the pleasure drawn from the Attic tragedy. The theatre stage was also Hume's frame of reference. Yet the apparent paradox has been a recurring topic in the philosophical thought on punishment, as exacted on other venues. I have chosen three cases of punishment: classical tragedies (ancient Greece), afterworldly punishments (medieval Europe), and public executions (early-modern Europe). The cases may not – apart from the last one – be immediately recognizable as punishment, on a modern understanding. Yet they were culturally intelligible as such to contemporaries. The observed suffering was understood as punishment imposed for rule violations. All three kinds of punishments were moreover identified as pleasurable to contemporary audiences, and the pleasure they were thought to provide was explicitly addressed by contemporary authors. There are also other commonalities between the cases, with respect to the basic mechanisms involved and the kind of pleasure being generated. Yet the experience of pleasure is assumed to be context-specific. The pleasure of tragedies refers to the experience of attending the Great Dionysia during the short democratic period of Athens. Modern theatre audiences may enjoy watching the same plays, but they will by necessity have a different experience, due to the world enacted through punishment (they are not likely to believe in the play of gods or in mandatory vengeance), through the institutional infrastructure of punishment (private vengeance is not the only option), and through particularities of the scene of consumption (the plays are not part of festivities or political manifestations). For the same reasons, while modern readers of Dante may enjoy the *Divine Comedy* and be fascinated by the worlds of heaven and hell, they will not experience the recognition of the medieval Christian community, which depended on the historically unique and collectively shared existential predicament being enacted in the punishment.

I will revisit some of the more noteworthy discussions on the paradoxical pleasure of watching pain, here represented by Aristotle and Aeschylus (ancient Greece), Thomas Aquinas and Dante Alighieri (medieval France/ Italy), and Thomas Hobbes and Jeremy Bentham (early-modern England). The problem has been framed differently, reflecting the widely shifting state of the discussion at the time of writing: as the paradoxical pleasure of watching tragedies, the beauty of divine justice in hell, the enjoyment of excessively painful executions, or as the modern predicament of disavowed atrocities and private pleasures. The basic problem, however, was essentially the same: how can the consumption of pain generate pleasure? There is no straightforward answer to this question since the satisfaction was embedded in assumptions and narratives. The spectacle of cruelty was not pleasurable per se. The satisfaction must be contextualized and re-inscribed in the corresponding world. The world-making quality of punishment is assumed to be the key to the paradox. It is necessary to look beyond the salient pain and suffering, and even beyond the specific domain of crime and punishment, and envisage the social world as a whole, and which challenges that world presented people at the time. Hence, to understand the pleasure, one needs to understand the world – three very different worlds – being enacted, first in the Attic tragedy, and then by divine punishment in medieval Europe and in the early-modern executions. I will undertake an attempt to reconstruct existential dilemmas, as they were experienced by the individual spectator. The aim is to understand the possible enjoyment provided to contemporary penal audiences. How did punishment in three pre-modern contexts satisfy the desire for social esteem among contemporary audiences? Analytically, this means a shift from desire to enjoyment. The desire for social esteem will be followed to the other side of the gap between desire and enjoyment. Given the complexities of *thumos*, how was it satisfied through the consumption of punishment?

Attic tragedy: enacting existential dilemmas

In what has been called the '*locus classicus* of tragic choice' (Goldhill 2004: 25), Agamemnon was ordered by Zeus to embark on a punishing expedition to sack the city of Troy. Zeus is king of the Olympian Gods, yet he issued the order in his capacity as the protector of proper family relations. Helen, the wife of his brother, had run away with the prince of Troy, or she had been abducted by him. It is not altogether clear why Helen left but, either way, the household's honour had been violated. Hence, Zeus's intervention. On his way to Troy, Agamemnon received a message from another Olympian God, Artemis. A seer had witnessed a pregnant hare being eaten by eagles, which meant that Agamemnon will have to sacrifice his own daughter Iphigeneia, should he proceed on the mission. Agamemnon was thus presented with two options. He will either exact the obligated revenge, and be forced to kill his daughter afterwards, or he will spare the life of Iphigeneia, his daughter, and passively endure the violation of social norms tied to his status as king of Mycenae.

> A heavy fate not to obey
> But heavy if I am to rend my
> child, glory of the household,
> Staining a father's hand
> With streams of virgin sacrifice near the altar.
> What of this is without disaster?
>   (*Agamemnon* 206–11, translated
>   by Goldhill 2004)

The choice between defending the 'glory of the household' and the life of his daughter Iphigeneia is tragic since there was no escape from the dilemma. Zeus demanded restoration of social esteem, while Artemis has held up the fleet and insisted on the sacrificial killing. Agamemnon was trapped in a hopelessly difficult situation, where all options had disastrous ramifications. What conferred the specifically tragic quality on the choice was that it would be impossible for him to live with the consequences, however he chose, as underlined by the last line; 'what of this is without disaster?' Convinced that he will have to kill Iphigeneia with his own hands 'near the altar', in a way reminding one of the contemporary religious sacrifices, Agamemnon nevertheless continued to sail toward Troy and impose an excessive revenge on the people of Troy. But he could not live with the consequences of the choice – literally not. Arriving home victorious, Agamemnon was eventually murdered because of it.

The *Oresteia* was built on events and characters from the Homeric poems. It was a blood feud in which any act of punishment led to a call for revenge. The logic of private vengeance propelled the story (Goldhill 2004; Sommerstein 2010). The cycles of revenge were disproportionate and endless, starting with a supposed adultery, continuing with murders, between two ruling families across generations, also affecting numerous ordinary citizens who were compelled to take part in the penal expeditions, or were otherwise affected by them, as soldiers, sailors, residents or citizens. Every atrocity was part of an ongoing vendetta, where the perpetrator was the next victim; 'the very act of taking revenge repeatedly turns the revenger into an object of revenge' (Goldhill 2004: 24). The *Oresteia* thus embraced the sacred duty to uphold honour through punishment. The absolute character of the duty was underlined by divine command. Zeus directed Agamemnon to Troy, Apollo commanded Orestes to murder his own mother, and so on, while they were the ones who later had to live with the consequences of their own actions.

Although cast in a dramatic form, the *Oresteia* reflected the social institution of punishment at the time. It was also clearly influenced by democratic ideas and practices. The surviving plays of Aeschylus, Sophocles and Euripides, the three great tragics, were all written and produced during the heyday of Athenian democracy, and would incorporate some of its institutional inventions. As often discussed in the literature, they were marked by the tension between the aristocratic virtues of the Homeric poems, which stemmed from a different time, before the evolution of the city-state, and the 'civic ideology' of the democratic political rule (Seaford 1994; Goldhill 1990). The *Oresteia*, in particular, reflected both the Homeric world in which punishment relied on private vengeance, and the tension with an embryonic system of public justice, which still largely obeyed the logic of private vengeance (Cohen 1995; Allen 2000). One of the most discussed modifications of the original Homeric narrative was Aeschylus's introduction of a court of law in the *Eumenides*, the final part of the trilogy, to settle the vendetta. Orestes was tried for the murder of his mother; the deities of revenge were infuriated by the acquittal but eventually mollified and integrated in the new judicial order. The trial of Orestes on stage mirrored the proceedings of the public court in Athens (Sommerstein 2013), as well as the evolution of democratic institutions. Areopagus, the place of Orestes's trial, was symbolic in this respect. It had recently been a central political body of the aristocratic regime. Yet a few years before the *Oresteia* was performed for the first time, in the spring of 458 BC, the political power had been transferred from Areopagus to the popular Assembly. The move has been assessed as a decisive step in the process of democratization (Meier 1990). No longer used for political decision-making, Areopagus was converted into a court of law that came to be specialized in homicide cases (Leão 2013). So, choosing Areopagus as the venue for the trial in the *Oresteia* underlined the close links to contemporary penal practices, at the same time as it reminded the audience of ongoing political change.

The Attic tragedy itself was a democratic institution, and as such hugely popular. As opposed to earlier stage productions – music or poetry commissioned for court consumption – the tragedies were produced for citizens, rich and poor, and many people attended the plays and the festivals of which they were a central part (Roselli 2011). Tragedies were performed each spring during Great Dionysia. Spectators turned out in large numbers to socialize, or to fulfil their public obligations. It has been estimated that a substantial minority, between 15,000 and 20,000 people, of the total population of Athens attended the yearly festival (Griffith 1995). The spectatorship reflected the composition of any important public event, with an overwhelming presence of men with some amount of social standing. Female citizens, slaves and foreigners were present to some extent and, particularly in the early days, large numbers of poor people were present (Roselli 2011). Tickets were distributed through existing political networks. The regime and a civic ideology were promulgated, and high-ranking militaries presided over the rituals attached to the plays (Goldhill 1990; 2000). Attendance was expected. Those who were invited to the festival were expected to show up. Attendance was considered along the lines of a civic duty; 'theater attendance', it has been remarked, was 'closely linked to citizenship' (Winkler and Zeitlin 1990: 4). But it could also have been sought for other reasons. The popularity of the plays must, in addition, be attributed to the enjoyment they provided. The tragedies were written with the intention of providing audiences with pleasure (Destrée 2014), and many of them seem to have been successful in this respect. The experiences of contemporary Athenians who took part in the yearly festivals belonged to the 'frustratingly undefined but essential category of pleasure' (Roselli 2011: 26). Sitting on the benches in the open-air amphitheatres, they were presented with a series of atrocities and dismay on stage, which evidently afforded pleasure. The pleasure must be understood in its historic context. As Mark Griffith (1995) has argued, the Attic tragedy was a cultural form that was born during and in the strict sense confined to Athens in the fifth century BCE. The satisfaction drawn from watching *Oresteia* in the festival of Great Dionysia may have little to do with the possible satisfaction of today's audiences. Although the same tragedies are still played on scenes around the world, and remain popular, the pleasure they once provided has to be understood in context. The spectators' experience was shaped by the immediate circumstances surrounding the play – it was part of a large festival with elements of eating and drinking, religious processions and public relations – as well as by the shared frame of reference between authors, actors and audiences (Griffith 1995; Goldhill 2000; Rosselli 2011).

Plato was concerned about the popularity of the tragedies. In the *Republic* (606a-b), he criticized dramatic poetry for producing the wrong kind of emotions among the audience: above all pity. To feel for the characters' misfortunes on stage was pleasurable, yet he dismissed pity on the grounds that it was bad for the spectators' character. Aristotle adopted a different approach to the emotions involved, revalued pity and turned tragic pleasure into a philosophical problem. It has been called the 'paradox of tragic pleasure' (Destrée 2014): that tragedy at one and the same time generates pain and pleasure for an audience. One common approach to the paradox was to assume that the painful experience transformed as the play unfolded; what started as pain evolved into pleasure (Destrée 2014; Williams 2014). This approach was encapsulated in the notion of *katharsis*. In the Aristotelian analysis of tragedy, the experience was the joint product of pity and fear. While often translated as purification, *katharsis* is better thought of as discharge of emotion (Nuttall 1996). It was an overwhelming sense of relief, evolving out of the pity and the fear experienced by the audience, as they felt with the characters on stage. On one reading of Aristotle, *katharsis* referred specifically to the satisfaction of *thumos* and status anxieties (Belfiore 1992). Witnessing the main characters acting out their *thumos* on stage, appreciating their anguish from the safe position of the spectators' seat, and sensing the violent character of the desire and its disastrous consequences, affected the desire of the audience. Over the course of the *Oresteia*, the everyday distress and status anxieties of the audience were alleviated, by living through the tragic choices of Agamemnon. Indirectly, their own status distress was experienced less intensely. Watching tragedies thus tempered rather than satisfied the spectators' desire, which was just as transgressive and obsessed with social esteem as the characters'.

Alternatively, the pleasure of tragedies was somehow related to what the world was like, or what it was depicted to be like, against the backdrop of a transcendental order that cast its shadows over the events, and the spectators' reminiscence of basic existential conditions. What Aeschylus offered the contemporary spectators of the *Oresteia* was 'a magnified reflection of their own lives' (Euben 1982: 24). It was the mark of a skilful playwriter to re-enact the order of the world, along with the existential implications of that order. The contemporary audiences would recognize the moral dilemmas in their lives, their existing options and the forces at work behind them, in the actions and the sufferings of the characters on stage (Halliwell 2002; Nussbaum 1992). On this reading, the satisfaction would have less to do with the pain of others. Instead, the world-making qualities of tragedies were decisive. Tragic pleasure would not be derived from the pain of the other, mediated by fear and pity and other emotional reactions within the audience, but would stem from the consumption of punishment in its entire moral and world-making capacities. The tragedies provided the spectators with satisfaction by including them in a moral order and by processing their existential dilemmas. The audience not only recognized the underlying order of the world, in the sense that they were familiar with it. They were moreover recognized by that order in return – or more accurately: they might recognize *themselves* as parts of that order. The spectators were not merely spectators of a stage production but participants in a ritual that enacted a socio-religious world, which included them as individual cogs and confirmed their place in the bigger scheme of things.

The Attic tragedy constituted a community of spectators and underpinned interpretations of the social world specifically in the dimension of justice and order. The *Oresteia* was exemplary in this respect (Goldhill 2004; Griffith 1995; Macleod 1982). Popular notions of justice played a pivotal role. Although the acts of vengeance were predominantly extra-legal and excessive, they were ordained by the gods, and in accordance with the principles of social morality (Goldhill 2004; Leão 2013). The transcendent order and the world of human affairs were not kept separate. The Olympian Gods frequently intervened on behalf of the struggling human royalties. The leading characters were called upon by Zeus, or by Apollo, to execute the revenge, and to restore the status that came with their social position. The principles of honour, in particular with respect to family relations – norms of sexuality, hospitality, or loyalty – directed the course of action on stage, just like in the public realm. The expectation to protect social status was pervasive, throughout the social body, extending to everyone, in principle. Yet the enacted moral universe above all addressed what it meant to be 'a male, a citizen, an Athenian' (Griffith 1995: 63). This social minority – making up approximately one-tenth of the total population in the city-state at the time – represented the bulk of the participants at the festival (Roselli 2011). To this audience of adult male citizens, the tragedies presented a world governed by private vengeance, forces beyond their reach and the centrality of social esteem. Slaves, female citizens and foreign residents were represented as characters in the play, and contributed in their respective roles to produce the world, with which one was familiar. Although the existential dilemmas belonged to male citizens, everyone was part of the enacted moral universe. The trilogy ended with the whole people of Athens on stage, representing the unity of the city-state.

Modern audiences have grown accustomed to cultural representations of penal practices targeting primarily people who are far removed from the ordinary arenas of power, glory and even respectability. During Great Dionysia in the fifth century BCE, however, it was the suffering and the agony of royals that were consumed, not the more profane suffering of a drug pusher, or a highwayman. The main characters belonged to the social elite. Those whose punishments were on display were rulers, who commanded armies and ruled societies. The choruses and the minor parts represented the common people. Especially the role of the chorus was decisive for the satisfaction provided to the audience. In the *Oresteia*, the choruses included old men, wives, visitors, slaves and servants. The chorus assumed the view from below, in social terms. Their view on the events came closest to the perspective of the audience. It was moreover significant that the chorus was safe – just like the audience (Griffith 1995). The chorus was never endangered by the unfolding events and gave voice to down-to-earth opinions. Its mood shifted back and forth, and its loyalties were unreliable. When Agamemnon was about to announce the victory over Troy, the chorus lamented those who once left their homes – 'but instead of human beings urns and ashes arrive back'. It reproached the king for the heavy war casualties, and for 'the slaughter' instigated because of the personal affairs of his brother. The chorus warned of the opinions of ordinary people, who had to live with the consequences of vengeance and whose hearts were filled with anger (*Agamemnon* 435–55). In other passages the chorus spurred the characters on to take revenge. After Agamemnon's death, for instance, it incited Orestes to avenge the murder, by killing his mother. The chorus was sometimes cheering and lauding, sometimes warning and reproaching, the actions undertaken by the main characters (Conacher 1974). It maintained an ambivalent relationship to the elevated status of the rulers who acted on the prevailing notions of anger and honour, and who were later struck down in acts of retribution.

From the vantage point of ordinary people, tragic pleasure has been associated with the satisfaction of watching lionized rulers stumble and fall based on their own mistakes. Royals such as Agamemnon were being punished for offences which were all the greater because of their standing, and therefore punished all the more ingeniously. The satisfaction of the audience was moral, and depended on the self-incurred misfortunes of powerful others (Eagleton 2003). Yet one may catch sight of a fuller satisfaction, by completing the shift of focus from Agamemnon to the chorus. Essentially, it was a story about them, the common people in the chorus. Rather than processing the spectators' relationship to their superiors, the tragedies may have enacted a social world in which they recognized each other, thereby satisfying their own specific desire for recognition. Picking up on Peter Euben's remark on the achievement of Aeschylus, to provide contemporary audiences with a magnified reflection of their lives, I want to suggest that the tragedies processed a widely shared existential dilemma in ways that could involve a collective recognition of social esteem.

In the context of Athens in the fifth century BCE, the *Oresteia* enacted an existential dilemma which may have satisfied the spectators' *thumos*-desire, by way of each other. On the one hand, there was the generally shared expectation to assert social esteem, and to do so privately – specifically in the face of flagrant violations of honour. This expectation was acted out by the main characters, to the fullest extent, as underlined by the chorus on stage. On the other hand, there was the inability to determine one's own fate, the agonizing lack of control of consequences, which was likewise experienced to the fullest by the main characters, and commented on by the chorus, in a world that was ruled by wilful gods and other forces beyond human control. Not even Agamemnon, despite his being the great warrior king, could determine the outcomes, since it was a world which escaped the control of the main actors, the chorus and the audience alike. 'What of this is without disaster?' – like Agamemnon, they could experience being caught between impossible options. The tragedies acknowledged the imperative of status-seeking as well as the basic futility of that endeavour, affirming the vulnerability of everyone and the location of power elsewhere. By acting out contradictions that were inherent in *thumos*-desire and which were further reinforced by the social conditions, the tragedies acknowledged the predicament of the individual spectator. They repackaged the contradiction between fatalism and vigilant self-assertion into a coherent message, which was conveyed to the festival participants. It became a story about them; you try hard to fulfil existing norms of social esteem, just like Agamemnon did, while success is beyond your control, just like it was for him. Still you try – like we all do, and in this striving, in precisely this existential predicament, you are one of us: a citizen, as good as anyone and fully part of society. Watching Agamemnon struggle with the play of gods and the duty to vindicate social esteem could provide relief from status concerns, primarily to the male citizens who were the overwhelming majority of the audience. It made them recognize each other, as struggling with the same basic predicament in social life, and hence equally part of the group. In this way, the tragedy offered temporary satisfaction of the perpetual desire for social esteem. The spectators were recognized in their day-to-day struggle to manage the tension between the expectations of social morality and their lack of control of outcomes.

Divine justice: watching hell

The paradox of tragic pleasure recurred in a cosmological setting in the thirteenth century. In the work of Thomas Aquinas, it appeared as a theological problem, posed within the context of divine justice. The punishments in hell were seen to provide contemporary audiences with a pleasure of contradictory nature. It was a pleasure in watching the pain of others, even though the pain was envisioned rather than observed. The envisioned afterworldly punishments were an integral part of the composition of the moral universe. Yet how could watching or contemplating hell provide spectators with pleasure? And how could it be enjoyed in such a manner that one did not turn into a future candidate for afterworldly punishment? The problem was explicitly addressed in *Summa Theologica.*

As opposed to the large numbers of spectators at the *Great Dionysia* festival, few people at the time would have read Aquinas, or anyone else writing on divine justice. The *Summa Theologica* comprised four thousand pages, which were inaccessible to the vast majority, because of its style of writing, the limited literacy and the manual copying techniques. By itself, his treatise could not satisfy a wider audience. Similar observations apply to Dante Alighieri and his masterpiece the *Divine Comedy* completed in 1320. Its literary qualities escaped most people at the time, for reasons of literacy and copying techniques. His vision of hell was nevertheless part of the contemporary culture, and corresponded to widely spread notions on the afterlife (Morgan 1990). There were many routes through which the principles of divine justice being developed in the theological writings would reach and possibly satisfy an audience of ordinary people. Aquinas's positions could count on institutional support from the Catholic Church (Chesterton 1943). The influence of the Church was unparalleled at the time, and, according to its written instructions, hell and divine justice were topics in the weekly sermons held throughout the European continent. As the church-goers listened to the preaching, they could contemplate the imminence of afterworldly punishment, while watching visual representations of the damned being boiled, impaired, or consumed by fire. In hundreds of medieval churches, the Last Judgement was portrayed in horrific detail on walls, windows and ceilings (Fudgè 2016). Hence, while the consumption of poetry and theological work was restricted to educated circles, visual art and sermons reached a larger audience. At the time, ordinary people may not have been familiar with all the twists and turns of the arguments, or with issues that strike modern readers of the *Summa Theologica* as rather particular, such as whether the worm tormenting those consigned to hell was corporeal or not, what the fire was like, or whether there was really place for everybody underground (ST suppl.-III, Q 97). Yet they must have been familiar with the fundamentals of afterworldly punishment. The originally Augustinian idea, that everyone deserved everlasting punishment, except for a small minority of individuals selected by God, remained influential (Talbott 1993). Many people may therefore have perceived themselves to be bound for punishment in the afterlife. The punishment was moreover thought to be self-incurred, in the sense that it was a consequence of the sins in life. During the Middle Ages, the idea of hell was supplemented with ideas on transitory punishment, which integrated popular beliefs about an intermediate place between heaven and hell (Le Goff 1983). The dogma on the purgatory was officially adopted by the Catholic Church in 1274: incidentally, the same year as Aquinas passed away and left the manuscript of *Summa Theologica* behind.

In *Treatise on the last things*, at the end of *Summa Theologica*, Thomas Aquinas discussed the special enjoyment provided by the consumption of hell, from a safe distance. It was one of the many questions raised by the relationship between the two extreme states of paradise and hell. Both paradise and hell were expressions of divine justice, yet one was the place of perfect happiness and the other was the site of horrific punishment. The saints inhabited paradise, and Aquinas broached the matter of whether they were aware of the fate of their fellow Christian companions. Were the saints in paradise able to see the sufferings of the damned in hell? Was there a clear line of sight? The answer was emphatically yes. Since their existence in paradise was perfect in every respect, one might think that the blessed should be spared the inconvenience. Or as one objection read: 'any deformity in the visible object redounds to the imperfection of the sight' (ST suppl.-III, Q 94, A 1, arg. 2). But that would have contradicted the postulate of perfection. Aquinas held that they – alternately referred to as the 'blessed' and as the 'saints' – must be able to see, precisely because their existence was perfect.

> Nothing should be denied the blessed that belongs to the perfection of their beatitude /.../ [and] in order that the happiness of the saints may be more delightful to them and that they may render more copious thanks to God for it, they are allowed to see perfectly the sufferings of the damned.
> (ST suppl.-III, Q 94, A 1, co.)

The saints should thus be allowed to watch everything in hell. They could see, if they wanted to. Yet one might still ask: did they have to watch? Would they not pity the wretched souls, or be disturbed by their endless pain? No, Aquinas responded; there must be a clear line of sight to hell since watching the torture and the torment enhanced the happiness of the saints. They had to watch, precisely for this reason. The souls of the righteous were able to draw pleasure from watching the exquisite sufferings in hell, thereby contributing to their state of perfect happiness. But the answer came with certain reservations, which showed that the theological problem was bound up with a moral one.

Punishment already generated pleasure in this world. It was a fact of life that 'an angry man takes pleasure in thinking much about vengeance' (ST I-II, Q 48, A 1, co.). This pleasure was morally problematic. Taking pleasure in the suffering of a fellow human could not be justified. It constituted a kind of hatred, which was contrary to the love of God and hence wrong (ST II-II, Q 108, A 1). The same principle applied to the consumption of divine punishment in the next world. The pleasure must not be tainted by passions such as hatred or pity. To enjoy the misery of the wretched souls in hell was a species of hatred, and ruled out as sinful. Nor could the pleasure involve compassion with the condemned since that would mean partaking in their unhappiness, and hence cease to be pleasurable (ST suppl.-III, Q 94, A 2 & A 3). At the same time, Aquinas noted, the Bible endorsed the pleasure of punishment; as it was written, 'the just shall rejoice when he shall see the revenge' (ST suppl.-III, Q 94, A 3, s.c.). How could such a pleasure be untainted by passion? Evidently, hell had to be enjoyed in a special way. At this point, Aquinas invoked the crucial distinction between direct and indirect enjoyment. To enjoy directly was to be carried away by emotions, whereas indirect enjoyment was intellectual: enjoyment mediated by reason. Only the latter provided the necessary safe ground. The distinction led Aquinas to deduce that God himself took pleasure in the torments in hell: 'God rejoices not in punishments as such, He rejoices in them as being ordered by His justice' (ST suppl.-III, Q 94, A 3, ad. 2). The punishments revealed the full extent of the love of god and of the beauty of divine justice. What might have appeared as only human misery and excessive pain was in fact evidence of the opposite: the perfection of the underlying order. In the same vein, the blessed in paradise did not enjoy the torture directly; instead, their pleasure was mediated by reason. It was a kind of intellectual enjoyment that bore the mark of a private insight into the build-up of the world. Hence, 'the saints will rejoice in the punishment of the wicked, by considering therein the order of Divine justice and their own deliverance, which will fill them with joy' (ST suppl.-III, Q 94, A 3, co.). Some people were able to see beyond the pain and beyond the torments in hell to instead appreciate the order and perfection of everything – and *that* was the object of their satisfaction.

The philosophical distinction between direct and indirect enjoyment was linked to practical outcomes. Like everything else, the pleasure of punishment was subject to divine justice and part of the final equation. Given the dual prospects of heaven and hell, the problem of the pleasure in watching the pain of others has perhaps never been posed more radically. Everlasting happiness and eternal pain were separated by the fine line between virtuous and sinful behaviour. The imposed suffering had to be perceived strictly through notions of divine justice; one could not be moved by the suffering as such, through pity or vengefulness, or through the sense of being better off than those who suffered, in hell or elsewhere. If the satisfaction of *thumos* more generally was a balancing act between worldly notions of social esteem and religious condemnation of pride, the pleasure of punishment involved a special balancing act. Derived in one way, the pleasure was a virtue, and derived in another way, it was a sin. If tainted by emotion, what was an intellectual joy for would-be saints, the contemplation of a perfectly ordered universe, would slip into a mortal sin, reducing them to ordinary sinners and diminishing their prospects at the Last Judgement. Everyone, without exception, was at the same time invited to contemplate the principles of divine justice. Nothing stopped ordinary Christians – referred to as 'wayfarers' – from appreciating the fundamental order of the world and the redemption to be found in punishment, although it was a task that presented them with much difficulty, 'because in a wayfarer the passions often forestall the judgment of reason' (ST suppl.-III, Q 94, A 3, ad 3). The saints were seen to be better off in this respect, as they were disposed to enjoy punishment through reason and much less likely to fall prey to passions.

The *Divine Comedy* belonged to a literature genre on the afterlife, which integrated popular beliefs with official Christian tenets. It presented a story about everlasting happiness and eternal damnation, and the ways to each according to the principles of divine justice. Dante was guided by the Roman poet Virgil through the long series of punishments in hell and in purgatory, before ascending to paradise. It was a demonstration of divine justice at work. The pain, in particular, was endorsed as an expression of divine justice, as the famous inscription on the gates to hell reminded the reader:

> Through me the way to everlasting pain,
> Through me the way among the lost.
> Justice moved my maker on high.
> Divine power made me,
> Wisdom supreme, and primal love.
>   (*Inf.* III: 1–6)

The institution of hell was in other words built on the same principles as the rest of the world: justice, wisdom and love. The afterworldly punishments forcefully demonstrated these principles – in ways that Dante sought to reconstruct from his horizon.

Whereas Aeschylus, in the *Oresteia*, had developed the implications of the Greek concept of justice simultaneously at the ontological and the interpersonal level (Leão 2013), in Dante's world the two kinds of justice were to be kept strictly separate. In Medieval Europe, the transcendent order was not conceived to intervene in the worldly business of punishment. The principles were of divine origin, and their import admittedly evaded human comprehension. At the same time, Dante implicitly passed hundreds of judgements in the *Inferno*, and the apparent lack of system in this part has puzzled interpreters of the *Divine Comedy*. As opposed to the penances in the *Purgatorio*, the punishments in hell did not cohere to established theological principles. Many individual encounters have given rise to speculation. Why, for instance, did Dante suddenly encounter his friend and teacher Brunetto Latini in the middle of hell? Was it because he knew that Latini was secretly homosexual and foresaw the outcome of the judgement upon his death (Ruud 2008)? Church doctrines at the time prescribed harsh penalties, and in some parts of Italy sodomy was punishable by death (Burgwinkle 2004). In addition to being thought of as acts of divine intervention based on unknowable principles, the pain inflicted in hell also seems to have been grounded in the social morality of Italy in the fourteenth century. The incorporation of social morality was precisely what made them intelligible to contemporary audiences as punishment. Consequently, the *Inferno* conveys a rather stereotypical image of sinners. Although everyone in the Christian community was supposed to be a sinner, and thus a likely candidate for eternal damnation, the actual population of sinners in Dante's hell – as well as, one might add, in the visual representations in the churches (Fudgè 2016) – were thieves, murderers, prostitutes, corrupt politicians, adulterers and heretics. They were punished in this world – and they were punished in the next world.

There are two answers to the central question, how the consumption of the envisioned punishments in the afterlife provided pleasure to contemporary audiences. One assumes that the audience were believers; that people who read Aquinas, or took part of the Thomistic framework via the weekly sermons, actually endorsed the cosmology and were able to fully appreciate the divinely ordered world. The other answer simply assumes that the audience were familiar with ideas of the inevitability of afterworldly punishment, and felt that there was little they could do about it.

1. Robin Kirkpatrick has argued that the *Divine Comedy* explored the ontological relationship between God and human beings in a way that turned the relationship into a personal one (Kirkpatrick 2004). To Dante, the cosmological order was not abstract, or indifferent to the strivings of individuals. The relationship was emphatically personal, as underlined at the very end of the *Paradisio* when Dante sees God face to face, and in a flash experienced the divine order in its entirety. He was overwhelmed by the immediate insight; 'O how all speech is feeble and falls short of my conceit' (*Par.* XXXIII: 121–2). The relationship was reciprocal. In the face-to-face encounter, he not only saw God but he was also seen by God. Dante was recognized by God, as a full member of His creation. After the long wandering, he was finally satisfied; 'the ardour of desire within me ended' (*Par.* XXXIII: 48). The encounter in paradise was painted in the brightest of colours, and was accompanied by feelings of joy. Dante's encounters in hell would not produce joy. They would not include the aspect of a deeply personal recognition, but could nevertheless

offer satisfaction of *thumos*. Following the inscription on its gates, one might discern the workings of God in the punishments in hell. They revealed a world shot through with meaning and emotional ties, entirely built on the principles of love and justice and wisdom. To see the punishments in that light may have provided satisfaction of the desire for recognition. The satisfaction required the indirect enjoyment advocated by Aquinas, and might in addition presuppose a particular vantage point, largely corresponding to the position of the saints in Aquinas's cosmology. Having managed to reach paradise, and thereby occupying the only available safe position in universe, the saints could contemplate the cosmological order, as they watched the never-ending torments far below. To them, the punishments in hell need not be a personal concern but could satisfy their desire for social esteem: the reassurance of their place – the best possible one – in a divinely ordered world.

2. To ordinary people, representations of hell were a reminder of what awaited. Their position in the enacted world had little resemblance to the saints' situation. Ordinary people could not avoid to sin, as they were, on occasion, envious, proud, licentious, or enraged. The audience, for instance church visitors listening to the preachings, or looking at the paintings of people being punished in hell, were sinners destined for hell, and they too – or most of them – could one day be punished in a similar fashion. Yet precisely because punishment in the afterlife seemed next to inevitable, they may also have experienced the satisfaction of *thumos*. They might do penance in life, or other things to survive the Last Judgement, such as purchasing counterfeited relics (Fudgè 2016). The wealthy could buy letters of indulgence. Yet not even kings or popes could escape the scrutiny at the Last Judgement. The outcome lay in the hands of forces beyond their comprehension as well as their control. The *Divine Comedy* enacted that dilemma, of being a good Christian – as good as anybody else – and of belonging to a community destined for damnation. You were expected to be a good Christian and live a virtuous life, without sin. Yet that was impossible except for a select few, so, despite their strivings, most people were destined for hell, or purgatory. That was a shared dilemma – the expectation to be a good Christian and the eventual futility of that striving, as you were doomed anyway, according to both Church doctrines and widely held popular beliefs. Ironically, this involved a recognition of full membership of the community. You may not be a good Christian in the eyes of God – such recognition was reserved for the saints. But you were recognized by other people as a full and worthy member of the Christian community, since your predicament was the same as everybody else's, on the road to damnation, yet leading a life in accordance with the social morality at the time, as far as anyone was concerned. In this way, the consumption of hell offered temporary satisfaction of the perpetual desire for social esteem. The wayfarers were recognized in their day-to-day struggle to manage the tension between the expectations of social morality and the expectations of the Catholic Church.

Early-modern capital punishment: theatres of recognition

On 5 January in 1757, Robert-François Damiens attacked and lightly wounded the French King Louis XV. His execution some months later made a lasting impression on contemporaries and was captured in gruesome detail by Michel Foucault on the very first pages of *Discipline and Punish*. The reactions of the audience can be glimpsed in the account.

> It is said that, though he [Robert-François Damiens] was always a great swearer, no blasphemy escaped his lips; but the excessive pain made him utter horrible cries, and he often repeated: "My God, have pity on me! Jesus, help me!" The spectators were all edified by the solicitude of the parish priest of St Paul's who despite his great age did not spare himself in offering consolation to the patient.
>
> (unnamed chronicler quoted in Foucault 1979: 3)

The torture was intended to end by Damiens being quartered. But the executioners were insufficiently familiar with the technique, and the horses, pulling each of the four limbs, failed again and again. The punishment was horrendous; unusually horrendous, in fact, as the crime was political and had been directed at the king. This was Foucault's foremost concern: the ceremonial cruelty. The shock effect of the opening scene made the reader appreciate the magnitude of the transformation which punishment undeniably went through in the first half of the nineteenth century. The protracted cruelty of the Paris execution differed markedly from the hidden pains of imprisonment. However, what the snapshot of Damiens and the priest also reveals is that the spectacle of cruelty was embedded in a story of possible redemption through suffering. The spectators were described by the unnamed chronicler to be edified. There was a moral lesson embedded in the spectacle of suffering. The lesson was not so much about what was right or wrong; rather, people were instructed what the world was like in the bigger scheme of things, and reminded of their own place in it.

Once again, the enacted world is the key to unlock the apparent paradox of how pleasure could be derived from the pain of others. David Hume's famous formulation of the problem concerned 'well-written' tragedies: stage productions, where the experience of pain to some extent relied on the powers of imagination on the part of the audience, and not the contemporary penal practices. But the paradox of tragic pleasure is equally applicable to public executions. It may have been more socially accepted to draw pleasure from watching a tragedy. Yet the paradox itself was merely underlined by the fact that the pain that confronted spectators at the execution was real, as opposed to the pain being enacted in the tragedies. The violence of early-modern punishment could be excessive, sometimes extending beyond death, when maimed corpses were put on display. Yet as indicated by contemporary observations to the effect that public executions reminded them of classic tragedies, desire may have been satisfied in a similar fashion. It was not the kind of penal pleasure that most readily springs to mind: the intense arousal at the scene, or the eye-witness accounts of carnivalesque excitement. Instead, it was a relief of *thumos*, in the sense of fully belonging to a community. Witnessing an execution during the early-modern period could satisfy the spectators' *thumos* by including them in a ritual, which demonstrated a shared existential predicament. The public executions enacted a world in which the common people, who made up the overwhelming majority of the audience, experienced unconditional protection and extreme vulnerability. Caught between the two forces of the sovereign state and imminent death, there seemed to be little they could do about it.

At the beginning of the period, especially in the sixteenth century, European executions were shrouded in a dense web of religious symbolism. Even the extremely cruel executions contained aspects of redemption. As several historians have pointed out, the first-hand experiences of horrific punishments were framed within a cosmological order where pain had a deeper religious meaning (Cohen 1989; Merback 1999; Groebner 2003). To the contemporary audience, the ritual on the scaffold seemed to re-enact the Christian cosmology, in which they too were condemned from the outset, yet were miraculously offered the prospect of redemption through the suffering on the cross. For this reason, it has been argued, the public executions could be comforting (Merback 1999). Contemporary audiences may have been no less horrified, but were at the same time reassured. Where modern audiences might primarily see cruelty, in the floggings, the mutilations and the hangings, contemporary audiences could also discern purification of sin and appreciate a deep-seated order of the world, as argued by Valentin Groebner (2003). He recapitulated the story of one papal envoy, who was travelling from Rome to Northern Europe in 1517. Having passed through the Alps, the envoy noted a proliferation of execution sites, as well as an abundance of exquisite paintings and statuettes of the crucifixion of Jesus. To travellers, such as the papal envoy, the connection was obvious. The punished bodies along the roads reminded them of the punished body of Jesus on the cross. The visible remains of public executions represented criminals who had violated the worldly laws. Yet they were also embedded in a story of possible redemption through the sacrificial suffering of Jesus. Thieves and murderers were punished, just like He had been punished. They suffered like He had suffered. The elements of death and pain in punishment were seen in a positive, even eschatological light – pain was purifying, even a gateway to heaven.

Notions of divine justice would continue to shape the meaning of pain, and the experience of spectators. Yet the rituals of public executions were above all tied to the processes of state formation in Europe. Punishment was secularized and centralized, transferred from lieges and ecclesiastical bodies and incorporated in the violence monopoly of the evolving nation states. The transformation found support in theories of sovereignty, elaborated by Jean Bodin, Thomas Hobbes and other political philosophers in the sixteenth and seventeenth centuries. At bottom lay a claim to uncontested superiority, primarily in matters of violence and coercion, to protect members of society from an even greater violence, eventually stemming from themselves. The sovereign claim came to define the era, until delimited by countervailing notions of the *Rechtsstaat*, which insisted on equipping individuals with legal protection against the sovereign. The religious origins of the idea of unconditional power were commented on by Carl Schmitt (2009), who described the claim to absolute power as a theological remnant: the transfer of sacred aura to the secular state. In practice, the exercise of the sovereign prerogatives was heavily circumscribed by, among other things, lack of administrative capacity. Only a restricted number of law-breakers could be processed through the existing framework of criminal justice. The organizational weakness of the state was compensated for by an excess of ritual – excess of pain and of symbolism, and a large audience. The excess of pain as 'the sovereign left his mark and brought down the effects of his power' on the body of the condemned was part of the ritualized bid for absolute power (Foucault 1979: 109). In that moment when punishments were exacted, the endangered order was ritually reinstated, and the power of the state appeared uncontested, towering over the social body.

The early-modern execution may be seen as a tragedy. In the most obvious sense, it was a grim and sad story; someone had to face the ultimate punishment for a horrific crime, or for the sake of a symbolic display of power. Yet the public execution might also have been a tragedy in the deepest sense of the word, enacting an existential dilemma of being caught between two impossible options. In the *Principles of Penal Law*, Bentham invoked the spectre of classic tragedy when characterizing public executions in the late eighteenth century.

> What is a public execution? It is a solemn tragedy which the legislator presents before an assembled people – a tragedy truly important, truly pathetic, by the sad reality of its catastrophe, and the grandeur of its object. The preparation for it, the place of exhibition, and the attendant circumstances, cannot be too carefully selected, as upon these the principal effect depends. The tribunal, the scaffold, the dresses of the officers of justice, the religious service, the procession, every kind of accompaniment, ought to bear a grave and melancholy character.
>
> (Bentham 1843: 404)

Bentham did not elaborate further on the observed similarities: the outward appearances and the meticulously staged character of the event. Yet by using the classic tragedy as the point of reference for an orderly execution, he may have been more accurate than he himself imagined. The public executions, just like the Attic tragedies, constituted a community of spectators and underpinned specific interpretations of the social world in the dimension of justice and order. All social positions were represented – the nobility, priests, merchants, legal officials, soldiers, farmers, vagabonds, and artisans – and the characters were expected to perform their roles in a rigidly hierarchical scheme, expressing their respective social standing and function, thereby enacting the entire social world, including the elevated status of the king and the symbolic subjection of the people, who had to watch. The element of carefully scripted display was significant. The condemned was expected to articulate remorse before death, asking for forgiveness. The priests, acting on behalf of the worldly as well as the divine justice, received the confession and prepared the soul for the passage to the next world. Executioners administered the actual violence. Officials and members of the local elite oversaw the events and acted as substitutes for the sovereign. Armed soldiers stood between the events on the scaffold and the audience, as visible reminders of the violence monopoly and ready to intervene, should things get out of hand.

The key figure was the common people who represented the bulk of the audience. In the early-modern executions, Foucault argued, 'the main character was the people', who were 'summoned as spectators'. They had to experience justice being done, at first hand; 'not only must people know, they must see with their own eyes' (Foucault 1979: 57f). The people had to watch, since the element of display was a crucial feature of sovereignty (Skinner 1989). Display was also a crucial feature of early-modern public executions, whose core meaning was 'the assertion, preservation and protection of the authority of the state' (Garland 2010: 76; see also Smith 2008). The symbolic display of excess made little sense without an audience. It was the indispensable main character in the ritual. The spectatorship was massive for the era, on all accounts. People from all walks of life and of all ages were present, and may have been attracted by curiosity, by social needs, or perceived obligation. Regardless of the spectators' motives, their mere presence at the scene ensured them a vital role, which went beyond watching the events unfold at the scaffold. The audience made the public execution into what it was: a demonstration of state power. To participate in the ritual was to be included as one cog in the larger build-up of state power, just as *Leviathan* was famously illustrated. On the frontispiece of Hobbes's original book, one finds the imposing figure drawn by Abraham Bosse, with a sword and a crown and a body made up of thousands of individuals, representing the protected yet disposable subjects of the king. Their attendance completed the sovereign ritual, at the same time as it turned the 'theatres of cruelty' (Evans 1996) into theatres of recognition, on the condition that they participated without interfering in the display of sovereign excess.

Throughout the period, the public execution was informed by the Hobbesian tale of the violent state as the bringer of order to chaos. In the state of nature, there was no society. There could be no culture, no navigation, no law, no commerce, no art, no security and no viable social organization. In this state, everyone wanted the same things, just waiting for the opportunity, and lived in constant fear of one another, since there was no institutional body with the capacity to intervene. Disorder, war and sudden death defined the condition (Hobbes 1996). The state of nature was not necessarily located in historical time, as it was perpetually looming over mankind, and threatened to bring pain and destruction to everyone. The postulated chaos, which required the deployment of unconditional power, may also have been derived from a religious framework of afterworldly punishments. The ultimate threat facing the audience was no longer understood as an otherworldly hell but as a this-worldly state of nature. Hobbes and other theorists of sovereignty could be seen to re-enact the medieval Catholic notion of hell in a secular setting, and in a much-diluted form. The rather concise account of the perpetual state of conflict and lack of personal security in the *Leviathan* did not compare with the elaborate images of hell in the *Divine Comedy*. Yet any shortcomings of the underlying vision were compensated for by the symbolism of the ritual itself. To purge evil and save social order from an imminent chaos has always been the promise of capital punishment (Smith 2008). Evil and chaos seem to be inherent in the very operation of the execution ritual – implied rather than explicitly stated. The very excess of punitive violence, it has been argued with respect to current conditions, gives rise to images 'of an even greater violence outside, or before, the law', thereby 'fueling our worst fears and nightmarish beliefs about ourselves and one another' (Sarat and Kearns 1993: 221–2). Similar observations could apply to early-modern conditions. The excessive violence at the scaffold conjured up a more violent chaos, which called for potentially transgressive violence to restore order and protect the subjects of the king.

The audience of mostly common people were caught between unconditional power and uncontrollable chaos. They were protected by one, and threatened by both. The public execution enacted a world in which the spectators were protected albeit constantly threatened by violent chaos and utterly disposable to the sovereign. The witnessed violence on the scaffold founded the community, defined the spectators as subjects of the king – subjects who were given protection by the violence on display. But while being offered protection, they were reminded that the state could turn on them. At any time, Leviathan, as the crowned guardian of the people, could shift into another incarnation of Leviathan, which was of a much older date: the biblical sea monster and its unrestrained and entirely arbitrary violence (Ericson 2007). As most likely would have been familiar to anyone living at the time, the monarchs could marshal people into conscript armies, they could wage wars on other sovereigns, or impose punishments after summary trials, in perfect accordance with existing theories of sovereignty. The subjects were offered protection against an imagined state of nature by a sovereign against whom they were wholly unprotected. The Hobbesian social contract could be seen to process that dilemma of vulnerability. The audience was trapped between the sovereign state, which enforced transgressions and enabled social existence, as the sole bulwark against imminent chaos, on the one hand, and a sovereign state that paid no attention to the individual subject, wilfully used them for wars and for punishment, displaying and proving their utter insignificance, on the other hand. The spectators participated in this ritual, which manifested the supremacy of the state and its powers to protect, but also its readiness to sacrifice without hesitation. During the early-modern period, or until the French revolution, there might not have seemed much to do about it. As subjects of the king, they could not escape the shared predicament that was being demonstrated at the scaffold, which paradoxically satisfied their desire for recognition. The spectators who were being reminded of their insignificance could at the same time recognize each other as fully part of the community of subjects, precisely because their predicament was the same as everybody else's, as protected by yet entirely disposable to machinations at the pinnacles of state power. In this way, witnessing public executions might have offered temporary satisfaction of the perpetual desire for social esteem. The spectators were recognized in their struggle to manage the tension between the experience of state protection and their own vulnerability, constantly threatened by the state of nature, or by the sovereign himself.

The problem of the pleasure of watching the pain of others has inspired discussion from ancient Greece and on to our days. In this chapter, I have revisited some of these discussions to account for the spectators' enjoyment. In three historical settings, all of them pre-modern, the key to the paradox of tragic pleasure was seen to lie in the world-making aspects of punishment. The Attic tragedy, the medieval visions of divine justice and the early-modern executions enacted a world in the dimensions of justice and order, along with a shared existential predicament of the audience, which was tragic in the original sense of presenting people with impossible options, or expectations. The classic tragedies addressed an existential dilemma, shared by above all the male citizens in the audience: the necessarily private assertion of social esteem while being at the mercy of powers beyond their control. The consumption of divine justice processed an existential dilemma for the medieval Christian community: the expectation to lead a life without sin and the futility of all striving to avoid being punished in the afterlife. The early-modern execution, finally, addressed the dilemma of being caught between state protection and utter disposability. The spectators were in each case included in the enacted world and recognized as fully part of it, as citizens of Athens, as members of the Christian community, or as subjects of the king. The recognition was in a significant sense indirect. There was no message being communicated to the audience that they were worthy, or valuable. To the contrary; in the eyes of the tragic heroes, in the eyes of God, or in the eyes of the king, the common people had little value. Instead, their recognition was mediated by the world and by the dilemmas that were being enacted. They all shared the same dilemma of being faced with impossible options, or expectations. For this reason, they could recognize themselves as inextricably part of the enacted world, and other people in the audience could recognize them as fully part of the community. To be recognized as fully part of the community was fundamental. Yet what more can be said about the nature of enjoyment? And which other kinds of pleasures may be at work in punishment? The next chapter will continue to discuss the enjoyment being produced.

References

Aeschylus (2008) *Oresteia: Agamemnon. Libation-bearers. Eumenides.* Trans. by Alan Sommerstein. Cambridge, MA: Harvard University Press.

Allen, Danielle (2000) *The world of Prometheus: the politics of punishing in democratic Athens.* Princeton: Princeton University Press.

Aquinas, Thomas (1941) *Summa Theologica.* London: Burns Oates & Washbourne.

Belfiore, Elizabeth (1992) *Tragic pleasures: Aristotle on plot and emotion.* Princeton: Princeton University Press.

Bentham, Jeremy (1843) Principles of penal law. *The Works of Jeremy Bentham.* Vol. I. London: Simpkin, Marshall & Co. pp 365–580.

Burgwinkle, William (2004) *Sodomy, masculinity, and law in medieval literature.* Cambridge: Cambridge University Press.

Chesterton, G. K. (1943) *St. Thomas Aquinas.* London: Hodder and Stoughton.

Cohen, David (1995) *Law, violence, and community in classical Athens.* Cambridge: Cambridge University Press.

Cohen, Esther (1989) Symbols of culpability and the universal language of justice: the ritual of public executions in late medieval Europe. *History of European Ideas* 11: 407–416.

Conacher, D. J. (1974) Interaction between chorus and characters in the Oresteia. *The American Journal of Philology* 95(4): 323–343.

Dante Alighieri (2002) *The Inferno.* Trans. by R. Hollander and J. Hollander. New York: Doubleday.

Destrée, Pierre (2014) Aristotle on the paradox of tragic pleasure. In J. Levinson (ed.), *Suffering art gladly.* London: Palgrave Macmillan. pp 3–27.

Eagleton, Terry (2003) *Sweet violence: the idea of the tragic.* Oxford: Blackwell

Ericson, Richard (2007) *Crime in an insecure world.* Cambridge: Polity.

Euben, Peter (1982) Justice and the Oresteia. *American Political Science Review* 76(1): 22–33.

Evans, Richard (1996) *Rituals of retribution: capital punishment in Germany 1600–1987.* Oxford: Oxford University Press.

Foucault, Michel (1979) *Discipline and punish: the birth of the prison.* New York: Vintage Books.

Fudgé, Thomas (2016) *Medieval religion and its anxieties: history and mystery in the other Middle Ages.* New York: Palgrave Macmillan.

Garland, David (2010) *Peculiar institution: America's death penalty in an age of abolition.* Oxford: Oxford University Press.

Goldhill, Simon (1990) Great Dionysia and civic ideology. In J. Winkler and F. Zeitlin (eds.), *Nothing to do with Dionysos? Athenian drama in its social context.* Princeton: Princeton University Press. pp 97–129.

Goldhill, Simon (2000) Civic ideology and the problem of difference: The politics of Aeschylean tragedy, once again. *The Journal of Hellenic Studies* 120: 34–56.

Goldhill, Simon (2004) *Aeschylus: the Oresteia.* Cambridge: Cambridge University Press.

Griffith, Mark (1995) Brilliant dynasts: power and politics in the Oresteia. *Classical Antiquity* 14(1): 62–129.
Groebner, Valentin (2003) *Ungestalten. Die visuelle Kultur der Gewalt im Mittelalter.* Munich: Hanser.
Halliwell, Stephen (2002) *The aesthetics of mimesis: ancient texts and modern problems.* Princeton: Princeton University Press.
Hobbes, Thomas (1996) *Leviathan.* Oxford: Oxford University Press.
Hume, David (1987) *Essays, moral, political, and literary.* Indianapolis: Liberty Fund.
Kirkpatrick, Robin (2004) *Dante, the Divine comedy.* Cambridge: Cambridge University Press.
Leão, Delfim (2013) The legal horizon of the Oresteia: the crime of homicide and the founding of the Areopagus. In E. Harris, D. Leão and P. J. Rhodes (eds.), *Law and drama in ancient Greece.* London: Bloomsbury Academic. pp 39–60.
Le Goff, Jacques (1983) *The birth of purgatory.* Chicago: University of Chicago Press.
Macleod, C. W. (1982) Politics and the Oresteia. *The Journal of Hellenic Studies* 102: 124–144.
Meier, Christian (1990) *The Greek discovery of politics.* Cambridge, MA: Harvard University Press.
Merback, Mitchell (1999) *The thief, the cross and the wheel: pain and the spectacle of punishment in medieval and Renaissance Europe.* London: Reaktion Books.
Morgan, Alison (1990) *Dante and the medieval other world.* Cambridge: Cambridge University Press.
Nussbaum, Martha (1992) Tragedy and self-sufficiency: Plato and Aristotle on fear and pity. *Oxford Studies in Ancient Philosophy* 10: 107–159.
Nuttall, A. D. (1996) *Why does tragedy give pleasure?* Oxford: Clarendon Press.
Plato (2013) *Republic Books 6–10.* Trans. by C. Emlyn-Jones and W. Preddy. Cambridge, MA: Harvard University Press.
Roselli, David (2011) *Theater of the people: spectators and society in ancient Athens.* Austin: University of Texas Press.
Ruud, Jay (2008) *Critical companion to Dante.* New York: Infobase Publishing.
Sarat, Austin, and Kearns, Thomas (1993) A journey through forgetting: toward a jurisprudence of violence. In. A. Sarat and T. Kearns (eds.), *The fate of law.* Ann Arbor: University of Michigan Press. pp 209 –273.
Schmitt, Carl (2009 [1934]) *Politische Theologie: vier Kapitel zur Lehre von der Souveränität.* Berlin: Duncker & Humblot.
Seaford, Richard (1994) *Reciprocity and ritual: Homer and tragedy in the developing city-state.* Oxford: Clarendon Press.
Skinner, Quentin (1989) The state. In F. Ball, J. Farr and R. Hanson (eds.), *Political innovation and conceptual change.* Cambridge: Cambridge University Press. pp 90–131.
Smith, Philip (2008) *Punishment and culture.* Chicago: University of Chicago Press.
Sommerstein, Alan (2010) *Aeschylean tragedy.* Bristol: Bristol classical press.
Sommerstein, Alan (2013) Orestes' trial and Athenian homicide procedure. In E. Harris, D. Leão and P. J. Rhodes (eds.), *Law and drama in ancient Greece.* London: Bloomsbury Academic. pp 25–38.

Talbott, Thomas (1993) Punishment, forgiveness, and divine justice. *Religious Studies* 29(2): 151–168.

Williams, Christopher (2014) On mere suffering: Hume and the problem of tragedy. In J. Levinson (ed.), *Suffering art gladly*. London: Palgrave Macmillan. pp 68–83.

Winkler, John, and Zeitlin, Froma (1990) Introduction. In J. Winkler and F. Zeitlin (eds.), *Nothing to do with Dionysos? Athenian drama in its social context*. Princeton: Princeton University Press. pp 3–11.

5 Two paradigms of enjoyment

The key question is how punishment produces pleasure. Given the problematic of desire, the question can be formulated in terms of how desire is transformed into enjoyment through punishment. How does punishment operate to transform distress related to social esteem – as an acutely experienced loss of status, a vaguely experienced sense of unease, or as unfulfilled ambition to distinguish oneself over against others – into experiences which, on all accounts, are radically different, conceived under the broad heading of enjoyment? Plato and Aristotle represent the two available paradigms of pleasure in Western philosophy. There does not seem to be any third alternative (van Riel 2000; Schuster 2016). So, with respect to the pleasure of punishment, in the sense of the enjoyment being produced, there are basically two alternatives: relief of distress (Plato), or being absorbed in unrestrained activity (Aristotle). In the last chapter, the audience was seen to be provided with relief of distress. Concerns related to the wish to be recognized as fully part of the community were alleviated through the consumption of punishment. The satisfaction was in essence Platonic: a temporary relief of unease related to social esteem. But what about the signs of enjoyment that do not seem to fit into the Platonian account, for instance the chanting and the laughter noticed in early-modern execution crowds? It would be wrong to suggest that all pleasure of punishment was a matter of feeling relief. In this chapter, I will briefly present the two paradigms of enjoyment – the Platonian relief of distress and the Aristotelian absorbed excitement – and then go on to discuss the evidence of Aristotelian absorbed excitement in the same selection of pre-modern cases: the tragedies in ancient Greece, afterworldly punishment in medieval Europe, and the early-modern public executions. There is most evidence available on the early-modern executions, and the experiences of the audience can be interpreted as sublime, or alternatively as carnivalesque, depending on whether the executions were orderly or not. The final section of the chapter introduces the idea of dynamic. The transformation cannot be conceived as a one-time occasion. The recognition of being fully part of a group facing a shared dilemma, derived from watching a tragedy, consuming afterworldly punishment or attending a public execution, was a passing experience. The process must be constantly repeated. Hence, the question concerns how punishment, seen as generic phenomena in any given society, is inserted into the dynamics of desire, which is perpetually moving back and forth from satisfaction. Hegel's master-and-slave dialectic, as presented in the *Phenomenology of Spirit*, provides a brilliant account of the tension between desire and enjoyment, and how it plays out in a social context. My re-reading concentrates on the inevitable mismatch between desire and enjoyment, a better understanding of which may help elucidate how punishment operates in the gap between the two.

Between partial relief and absorbed excitement

In *Gorgias*, Plato illustrated pleasure with the satisfaction of eating. Pleasure could be the experience of eating a meal of food after being hungry. The experience involved relief of distress. Considering a hungry person, it was obvious that the body was in a state of distress. The body was missing something. Such was the experience of desire. Desire was satisfied when one was no longer hungry. Bridging the gap between desire and enjoyment involved a transition from pain to pleasure: being hungry was painful, and eating when hungry was pleasurable. When the meal was over and one had eaten enough, the body was in a state of satisfaction. The food need not taste good, it just had to be sufficient to quell the hunger. After some time, the body became hungry again, and the process was repeated; once again, one must eat to be satisfied. The natural state was balance, or not being hungry. Consequently, satisfaction involved a return to equilibrium, by filling a lack (*Gorgias* 496–7).

The paradigm was modelled after the satisfaction of bodily needs (van Riel 2000). Pleasure in the context of punishment can be understood in the same manner. The satisfaction experienced while watching a classic tragedy, contemplating afterworldly punishment or attending a public execution was consistent with the Platonic notion of pleasure. In each case, punishment forged a community of spectators who shared the same predicament, and confirmed their place in the bigger scheme of things, caught between forces beyond their control and the necessity to gain recognition from their own community. While the worlds were markedly different from another, the dilemmas facing contemporary audiences appear to have shared some general characteristics. The spectators struggled with the impossible requirements of the enacted world. They strived to satisfy the desire for social esteem, derived from the prevailing social morality, while the satisfaction was elusive due to powerful agents of justice and other forces beyond their control. At the same time, they were recognized by other people in the audience as one of them, precisely because their predicament was the same as everybody else's. The consumption of punishment thus offered a temporary and partial relief of distress. In terms of the nature of enjoyment, punishment was consistent with the paradigm elaborated by Plato. The satisfaction of being recognized as fully part of the community meant a temporary relief of distress, rather than a sense of exaltation or achievement of a positive state of happiness. A lack was filled, worries disappeared, or a balance was restored. The spectators were more at ease. Satisfying the desire for recognition involved cessation of stress; for a brief moment one stopped thinking about status. The audience was not included in the enacted world in any deeper sense; they were not necessarily empowered to do anything, or better off in any more tangible respect, but they were a bit more at ease, since their desire for social esteem was satisfied, for the moment.

The satisfaction of punishment would thus correspond to the notion of pleasure as relief of distress. In each of the three pre-modern cases, the pleasure was Platonic. But not all pleasures of punishment were necessarily Platonic, or involved a return to equilibrium. Each of the three pre-modern cases contains traces of another kind of pleasure. The early-modern execution may actually seem to provide firmer ground for arguments on Aristotelian pleasure. Evidence from different countries talks about shared expressions of enjoyment at the execution site, corresponding to intense excitement, or captivated arousal. Many first-hand accounts mentioned laughter, cheering, drunkenness, or other signs of excitement among the audience. As can be taken from the quotes reproduced in Chapter 1, some eye-witnesses used words that explicitly indicated enjoyment. Francis Grose likened an eighteenth-century execution to 'a fair of merry-making' against the backdrop of 'solemn and dreadful scenes', the French envoy in Stockholm was reminded of a 'comical farce', whereas Charles Dickens saw 'nothing but ribaldry, debauchery, levity' in a London execution of the mid-nineteenth century. One can find further evidence of shared excitement in the archives. The Quaker J. J. Gurney, for instance, reported 'a feeling of pleasure in the excitement' at an execution in 1816 (quoted in McGowen 1986: 319). Such testimonies appear inconsistent with the Platonic return to equilibrium, and point toward the Aristotelian paradigm of pleasure.

Aristotle stood for a different conception of pleasure. In the *Nicomachean Ethics*, the Platonic model was criticized on the grounds that it did not assure pleasure a role in the good life. If pleasure was part of the good life, it could not involve relief of distress, and hence a change away from an undesirable state. It should rather be about attaining a positive, or more perfect state. Aristotle conceived of pleasure as a sort of perfection: the actualization of a natural state (Taylor 2008). His notion of pleasure left more space for interpretation compared to the Platonic model. Admittedly, what offered relief of distress could be more or less anything, and hence open to interpretation. But the image of eating when hungry was easy to grasp, and relief of distress was an everyday experience which everyone could relate to. On the Aristotelian model, on the other hand, pleasure was immediately generated by certain forms of activity. Pleasures were 'species of activity' as opposed to processes with a separate goal (*Nicomachean Ethics* 1153a). Pleasure was not a separate experience which involved a previous state of distress, or any process leading up to the experience. It was immediate and accompanied activities that were unimpeded. Aristotelian pleasure has been described as 'an additional element' of activities performed without impediment (van Riel 2000: 2). Aristotle stressed the striving for perfection and intellectual enjoyment, as rational activities represented the highest form of pleasure in life. Yet strictly speaking, pleasure was not necessarily tied to reason, or to the attainment of perfection. 'Unimpeded' is the crucial word (*Nicomachean Ethics* 1153a), and it simply meant the absence of any kind of obstacles: an absence which allowed the activity to unfold uninterrupted. Unimpeded activities could involve literally anything. One of Aristotle's many examples involved manual labour. Under certain conditions, building a house afforded pleasure. If the construction went uninterrupted, if the builder was skilled and the work flowed smoothly, pleasure was generated (Taylor 2008). This pleasure could not be understood as a separate experience, like relief of distress, but must be thought of as an experience that was intimately tied to the uninterrupted flow of activity. It may likewise correspond to an everyday experience which everyone can relate to: the experience of being carried away, for a moment oblivious of other concerns or commitments. Paul Moyaert (2010) has suggested that the rather formal delineation of pleasure as the additional element of unimpeded activities should be conceived along the lines of abandon, enthusiasm, and absorption. The Aristotelian, piggy-backing approach to pleasure could thus involve more than one element: absorption and forgetfulness, as well as enthusiasm and excitement, depending on the experience-carrying activity. Hence there might be an alternative pleasure in the consumption of punishment. Not all pleasures of punishment would be reducible to the recognition of social esteem. In the scholarly literature on each of the three premodern periods, there are indications of abandon, enthusiasm, and absorption.

The Platonic relief of distress may not have been the only kind of pleasure of punishment in ancient Greece. It has been argued, first by Friedrich Nietzsche and then in more recent times, most eloquently by Terry Eagleton, that ancient Bacchic cults provided the intense excitement of ritualistic cruelty. The cruelty was supposed to have performed religious functions, rather than punitive. It may not have been understood as punishment by contemporary audiences, and if so, it is not a good example for that reason. In addition, many claims made about the ancient Bacchic rituals can been criticized for being speculative (Heinrichs 1984). The terror-induced enjoyment in the Bacchic cults may be no more than a tale. Yet it nevertheless played a significant role in later discussions, as the Dionysic principle. In the *Birth of Tragedy*, Nietzsche wrote about the intoxicating mix of cruelty and pleasure as a universal aspect of human experience rather than as a specific historic event. It was the aspect of ruthless self-assertion. In the modern reception of Dionysus, the Greek deity represented the terrifying consequences of unrestricted enjoyment, what happened when collective self-assertion was followed to the bitter end. The violence that transgressed the boundaries of enacted laws gave rise to transcendence and assumed a sacred character. Utter terror and unbounded enjoyment were by nature divine attributes. With respect to the character of the spectators' enjoyment, apparent opposites merged, such as subject and object, pleasure and pain, law and excess (Eagleton 2005). The experience was conceived along the lines of the Aristotelian kind of pleasure as excitement, arousal, the loss of self or unrestrained assertion. In the *Will to Power*, Nietzsche explicitly rejected the Platonic conception of pleasure as satisfaction of lack. 'It is *not* the satisfaction of the will which causes pleasure', instead, 'the cause of pleasure is the fact that the will presses onwards and prevails against all that stands in its way' (Nietzsche 2017: 696, emphasis in original). In other words: desire stops at nothing, and will not disappear even if a point of balance has been reached. Desire pushes forward beyond all boundaries, and pleasure occurs when the process of self-assertion is unimpeded, or, in Nietzsche's case, when obstacles are successfully overcome.

One and the same kind of event could generate both satisfaction of status concerns and excitement of being carried away by the activities. Great Dionysia may have been such an event. The Attic tragedies were performed during the five-day festival, which also included ritual processions and opportunities to drink and socialize. Great Dionysia could have been a venue for both kinds of pleasure, as revealed by the scholarly discussion on the nature of the event. There are two main positions: one emphasizing the orderly (Goldhill 1990; 2000) and the other the rowdy aspects (Griffith 1995; Roselli 2011). As argued in the last chapter, the Attic tragedy constituted a community and enacted a social world in the dimension of justice and order, which offered recognition to spectators. In the rituals attached to the plays, a civic ideology was promulgated in a solemn fashion, overseen by high dignitaries (Goldhill 1990; 2000). This generated one kind of pleasure, the Platonic relief of distress, which was different from the intense excitement of the Aristotelian pleasure. At the same time, Great Dionysia could become carnivalesque, simultaneously transgressing and reinforcing social order in much the same way as the popular festivals of medieval Europe (Griffith 1995; Roselli 2011). While the festival was no doubt used to glorify the city-state, it was also, as suggested by the name, held in honour of Dionysus, who was the god of wine, theatre, fertility, suffering and excess, amongst other things. The audience could adopt several roles. Sometimes the spectators would be drunken participants in the festival, sometimes sober adjudicators of the plays. They could be taking part in heavily scripted expressions of the Athenian political regime, or the very opposite: exploring and subverting given social roles (Griffith 1995; Goldhill 2000; Roselli 2011). Events could thus unfold both ways, questioning or reenforcing given social conventions. Without choosing sides in the debate, it may be concluded that in each case, pleasure was guaranteed. An orderly tragedy performance was likely to offer recognition, whereas the disorderly and carnivalesque was more likely to generate absorbed excitement.

The many representations of divine justice in medieval Europe may also have offered a venue for both kinds of pleasure. As argued in the last chapter, Dante and Aquinas articulated the expectation to be a good Christian as well as the futility of that striving, as in principle everyone in the audience was doomed anyway, which ironically provided a recognition of full membership of the community. If that argument holds, the resulting pleasure was Platonic. Yet what about the other kind of pleasure, the intense excitement that the punishment may have generated? Was not the encounter with hell, even if only in contemplation, likely to produce an intense existential awareness, or even an elevated arousal? Little is known about the actual response of the audience. Yet some scholars have argued that the intimate connection between suffering and transcendence gave rise to awe, reverence and excitement among the medieval audience. Their evidence relies on preserved artistic representations and biblical plays rather than on eyewitness accounts. The suffering of Christ on the cross, as reproduced in paintings and mosaics, or as enacted in the passion plays, was seen to generate pleasure. In medieval visual art, the 'punished body-in-pain' articulated 'certain kinds of pleasure' – a religiously elevated pleasure, partaking in the suffering of Christ (Mills 2005: 202). The elevation of pain into pleasure relied on the basic assumptions of divine justice and beliefs about cleansing of sin through suffering. The joy was moreover perceived to be an effect of the mode of presentation. Dramatists intentionally reconfigured 'the spectacle of brutality as joyful' (Enders 1999: 172; see also Ciobanu 2018). The eschatologically coloured experience extended into the consumption of worldly punishment, above all in the public executions of law-breakers. Given the religious framework, there was a 'feeling of kinship between the criminal on his way to the gallows and the saint in search of God' (Cohen 1989: 409). On this line of reasoning, the 'punished body-in-pain' in medieval culture produced excitement, reverence and joy among the audience, which was entirely consistent with the Aristotelian notion of pleasure.

The early-modern executions may, likewise, have produced both recognition and enjoyment. As often noted, there was a tension between the tragic and the Dionysic in the public executions. Historians have discussed which element was the most predominant – whether early-modern executions were solemn theatres of terror, or Dionysic carnivals of popular debauchery (Garland 2010; Spierenburg 1984; Ignatieff 1978; Evans 1996; Lacqueur 1989). The conclusions differed according to the sites being researched. The executions in London, for instance, seemed to have been rowdier than those in Amsterdam. The disagreement among historians also meant that both outcomes are well supported by empirical evidence; some executions were no doubt silent and orderly, and other executions were characterized by laughter and chanting, or public unrest. The findings are highly relevant for any discussion of pleasure, since the orderly and the disorderly outcomes can be seen to correspond to different kinds of pleasures among the audience. The tragic would correspond to Platonic pleasure whereas the Dionysic would correspond to Aristotelian pleasure. In the literature, only the Dionysic aspects have so far been discussed in terms of pleasure. One kind of pleasure (the collectively shared excitement) has dominated discussions on the early-modern executions over against the other (the recognition of social esteem), either because Norbert Elias's main frame of the process of civilization was tacitly endorsed, or for more easily recognizable reasons. The visible and very audible signs of enjoyment were difficult to ignore, whereas relief of distress – the silent recognition of status – was less likely to catch the attention of writers who happened to be part of an execution crowd, with which they often felt little sympathy. One might even doubt whether it was at all possible to capture this kind of pleasure phenomenologically. Given the assumptions of the Platonic model, pleasure involved an absence rather than a presence, it was silent rather than audible, and the satisfaction was not necessarily consciously experienced as such. It was a satisfaction that had to be inferred, rather than observed, from the world as people knew it, at the time. There were no self-evident exterior signs. Even silence and orderly performance were unreliable, since how do you interpret silence? Take for instance the 1802 execution of the colonial governor Joseph Wall, who was notorious for the cruel treatment of the British soldiers he once commanded. Robert Southey, writing under the pseudonym of a fictitious Spanish tourist, distanced himself from the crowd, which was reproached for being inhuman, unchristian and disgraceful. But in the moment of hanging, its mood changed. He noted 'the sudden extinction of that joy, the feeling which at one moment struck so many thousands, stopped their acclamations at once; and awed them into dead silence when they saw the object of their hatred in the act and agony of death' (Southey 2016: 116). Yet it is not clear what are we to make of the 'dead silence' of the audience. Was it a sign of recognition and relief of distress, or was it a sign of speechless awe and excitement? The silence was no doubt open to both interpretations.

The available evidence on ancient Greece and medieval Europe can be seen to offer leads for further research on absorbed arousal in the context of punishment. At present, however, it seems insufficient to warrant any conclusions that go beyond fairly reasonable assumptions. Only starting with the early-modern period, the traces of Aristotelian pleasure become more conclusive. The well-documented excitement and rowdy behaviour of early-modern execution crowds, which have served as the point of reference in many discussions of the pleasure of punishment, cannot be understood merely as relief of distress. While the desire may have been the same, the nature of the enjoyment was markedly different from status recognition. The next section will move on from the immediate eyewitness accounts, while remaining with the early-modern executions. Recent historical accounts of a carnivalesque popular culture at the scaffold, in conjunction with the emergence of a philosophical discussion on the sublime during the eighteenth century, may further elucidate the shared pleasure as absorbed arousal among the audience.

Early-modern excitement: between the carnivalesque and the sublime

The eye-witness reports on popular expressions of enjoyment suggest a very different kind of pleasure from the Platonic relief of distress. Yet how

should the broad category of Aristotelian pleasure of punishment be spe-
cified in an early-modern context? The experience can be approached from
two angles: from the contemporary discussion of the sublime, in essence an
intense excitement and a heightened existential awareness in the experience
of power from a safe position (Burke 1997), or from latter-day discussions of
the carnivalesque (Bakhtin 1968), an experience which came from momentary
transgression of otherwise rigid rules and social hierarchies.

During the carnival season, behaviour that was otherwise prohibited was
allowed, as people were singing and drinking and settling all sorts of scores
in public, with abusive spouses or with local potentates. The world was temporarily turned upside down (Hill 1972). The public executions presented one
crucial venue for the carnivalesque, as they were designed to be pillars of the
established order. Precisely because executions were an occasion for articulate
display of official rank and social prestige, when overturned, the experience
of liberation was powerful and captivating: 'the suspension of all hierarchical rank, privilege, norms and prohibition' (Bakhtin 1968: 10). In contin-
ental Europe, executions and other established rituals, such as sermons and
weddings, were mocked and inverted. The figure of 'Carnival', often portrayed
as a cheerful fat man, could be exposed to a mock trial followed by a mock
execution, in one place by burning. In other places, pigs were ceremonially
beheaded, mimicking the rituals of capital punishment, and invoking the
entire symbolism of criminal justice (Burke 2009). In the protracted discussion on the nature of early-modern executions, the carnival and the carnivalesque have been invoked by writers who claimed that the sovereign exercise
of power was often subverted by the crowd. Michel Foucault maintained that
French executions in the eighteenth century encompassed 'the whole aspect
of carnival, in which rules were inverted [and] authority mocked' (Foucault
1979: 61). Public executions in Britain were explicitly addressed as carnivalesque in Bakthin's sense; scorn, laughter, defiance, violence and blasphemy
were part of the ritual, as the crowd saw it (Lacqueur 1989). In a similar vein,
Michael Ignatieff referred to usurped execution processions through London
as the 'poor people's carnival' (Ignatieff 1978: 88; see also Linebaugh 1991). On
such occasions, when solemnly designed rituals of justice were subverted and
ridiculed by spectators, executions seemed to borrow traits from the medieval
carnival. The carnivalesque may thus have captured the Aristotelian pleasure
of disorderly executions. It was the excitement of transcending a deeply felt
and rigidly unequal social order, mixed up with partying, aggression and violence, and a reawakened sense of collective power.

If, on the other hand, the executions proceeded as planned, without
popular disturbances, the carefully scripted display of sovereign power may
have produced intense excitement of a different nature – while still being
pleasure in the Aristotelian sense. It was the awe and the fascination in the
face of unrestrained power. As generated by the safe consumption of terror,
the excitement was in many respects the opposite of the carnivalesque. The
experience relied on passive consumption rather than active participation. It

was sovereign rather than plebeian in orientation, involving shared power-lessness rather than collective empowerment of the audience. As opposed to the carnivalesque, it was moreover a kind of intense excitement that was discussed as such at the time, although rarely in conjunction with punish-ment. Contemporary philosophers analysed the experience in terms of the sublime to understand the impact on the audience.

The concept of the sublime was rediscovered at a point in time when public executions reached a peak in many European countries. In the late seven-teenth century, the classic text *On the Sublime* was simultaneously translated into English and French (Albrecht 1975; Battersby 2007). The original text was written by an unknown author, often referred to as Longinus, during the Roman period. In antiquity, the sublime was a concept in rhetoric. It referred to the power of the orator to produce amazement and overwhelming emotional effects, rather than persuasion through reasoning, in the audience (Heath 2012; Porter 2016). The effect was inexplicable and irresistible. When the notion of the sublime re-appeared in the late seventeenth century, the extreme sensual impact on an audience, its sense of excitement, remained in focus but was no longer linked to public speech. Instead, terror was seen as the source of the sublime. The translation of Longinus's text was followed by a string of British writers in the eighteenth century, starting with John Dennis, who characterized the sublime experience as 'enthusiastic terror', induced by, among other things, 'gods, dæmons, hell, spirits and souls of men, miracles, prodigies, enchantments, witchcrafts, thunder, tempests, raging seas, inundations, torrents, earthquakes, volcanoes, monsters, serpents, lions, tigers, fire, war, pestilence, famine' (Dennis 1996: 38). Witnessing or contemplating the various manifestations of terror produced absorbed elevation, admiration and wonder among the audience. The sensation was inextricably linked to the sacred, or the idea of a transcendent order manifesting itself in hell, vol-canoes, pestilence and miracles. The sublime captured the sacred dimensions within an evolving secular context. But at the beginning of the eighteenth century, the experience was embedded in a Christian cosmology. Referred to as the 'great universal monarch', God was the ultimate source of the sublime (Dennis 1996: 38).

In his highly influential *Philosophical Enquiry into the Origin of Our Ideas of the Sublime and the Beautiful*, published in 1757, Edmund Burke discussed terror in what was essentially a phenomenological analysis. Terror was the power-house of the sublime. Due to its capacity to induce the strongest emotion, terror was 'the ruling principle of the sublime' (Burke 1997: 231). There was a shared excitement of being close to terror and unbounded vio-lence, provided that it was experienced from a safe position. 'When danger or pain press too nearly, they are incapable of giving any delight, and are simply terrible, but at certain distances', he said, invoking everyday experiences, 'they may be, and they are, delightful' (Burke 1997: 217). Should one be directly exposed to violence, death or degradation, there is only fear and suffering, and no pleasure. When experienced from the spectators' seat, however, terror was delightful. But the pleasure was never pure. The sublime was delightful in itself, yet the experience was mixed up with the seemingly contrary emotions of pain and fear. That was the paradox of the sublime, in Burke's theory of sensory impression. It was the classic problem of the pleasure of watching the pain of others, compounded with a further opposition: between degradation and a sense of elevation. The early-modern sublime was built on this twin contradiction. It articulated a kind of absorbed arousal with transcendent implications. The audience were on the one hand absorbed in the unfolding scenes, experiencing an almost irresistible attraction to violence, death or degradation, while at the same time experiencing a kind of elevation: awe, reverence, and respect.

In the aesthetics of the eighteenth century, the sublime represented a different approach to the paradox of the pleasure of watching the pain of others, compared to previous interpretations through the lens of tragedy. The pleasure was first of all seen to be different. The encounter with terror, or unrestrained power, produced intense arousal rather than satisfaction. It was the Aristotelian kind of pleasure – absorbed excitement, not the relief of the desire for recognition. There was moreover no space for reason, or for ritual enactment of dilemmas: mechanisms that were crucial for tragic pleasure. The overwhelming sensory arousal bypassed conscious thought to produce a sense of elevation and higher meaning. This aspect was stressed most explicitly by Immanuel Kant, who argued that the sublime was per se unintelligible. It was a totally overwhelming sensation, which escaped the understanding, and constituted a mix of pleasure and pain. The breakdown of representation was intensely exciting as well as deeply disturbing (Kant 1914; Lyotard 1994). Transcendence was inherent in the experience. The sense of elevation was a product of the excitement induced by terror. A system of religious beliefs was never called for. Instead, from the safe position of the spectator's seat, the encounter would by itself produce an intense existential awareness and pointed toward something larger than life, underlying the experience.

During this period, the sublime was mainly discussed in relation to the vastness of nature, exceptional art, or beauty (Battersby 2007; Eagleton 2003). But the constitutive experience of terror could be grounded in anything. John Dennis's list encompassed everything between outbreaks of pandemics and of volcanoes. At heart, or as an early-modern theory of the sensory impact on an audience, its basic principles were just as applicable to punishment as to art, although rarely done. The sublime could thus describe sensations far beyond what we today consider to be the domain of aesthetic experiences. In one short passage in the *Enquiry*, Burke argued that a public execution was a more powerful source of the sublime than a classic tragedy. To prove the point which pleasure would prevail, if put to the test, he designed a thought experiment. Imagine, he suggested, an audience in a theatre as they are watching a tragedy. During the show, they are being told, presumably from the stage, that a well-known criminal was about to be executed in a nearby square. What would happen; would the audience stay and watch the stage performance to the end or would they leave the theatre? He was confident – everyone would rush out immediately; 'in a moment the emptiness of the theatre would demonstrate the comparative weakness of the imitative arts' (Burke 1997: 223). The terror in real life was superior. On this line of reasoning, one might think that punishment as a source of the sublime would automatically qualify as a topic in his aesthetics. The very point of the amalgam of ritual and cruelty at the scaffold was intimidation. But for some reason, punishment was not a topic in the *Enquiry*. Decades later, however, Burke would make use of his theory of sensory impression in discussions of the death penalty. Following the Gordon Riots in London, June 1780, more than one hundred people appeared for trial, facing the risk of execution. The trials went on all summer, and eventually 62 people were sentenced to death (Rudé 1956). In a short text written during the trials, *Some Thoughts on the approaching Executions*, Burke argued against mass executions of rioters based on his aesthetic theory. A limited number of rioters should, he suggested, be singled out based on a full investigation of the events, and then be executed one by one:

> Six, at the very utmost, of the fittest examples may then be selected for execution, who ought to be brought out and put to death, on one and the same day, in Six different places, and in the most solemn manner that can be devised.
>
> (Burke 1996: 613)

Awe and terror could be derived from the singular event, especially if the execution was staged to achieve that end. Mass hangings, on the other hand, tended to produce a numbing effect and sensory overload; 'the sense of Justice in Men is overloaded and fatigued with a long series of executions' (Burke 1996: 614). More people than one could be executed, but not at exactly the same time and place. If the primary concern of his aesthetics was to secure the emotional grounding of political power (O'Neill 2012; Eagleton 1995), the proposed punishment made sense. To watch malefactors being hanged, one by one, 'in the most solemn manner that can be devised' might produce an intense excitement that reinforced the bond between the audience and the state. Individual guilt was secondary, and large-scale terror was ruled out on political grounds. As to how many were appropriate, he came up with the figure of six before the trials were finished. The execution of six people appeared to strike a balance within the context of the Gordon Riots. It was not a massacre, Burke emphasized, and anyway fewer than the 25 people who were eventually hanged, after all appeals had been made. At the same time, the law lost nothing of its terror in the minds of the population. On the contrary, the one-by-one approach to hanging promised to be quite effective, since 'the execution of one Man fixes the attention and excites awe' (Burke 1996: 614).

During the nineteenth century, the focus on terror faded, and was replaced by an interest in natural phenomena and the 'romantic sublime' (Brady 2013). The telegraph and imposing bridges, electric lights and skyscrapers were likewise seen as sources of the sublime. David Nye (1994) has written about the 'technological sublime' in the United States. The new inventions inspired awe and wonder among the audience, and seemed to retain a link to the otherworld despite being man-made. The awe which they expressed was also an awe at the progress and the promises of science, far from the sublime experiences of terror derived from uncontrollable natural events such as earthquakes and volcanoes in the preceding century. The technological sublime was an experience of transcendence based on inventions made by scientists and engineers. The visual effects of electricity impressed audiences unfamiliar with bright lights of different colours. During light-shows in the big US cities, spectators were reported to fall on their knees, as if the electric lights were from another world. Electricity allowed the creation of phenomena that widely surpassed gas lighting, and appeared, perhaps more than any other invention, to incorporate elements of the supernatural and the inexplicable (Nye 1994; 2018).

At the end of the nineteenth century, the technological sublime was perfectly illustrated by the electric chair, located as it was at the intersection of natural wonder and supernatural power (Martschukat 2002; Ruddick 1998). The original argument for the electric chair was scientific and humanitarian. It promised a swift and painless death in a controlled environment, against the background of growing public concern about unnecessarily painful hangings. After years of experimenting and following an intense discussion of the benefits of electrocution, the state of New York decided to use the electric chair. William Kemmler, a 28-year-old vegetable peddler from Buffalo, would be the first one ever to be officially electrocuted. In the legal process before the decision, medical experts had ascertained that his death would be instantaneous and painless. On the evening of 5 August 1890, a crowd of people gathered at the gates of the Auburn prison. The execution was to take place inside the prison, the following morning. Jürgen Martschukat (2002: 917) quoted one reporter who was present and captured the mood of the audience. ' "There was no noise. There was no loud talking /.../ Everybody spoke in a subdued way as though a feeling of awe had settled upon them." ' Expectations were high on the wonders and the deadly powers of electricity. In the early morning, Kemmler was strapped to a chair powered by an AC dynamo that supplied up to 1680 volts (Ruddick 1998). How events evolved would hugely surprise witnesses, according to the following day's account in the *New York Times*.

> At 6:42 A.M. the electricity was turned on for seventeen seconds, and afterwards no one doubted the death of the experimental object. But Kemmler had not died. The current had to be switched on again; the carefully controlled situation gave way to chaos. /.../ According to the press, the witnesses, "horrified by the ghastly sight," could not turn their eyes from the obviously suffering man in the agony of death. /.../ The electricity flowed, Kemmler's blood vessels began to burst, the hair and skin

under the electrodes burned, "the stench was unbearable," and people collapsed.

(Martschukat 2002: 918)

The operators lost track of time after the electricity was turned on the second time – estimates vary between one minute and four and a half minutes – and when the body was finally proclaimed dead, witnesses left the room 'weak-kneed and nauseated' (Ruddick 1998: 85) Electricity, the powerful symbol of modernity, merged with the arcane symbolism of death. What was expected to be a triumph of science and civilization turned out as yet another 'spectacle at the scaffold', a repetition of the ritualistic cruelty of the early-modern era. Given the expectations of a fully controlled, swift and painless death, which would leave the body of William Kemmler unscathed, the outcome came as a shock to everyone present: all the blood, the smell, the visible pain, the disorder of operators losing control and people collapsing. Subsequent investigations revealed that the execution was botched due to technical failure; the electric pressure from the dynamo was heavily reduced and the electrodes moreover failed to make full contact with the body. The protracted agony was entirely unintended. But if Edmund Burke had been concerned by sensory fatigue and lack of novelty when people were hanged collectively, the execution certainly did not fail to impress the audience. Judging from the journalistic accounts, the audience consumed the scenes of terror with intense excitement; the immediate eye-witnesses were unable to turn their eyes from the agony, watching the extraordinary and unexpected effects of electricity from a safe distance.

A year later, the electric chair was used again in another New York prison. Everything went according to plan, and the public response was enthusiastic; some were celebrating the execution as one of the most humane of all times (Martschukat 2002). The sublime at Kemmler's execution turned out to be somewhat of an anomaly. What was the first time in one sense might have been the last time in another sense. The electric chair was inaugurated on the threshold of modernity, when the conditions for pleasure were changing, including those associated with intense terror-induced excitement. In the accounts of Kemmler's execution, little suggests that the response of the audience was considered inappropriate. The absence of shame was typical of the early-modern sublime. Edmund Burke discussed the delight in the face of terror without second thoughts, or without mentioning that it could be shameful or inappropriate. The excitement in the encounter with terror was embraced, as overwhelming and ennobling, as it brought the spectators into contact with the sacred, or allowed them to catch a glimpse of a transcendent reality. Terror-induced arousal was the source of the sublime – and not a source of shame. But at the end of the next century, this kind of absorbed arousal had become problematic, and evolved into a different experience. Freud started discussing sublimation in the 1890s, the same decade as the electric chair was adopted as an execution technique. Despite the etymological kinship between the two terms, the sublime and sublimation, the corresponding experiences were miles apart (for the opposite view, see Civitarese 2016). The sublime was the innocent excitement of the unmediated encounter with sovereign terror, whereas sublimation involved its denial and transformation into something else. Shame and prohibition induced by social morality refashioned the enjoyment. Immediacy, absorption and abandon – central elements in the early-modern sublime – were disrupted by prohibition. The *fin de siècle* social morality was rendering shared excitement and absorption increasingly difficult. Punishment was enjoyed in the company of others only on condition of its public disavowal. The Freudian concept of sublimation captured the transformation. The experience of the sublime was being supplanted by the mechanisms of sublimation, thus encapsulating the problematic character of the pleasure of punishment as a modern experience. Obscene enjoyment came to incorporate the Aristotelian features of abandon, absorption and arousal, and replaced the sublime, as well as replacing the carnivalesque experience of the audience. The nature of that particularly modern pleasure will be further discussed in Chapter 7.

Punishment in the gap between desire and enjoyment

Essentially two kinds of pleasure are available to any audience, with respect to punishment. It is either Platonian (relief of distress) or Aristotelian (absorption and excitement). They may be seen as different satisfactions of the same family of desires centred on social esteem. The two kinds of enjoyment would, on this analysis, be expressions of a desire which is inherently dualistic, shaped by social morality and by calculated concern, and predisposed to conformity and to excess. After having provided provisional answers to the questions 'what kind of desire?' and 'what kind of enjoyment?', we are now in a position to approach the dynamic: how desire transforms into satisfaction, through actions and interventions, and then recedes into desire. What needs to be understood is the relationship between desire and enjoyment, and how the consumption of punishment operates in the gap. Hegel's master-and-slave dialectic offers one account of the tension between desire and enjoyment, and how it plays out in a social context. My re-reading concentrates on the volatile nature of desire and the precarity of satisfaction, a better understanding of which may help elucidate how punishment operates in the gap between the two.

The short section in the *Phenomenology* on the struggle for recognition between Master and Slave must be among the most well-interpreted in the history of philosophy. Hegel's immediate concern was to account for a stage in the evolution of self-knowledge (Hegel 2018). From within the problematic of subject formation, it has been seen as a decisive stage in the evolution of the autonomous subject (Honneth 1992; Habermas 1963; Taylor 1975; Butler 1987). The complexities of subject formation have been at the centre of many interpretations. But the section can also – given the problematic of desire – be read as a story about the predicament of already constituted subjects who try to acquire recognition from one another. That is also my concern in this section. The master-and-slave dialectic shows the predicament of people who are moved into action by the incessant tension between ambiguous status concerns and an always partial and precarious recognition. Satisfaction was at best a passing state. No one caught the contradictory dynamics – the desire that pushed for relief and what the satisfaction momentarily entailed, the impossibility of full recognition, and hence the renewed distress, renewed recognition, and so on – better than Hegel.

It started as an encounter between two parties, both of whom were figures of the same consciousness, who desired the same thing: to be recognized by the other for what they were, or aspired to be. As opposed to the first version, in the *Phenomenology* the struggle for recognition was presented as already ongoing, fraught with tension and distress yet triggered by nothing. Both of them just wanted to be recognized by the other. The struggle was not a response to any specific status anxiety, such as the fear of falling in social terms; nor was it a response to concrete status violations, such as the theft which triggered the struggle in *System der Sittlichkeit*. Hegelian desire (*Begierde*) cannot be identified with a specific source. It was rather an existential condition, which necessitated action. None of the two parties could refrain from taking part in a struggle that was anyway inevitable. At stake was the entire social being. To be acknowledged as fully part of society was more precious than one's life. Hence both parties put their lives on the line to gain full status. The two parties took turns vindicating their claims for recognition and ended up in a struggle for life and death in which both parties do their utmost to assert themselves over against each other, through determination, violence, sacrifices, and a readiness to risk everything. This phase is necessary, as 'it is through a life and death struggle that each *proves its worth* to itself, and that both *prove their worth* to each other' (Hegel 2018: 111, emphasis in original). They seek to prove themselves, motivated by the desire to be recognized by the other as a full and worthy part. Out of the life and death struggle, there emerged a Master and a Slave, or more closely defined social roles. The Master acquired the privileges of power and had the capacity to make the Slave work and fulfil the Master's wishes. Yet none of them were successful in gaining recognition. The Slave did not acquire recognition, despite working hard, and the Master did not acquire recognition, despite being apparently able to realize every wish. The desired recognition eluded them both. For my purposes, the failure of the Master is the most instructive, as it includes the position of power and consumption. The Master was said to satisfy desire through *Genuss*, which carried the double meaning of both enjoyment and consumption. The Master could enjoy whatever the Slave produced. But no amount of coercion could secure recognition. The Slave could be forced into submission, and the Slave could be forced to acknowledge the superior social status of the Master. But it was a recognition that failed to satisfy, since it did not mean anything. The act of recognition did not confer any social esteem, since the Slave had no esteem to offer. Everything had been devalued through the one-sided assertion of the Master.

The Master and the Slave remained caught in a struggle for recognition, and their unfulfilled desire continued to push them beyond existing restraints. None of them were successful, and none of them could escape the mutual dependence. Enjoyment was inextricably dependent on the other, who granted recognition, or, alternatively, withheld it. To gain recognition, one had to match the expectations and the demands of the other, who could offer recognition while at the same time being the antagonist against whom the subject proved his worth. The other had the contradictory role of being both potential provider and antagonist. This line of reasoning was adopted and further elaborated in Lacanian psychoanalysis. Jacques Lacan suggested that enjoyment was altogether 'of the other'. Just as 'desire is the desire of the Other' (Lacan 1977: 235), enjoyment is of the other. The subject feels compelled to comply, according to what is perceived to be the expectations of others, and undertake actions which may generate satisfaction, or recognition of social esteem, as they satisfy these expectations. The satisfaction need not be consciously experienced as such. People may enjoy without being aware of it. Enjoyment can – but need not – include a state of conscious happiness, or sense of relief. It can also be a brief and partial break from a state of distress. Conscious satisfaction may be accidental. Enjoyment can even be seen as the price to be paid for conformity (Freud 1931). It can be the very opposite of joyous feelings. As Slavoj Žižek pointed out, 'to enjoy' is rather 'something we do as a kind of weird and twisted ethical duty' (Žižek 2006: 79). Desire has been satisfied. But it does not feel satisfying but rather as a fulfilment of duties, as something we have to do: the compulsion to satisfy moral expectations and the awkward sense of relief when these expectations are being met.

The precarious nature of recognition has been seen as central for the specifically modern experience of recognition. The two central strands in the re-articulation of the Hegelian concept of recognition in the early 1990s, the communitarian reading of Charles Taylor and the recognition-oriented reformulation of German Critical Theory made by Axel Honneth, both offered a historicizing interpretation of the master-and-slave dialectic. On their analysis, the *Phenomenology*, published in 1807, indicated that a change was under way. Recognition could no longer be taken for granted. 'What has come about with the modern age', Charles Taylor argued, 'is not the need for recognition but the conditions in which the attempt to be recognized can fail' (Taylor 1992: 35; see also Taylor 1989). Recognition had turned into an individual project without definite end in sight. The traditional sources, based on estates, birth-right, or a piece of land, were called into question, and status anxiety became a generally shared experience, traceable to the emergence of capitalism and the disintegration of stable estates. As a consequence, recognition had to be achieved, or actively secured; it was no longer an automatic reward for conformity (Taylor 1992; Honneth 2003; Welskopp 2013).

Another influential line of reception, starting with the reading of the master-and-slave dialectic developed by Alexandre Kojève in his 1930s lectures, and later elaborated in a psychoanalytic direction by Jacques Lacan, offered an existential reading of the same section. The struggle for recognition was seen as indicative of what it meant to be human, and thus not tied to a specific historic situation. Recognition was precarious because each individual desire operated defensively. There is, in any society, a multiplicity of desires, 'each of which wants to negate, to assimilate, to make its own, to subjugate, the other Desire as Desire' (Kojève 1969: 40). Everyone desperately wanted to be desired by another desire, in an environment where everyone else was just as anxious, creating constant distress and making recognition inherently diffi-cult to attain. On this analysis, Hegel did not articulate a specifically modern experience. To the contrary, recognition will be precarious and fundamentally uncertain in any society – in ancient Greece, or in medieval Europe – in which people are motivated by a desire for social esteem.

Punishment is conceived to operate right in the middle of this dynamic, in the gap between desire and satisfaction. Unlike the Slave in Hegel's tale, it has the power to provide recognition. Inserted in between desire and enjoy-ment, punishment could offer relief of the status concerns of an audience which experienced just a slight sense of unease or, alternatively, a pervasive awareness of being denied acknowledgement. The audience is driven by a desire to be acknowledged as fully part of society, or to assert their status over against other groups, and when they are successful in any of these respects, when recognition is momentarily provided through punishment, it involves a relief of distress, which is precisely pleasure in the Platonic sense. Nothing was direct. With respect to the three pre-modern contexts, the penal rituals did not communicate that the spectators were valuable; if anything, pun-ishment was a reminder that they were no more than cogs in a world that proved them to be expendable. As opposed to the Aristotelian exaltation, the pleasure was mediated by conceptions about the world and by the dilemmas that were being enacted. The world and its existential dilemmas were central, underlined by the witnessed pain and suffering. The early-modern executions, for instance, enacted the predicament of being entirely disposable and at the same time entirely protected subjects of the king. By being part of the ritual, everyone's desire for belonging was satisfied, since they recognized themselves as being in the same position, squeezed between vulnerability and protection. The spectators recognized *themselves* as part of the enacted world, and they moreover recognized *each other* as fully part of a group with a common pre-dicament. In this way, punishment latched on to the desire for social esteem and bridged the gap to enjoyment.

While conveyed by other people in the audience, the recognition was essen-tially institutional, embedded in institutionalized social practice. To catch sight of it requires an abstraction from the interpersonal focus of the master-and-slave dialectic, which was tailored around face-to-face interaction: two actors who try to gain recognition from each other. In his later work, in the

Philosophy of Right, Hegel employed an institutional perspective, which might include punishment. On this analysis, there was by and large congruence between the lived morality and social institutions at any given time. Habits and ideals which were valued within a community were seen to be institutionalized in existing social institutions – punishment, education, religion, family – which in turn could satisfy the desire for recognition (Hegel 1952). The basic congruence made people susceptible to what the institutions had to offer, in terms of recognition. Desire and satisfaction were shaped by the available institutional provision. In a modern context, there are a range of different institutional providers, which can provide other kinds of recognition, beyond the primordial recognition of status. Axel Honneth has, most notably, distinguished three modes of recognition, each tied to a particular social sphere. The family satisfied the desire for recognition by offering love and emotional support, whereas the state offered recognition by providing equal opportunity and respect for legal rights and safeguarding the sanctity of individuals. Recognition of social esteem was attributed to the institutions of civil society, which acknowledged individual achievements and conferred social status (Honneth 1992; 2011; Honneth et al. 2013). Punishment may offer recognition of social esteem (although primarily located within the state). Like a number of other social institutions, punishment may bridge the gap between the desire for social esteem and the satisfaction of this desire. Education and religion, the family and the workplace may, likewise, activate the desire for status recognition and offer opportunities for its satisfaction. In several respects, punishment resembles other social institutions. Like them, it embodies rituals, morality and beliefs, and is engaged in 'ways of world-making' (Goodman 1978).

Punishment was also uniquely positioned to satisfy specifically the desire for social esteem. The world was laid out particularly in the dimension of justice and moral order. The performative function of penal practices was brought out in the programmatic statements on punishment as a social institution made by David Garland in an overlooked article from 1991, and at the end of *Punishment and Modern Society*. Elaborating on Durkheim's idea of punishment as symbolic communication, he argued that penal practices shape worlds by enacting basic moral and social distinctions (Garland 1991). Punishment can 'tell us where to locate social authority, how to preserve order and community, where to look for social dangers and how to feel about these matters' (Garland 1990: 252/3). It provides answers to questions that are moral and existential. How are we, or the penal spectators in any given community, rectified or safeguarded, and where is our place in the total scheme of things? It is not simply a matter of who is the criminal, or a statement on how order and community are best preserved. It is also about the composition of what is being defended: the social hierarchies, the underlying order, and the spectators' own position. Punishment is never a sideshow; it enacts a whole world in the key dimensions of order and morality. The enacted world is moreover authoritatively underlined by pain and ritualistic violence. Punishment is a peculiarly charged arena. The intentional infliction of pain may be prohibited in other areas of life but is in this specific context backed by social morality. Punishment may for these reasons be uniquely positioned, to activate a desire, which from the outset has been defined by vengeful passions, prevailing notions of justice and standards of social esteem, and to satisfy this desire, in addition. Potentially everyone was included. Punishment manifested a shared social world and lived morality, which was liable to provide recognition to individuals who had been and continued to be immersed in that world and that morality. Because of the congruence, any member of the community could effortlessly partake in the consumption of punishment and access the shared world which was being enacted in the dimensions of order and morality. The dependence on specific others appeared to vanish, allowing them to recognize *themselves* in that order, as full members. On the face of it, it was recognition for free. One just needed to be part of the audience.

The argument just advanced, that punishment provided satisfaction by enacting a world in the dimensions of justice and moral order, which made individuals in the audience recognize themselves as fully part of a group, is open to discussion and numerous objections can be made. The enacted worlds and their interpretations will always vary, historically, across social divisions, and otherwise, and the pleasure of the audience – as an actual experience – will always, in the final analysis, elude any attempt to reconstruct it. With respect to the early-modern period, Bentham above all saw the repeated tragedy. Yet that may not have been how everybody experienced the public execution, regardless of how events unfolded in other respects around the scaffold. Some people may not have seen their own utter disposability and instead felt the power and the protection of the sovereign – the sublime experience – or experienced the absorbed arousal of the carnivalesque. In that case, their pleasure would probably have been different, less a relief of status concerns and instead the absorbed excitement of terror at a safe distance, of popular acts of defiance, or the enthusiasm of self-assertion. In addition, punishment may not necessarily have provided pleasure at all. To some people in the audience it was a discomforting experience. Several contemporary observers of the early-modern executions were appalled, or morally alienated. There is no necessary pleasure, and any attempt to reconstruct the mechanisms carries a tentative character, including this one.

How is punishment to be situated with respect to pleasure's seemingly incompatible duality, stretched out between the desire for recognition and its elusive, uncertain and always partial satisfaction? I have argued that punishment operates in a specific way, as an intervention bridging the gap between desire and enjoyment. The consumption of punishment promises to satisfy the incessant and never satisfied desire for status recognition, at the same time as it provides enjoyment, by recognizing spectators as fully part of the community or, alternatively, through the excitement of taking part in collective self-assertion. With respect to the character of experience, these are very different kinds of enjoyment. On one account, punishment offers relief of distress by shaping social worlds in the dimension of justice and order. On the other account, punishment creates immediate excitement through an unrestrained display of violence and morality. So far in the book, the examples have been exclusively pre-modern, and it is now time to start discussing the pleasure of punishment in a modern context. As traceable in Nietzschean philosophy and Freudian psychoanalysis at the end of the nineteenth century, with the passage to modernity, the conditions for the consumption of pleasure were transformed. Shared excitement and immediate absorption were rendered increasingly difficult at the scenes of punishment; there was a shift of focus from anger to pleasure as the prime disruptive element in punishment; and social prohibitions changed, which necessitated sublimation of the enjoyment. All these changes have been covered so far. In addition, the evolution of the state-administered criminal justice system seemed to support the novel idea of punishment as something representing the audience (Durkheim 1997; Lenin 1965). During the early-modern period, the audience must have felt that the justice being done was not theirs, but rather a justice representing either gods or monarchs. But the evolution of modern police forces and correctional services, in combination with the gradual evolution of democratic practices, placed punishment within reach of the audience. Punishment could be *their* punishment, used for rehabilitative ends, or as an expression of their terror.

These changes fundamentally affected the modern experience of pleasure, both as the Platonian relief of distress and as the Aristotelian absorbed excitement. The Platonian pleasure will be treated in the next chapter. The recognition which had been readily accessible in the consumption of the world and the shared dilemmas of impotence being enacted now evolved into *ressentiment*, as status hierarchies and status expectations were unsettled, and the idea of punishment as a representation of the popular majority gained ground. The last chapter will discuss Aristotelian pleasure. The carnivalesque excitement and the sublime abandon evolved into obscene enjoyment, due to the difficulties of expressing unrestrained excitement in public, and the possibility of terror as an expression of the social morality of the group. There were also other dislocations, which justify the choice of presenting the specifically modern Platonian and Aristotelian pleasures in separate chapters. The division corresponds to different experiences of punishment, but also to different kinds of punishment. With respect to pre-modern conditions, one and the same type of punishment could provide different kinds of enjoyment: sometimes unconscious satisfaction and sometimes visible exaltation. The desire for social esteem could find satisfaction in the collective recognition of social worth or, alternatively, develop into excitement and absorption in excessive punishment, in the consumption of Attic tragedies, afterworldly punishment and public executions. With the passage to modernity, however, the two kinds of pleasure appeared to be provided by different kinds of punishment: punishments which moreover have been discussed separately, in different strands of research. *Ressentiment*, which provided recognition of social esteem through an imaginary revenge in the projected world of order and morality, relied mainly on ordinary punishment, or punishment that was legitimate in the Weberian sense. Obscene enjoyment, on the other hand, the intense excitement of asserting desire without paying heed to conventional normative constraints, was considered as the domain of excessive or illegitimate punishment.

References

Albrecht, William (1975) *The sublime pleasures of tragedy: a study of critical theory from Dennis to Keats*. Lawrence: University Press of Kansas.

Aristotle (1976) *Nicomachean ethics*. Trans. by J. Thomson. Harmondsworth: Penguin.

Bakhtin, Michail (1968) *Rabelais and his world*. Cambridge, MA: M.I.T. Press.

Battersby, Christine (2007) *The Sublime, terror and human difference*. Abingdon: Routledge.

Brady, Emily (2013) *The sublime in modern philosophy: aesthetics, ethics, and nature*. Cambridge: Cambridge University Press.

Burke, Edmund (1996) *The writings and speeches of Edmund Burke. Vol. 3, Party, parliament, and the American War, 1774–1780*. Oxford: Clarendon Press.

Burke, Edmund (1997) *The writings and speeches of Edmund Burke. Vol. 1, The early writings*. Oxford: Clarendon Press.

Burke, Peter (2009) *Popular culture in early modern Europe*. Farnham: Ashgate.

Butler, Judith (1987) *Subjects of desire: Hegelian reflections in twentieth-century France*. New York: Columbia University Press.

Ciobanu, Estella (2018) *Representations of the body in Middle English Biblical drama*. Cham: Springer International Publishing.

Civitarese, Guiseppe (2016) On sublimation. *International Journal of Psychoanalysis* 97: 1369–1392.

Cohen, Esther (1989) Symbols of culpability and the universal language of justice: the ritual of public executions in late medieval Europe. *History of European Ideas* 11: 407–416.

Dennis, John (1996) The grounds of criticism in poetry. In A. Ashfield and P. de Bolla (eds.), *The sublime: a reader in British eighteenth-century aesthetic theory*. Cambridge: Cambridge University Press. pp 35–39.

Eagleton, Terry (1995) *Heathcliff and the great hunger*. London: Verso.

Eagleton, Terry (2003) *Sweet violence: the idea of the tragic*. Oxford: Blackwell.

Eagleton, Terry (2005) *Holy terror*. Oxford: Oxford University Press.

Enders, Jody (1999) *The medieval theater of cruelty: rhetoric, memory, violence*. Ithaca, NY: Cornell University Press.

Evans, Richard (1996) *Rituals of retribution: capital punishment in Germany 1600–1987*. Oxford: Oxford University Press.

Foucault, Michel (1979) *Discipline and punish: the birth of the prison*. New York: Vintage Books.

Freud, Sigmund (1931) *Das Unbehagen in der Kultur*. Wien: Internationaler psychoanalytischer Verlag.

Garland, David (1990) *Punishment and modern society: a study in social theory*. Oxford: Clarendon.

Garland, David (1991) Punishment and culture: the symbolic dimensions of criminal justice. In A. Sarat and S. Silbey (eds.), *Studies in law, politics and society*. Vol. 11. London: JAI Press. pp 191–222.

Garland, David (2010) *Peculiar institution: America's death penalty in an age of abolition*. Oxford: Oxford University Press.

Goldhill, Simon (1990) Great Dionysia and civic ideology. In J. Winkler and F. Zeitlin (eds.), *Nothing to do with Dionysos? Athenian drama in its social context*. Princeton: Princeton University Press. pp 97–129.

Goldhill, Simon (2000) Civic ideology and the problem of difference: the politics of Aeschylean tragedy, once again. *The Journal of Hellenic Studies* 120: 34–56.

Goodman, Nelson (1978) *Ways of worldmaking*. Hassocks: Harvester Press.

Griffith, Mark (1995) Brilliant dynasts: power and politics in the Oresteia. *Classical Antiquity* 14(1): 62–129.

Habermas, Jürgen (1963) *Theorie und Praxis: sozialphilosophische Studien*. Neuwied am Rhein: Luchterhand.

Heath, Malcolm (2012) Longinus and the ancient sublime. In T. Costelloe (ed.), *The sublime. From antiquity to the present*. Cambridge: Cambridge University Press. pp 11–23.

Hegel, Georg Wilhelm Friedrich (1952) *The philosophy of right*. Oxford: Oxford University Press.

Hegel, Georg Wilhelm Friedrich (1998) System der Sittlichkeit. *Gesammelte Werke, Band 5. Schriften und Entwürfe (1799–1808)*. Hamburg: Meiner.

Hegel, Georg Wilhelm Fredrich (2018) *The phenomenology of spirit*. Cambridge: Cambridge University Press.

Henrichs, Albert (1984) Loss of self, suffering, violence: the modern view of Dionysus from Nietzsche to Girard. *Harvard Studies in Classical Philology* 88: 205–240.

Hill, Christopher (1972) *The world turned upside down: radical ideas during the English revolution*. London: Maurice Temple Smith.

Honneth, Axel (1992) *Kampf um Anerkennung: zur moralischen Grammatik sozialer Konflikte*. Frankfurt am Main: Suhrkamp.

Honneth, Axel (2003) Redistribution as recognition. A response to Nancy Fraser. In N. Fraser and A. Honneth. *Redistribution or recognition?: a political-philosophical exchange*. London: Verso. pp 110–197.

Honneth, Axel (2011) *Das Recht der Freiheit: Grundriss einer demokratischen Sittlichkeit*. Berlin: Suhrkamp.

Honneth, Axel (2013) Recognition and Critical Theory today: an interview with Axel Honneth, by Gonçalo Marcelo. *Philosophy and Social Criticism* 39(2): 209–221.

Ignatieff, Michael (1978) *A just measure of pain: the penitentiary in the industrial revolution, 1750–1850*. London: Macmillan.

Kant, Immanuel (1914a) *Kritik der Urteilskraft. Immanuel Kants Werke. Band V*. Berlin: Cassirer.

Kojève, Alexandre (1969) *Introduction to the reading of Hegel*. New York: Basic Books.

Lacan, Jacques (1977) *The four fundamental concepts of psycho-analysis*. London: Hogarth.

Laqueur, Thomas (1989) Crowds, carnival and the state in English executions, 1604 – 1868. In A. Beier, D. Cannadine and J. Rosenheim (eds.), *The first modern society: essays in English History in honour of Lawrence Stone*. Cambridge: Cambridge University Press. pp 305–356.

Lenin, Vladimir (1965) *The state and revolution: Marxist teaching on the state and the tasks of the proletariat in the revolution*. Peking: Foreign Language Press.

Linebaugh, Peter (1991) *The London hanged: crime and civil society in the eighteenth century*. London: Allen Lane.

Lyotard, Jean-François (1994) *Lessons on the analytic of the sublime: (Kant's Critique of judgment, §§ 23–29)*. Stanford: Stanford University Press.

Martschukat, Jürgen (2002) 'The art of killing by electricity': the sublime and the electric chair. *Journal of American History* 89(3): 900–921.

McGowen, Randall (1986) A powerful sympathy: terror, the prison, and humanitarian reform in early nineteenth-century Britain. *Journal of British Studies* 25(3): 312–334.

Mills, Robert (2005) *Suspended animation: pain, pleasure and punishment in medieval culture*. London: Reaktion Books.

Moyaert, Paul (2010) What is frightening about sexual pleasure? Introducing Lacan's jouissance into Freudian psychoanalysis via Plato and Aristotle. In E. Dorfman and J. de Vleminck (eds.), *Sexuality and psychoanalysis: philosophical criticisms*. Leuven: Leuven University Press. pp 21–33.

Nietzsche, Friedrich (1967) *The birth of tragedy*. New York: Vintage Books.

Nietzsche, Friedrich (2017) *The will to power*. London: Penguin Books.

Nye, David (1994) *American technological sublime*. Cambridge, MA: MIT Press.

Nye, David (2018) *American illuminations: urban lighting, 1800–1920*. Cambridge, MA: MIT Press.

O'Neill, Daniel (2012) The sublime, the beautiful, and the political in Burke's work. In K. Vermeir and M. Funk Deckard (eds.), *The science of sensibility: reading Burke's Philosophical Enquiry*. Dordrecht: Springer. pp 193–221.

Plato (1959) *Gorgias*. Trans. by E. R. Dodds. Oxford: Clarendon Press.

Porter, James (2016) *The sublime in antiquity*. Cambridge: Cambridge University Press.

Roselli, David (2011) *Theater of the people: spectators and society in ancient Athens*. Austin: University of Texas Press.

Ruddick, Nicholas (1998) Life and death by electricity in 1890: the transfiguration of William Kemmler. *Journal of American Culture* 21(4): 79–87.

Rudé, George (1956) The Gordon Riots: a study of the rioters and their victims. *Transactions of the Royal Historical Society* 6: 93–114.

Schuster, Aaron (2016) *The trouble with pleasure: Deleuze and psychoanalysis*. Cambridge, MA: MIT Press.

Southey, Robert (2016) *Letters from England: by Don Manuel Alvarez Espriella*. Abingdon: Routledge.

Spierenburg, Pieter (1984) *The spectacle of suffering: executions and the evolution of repression: from a preindustrial metropolis to the European experience*. Cambridge: Cambridge University Press.

Taylor, Charles (1975) *Hegel*. Cambridge: Cambridge University Press.

Taylor, Charles (1989) *Sources of the self: the making of the modern identity*. Cambridge: Cambridge University Press.

Taylor, Charles (1992) The politics of recognition. In A. Gutmann (ed.), *Multiculturalism and the politics of recognition*. Princeton: Princeton University Press. pp 25–74.

Taylor, C. C. W. (2008) Pleasure: Aristotle's response to Plato. In *Pleasure, mind, and soul: selected papers in ancient philosophy*. Oxford: Oxford University Press. pp 240–264.

van Riel, Gerd (2000) *Pleasure and the good life: Plato, Aristotle, and the Neoplatonists.* Leiden: Brill.

Welskopp, Thomas (2013) Anerkennung – Verheissung und Zumutungen der Moderne. In A. Honneth, O. Lindemann and S. Voswinkel (eds.), *Strukturwandel der Anerkennung. Paradoxien sozialer Integration in der Gegenwart*. Frankfurt am Main: Campus. pp 41–73.

Žižek, Slavoj (2006) *How to read Lacan*. London: Granta.

6   *Ressentiment*
Moral elevation through punishment

As indicated by the Hegelian master-and-slave dialectic, satisfaction of desire was precarious, passing, partial, potentially harmful, socially conditioned and dependent on others. Under modern conditions, desire was no less persistent than before, while recognition appeared more elusive. The reinforced tension between the desire for social esteem and its satisfaction was explicit in the theories of *ressentiment* by Friedrich Nietzsche and Max Scheler. They formulated the idea of a general societal condition, which shaped the very experience of satisfaction, after the passage to modernity. *Ressentiment* changed the conditions for pleasure, affecting everyone, although some were more affected than others. In certain respects, the difficulties in acquiring recognition were compounded. The tension was acutely experienced among significant sections of the population, painful and pervasive, as a result of the combined impact of destabilized status hierarchies and the new contradictions of capitalism. Punishment, along with other institutions, could no longer provide recognition by re-enacting a world in the dimensions of order and morality, since that world had lost some of its ontological weight. Due to socio-political changes conceived of as historical injustices of monumental proportions, the world had to be radically restored, or reshaped. Not even punishment could be trusted, and had to be reinvented. In one respect, however, recognition of status was facilitated. Recognition through punishment was direct. It was no longer mediated through the other spectators, as a shared predicament, but immediately provided by a punishment which audiences felt to be their own. In all these three respects, *ressentiment* constituted an adaptation to the changed conditions for the experience of pleasure in the late-nineteenth century.

In the *Genealogy of Morals*, Friedrich Nietzsche offered a ground-breaking analysis of *ressentiment* as a mechanism for self-valuation through proxy, or a way to access recognition of status in a situation when recognition was perceived to be actively, durably and unjustly denied. Once again, the issue was how pain was transformed into pleasure. As opposed to most later commentators on *ressentiment*, Nietzsche accorded a central role to punishment. To him, it was a central mechanism that would transform the spectators' pain into pleasure. It had the power to release the accumulated tension and provide pleasure to angry and humiliated spectators. All of a sudden, the tension would be released. The transition was affected through a revenge, which was not of their own making but administered through the criminal justice system of the state. Still, it was perceived to be their revenge and, in the process, spectators were morally elevated – in their own eyes and in the eyes of the fellow members of the group. The transformation appeared paradoxical. On the one hand, there was a pervasive sense of powerlessness, a fair share of culturally devalued feelings such as bitterness and envy, as well as the less than reassuring belief that the world was crumbling at the seams; on the other hand, there was a sense of relief, the experience of being rectified and seen as being the backbone of society, in the key dimensions of order and morality. How could embittered observers of a crumbling order be transformed into esteemed pillars of a restored order through punishment? This apparent paradox will be approached in the same way as the problem of tragic pleasure, the popular representations of Hell, and the satisfaction of public executions. Instead of focusing on the promised blood, one should direct attention to the world being enacted. In this chapter, I will discuss *ressentiment* as a contemporary experience. Criminological research on the evolution of criminal justice in the post-1960s Western world offers a wealth of examples on both the build-up and the release of tension, which can be used to shed light on how punishment operates in the gap between desire and enjoyment, under conditions of *ressentiment*. As before, the relationship between the audience and the world projected through punishment provides the key to the transformation of pain into pleasure.

The build-up of tension: way of life and no way out

The idea of *ressentiment* as a general condition, which shaped the very experience of satisfaction, emerged with the modern period. In *The Present Age*, originally published in 1846, Søren Kierkegaard used the French term *ressentiment* to describe a psychological reaction of envy and the denial of distinction (Kierkegaard 1962). The reaction was conceived of as a general mood, shared by many, and rooted in the contemporary experience of status uncertainty and lack of recognition. Max Scheler later elaborated the experience phenomenologically in *Das Ressentiment im Aufbau der Moralen*, published in 1912. He treated *ressentiment* as an inner-psychological mechanism, which some people were more prone to adopt than others, because they were more exposed to the tension between rising status expectations and existing relationships of power. From the outset, *ressentiment* was driven by pain: the simultaneous experience of injustice and the inability to make it go away. Desire for status recognition could not be satisfied, and pressure was mounting. The injustice was deeply felt and rectification beyond reach. The experienced dilemma was accompanied by a host of emotional reactions. Bitterness, envy, *schadenfreude*, malice, hatred, and jealousy were typical symptoms of a seemingly unbridgeable gap between desire and enjoyment.

Like Kierkegaard before him, Scheler saw *ressentiment* as an expression of the age, in this case Europe before the First World War. The experience was described as something specifically modern, widespread, and unthinkable in pre-modern times. The feelings of bitterness and impotence ironically presupposed hope and privileges. The causes were located in the dissolution of old hierarchies. *Ressentiment* grew out of perceived powerlessness, combined with unfulfilled status expectations, and was set in motion by the French revolution, which had affected the horizon of expectations. The expectations among broad sectors of the population were severed from rigid status hierarchies and moved slowly upwards as they became citizens with rights as well as obligations in a nation state, while they at the same time were being squeezed between unlimited goals and general expectations and the limited means at disposal, a contradiction that was foregrounded by the advent of capitalism. The raised expectations could not be matched. The result was experienced as durably denied or even as actively withheld recognition, with little prospect of change in sight (Scheler 2017). Satisfaction is in one sense always uncertain, potentially harmful and dependent on others' gratification; it may be endemic in the modern condition (Taylor 1992; 1989), or even be part of what it means to be human, as suggested by Kojève (1969). Yet this was different; the lack of recognition was acutely experienced, and ever more so. As tension was mounting – there was no outlet of desire, no bridge to enjoyment – the situation became unbearable. Scheler called it 'psychological dynamite' (*seelisches Dynamit*) which threatened to detonate (Scheler 2017: 25).

The idea of *ressentiment* as a general condition has recurred several times during the modern period. Each time, the main objective was to understand the allure of political movements which came across as problematic, rather than the impact of punishment. Max Scheler was deeply concerned by the progress of the labour movement in the beginning of the nineteenth century, and accorded a role to the criminal law only at the margins of his account. The focus on political mobilization has characterized most analysis of *ressentiment* in social science and cultural theory. In the 1990s, Wendy Brown discussed *ressentiment* from a Left-wing perspective, and keenly diagnosed its pervasive impact; 'starkly accountable yet dramatically impotent, the late modern liberal subject quite literally seethes with *ressentiment*' (Brown 1995: 69). It was exemplified with the identity politics that was being articulated on behalf of oppressed groups, influential at the time, spreading from Western universities and beyond. The experience of living in an age of *ressentiment* was articulated once again in the 2010s (Dolgert 2016; Tomelleri 2017). This time, writers tended to see *ressentiment* as one main cause for the rise of authoritarian populism, organized around a core of predominantly white working-class males on both sides of the Atlantic (Dolgert 2016; Harper and Schaaf 2018; Oudenampsen 2018; Gidron and Hall 2017). The mobilizations were linked to shifting political agendas and social compositions. Yet they were all informed by the idea of historical injustice and the non-recognition of rights. Everyday experiences of frustration and perceived status infraction blended with existing narratives to the effect that recognition was being actively withheld, as opposed to just missing. The powerful idea of historic injustice, which had to be avenged, was the hallmark of *ressentiment*. The idea of injustice did not seem to be wedded to any particular values. In this sense, *ressentiment* was politically colour-blind. But it was inevitably political. Each mobilization was powered by political demands for justice, and was successful to the extent that it articulated the wish of significant sections of the populations to be recognized and rectified as victims of injustices (Brown 1995; Dolgert 2016; Elgat 2017).

Some of the more prominent narratives in the post-1968 era have been organized around crime – as a shorthand for the key drivers of *ressentiment* – with punishment as the natural counterpoint. Individual acts of crime made the denied recognition intelligible, as they were inserted in a wider tale of breakdown of socio-moral order. On the 5 November 1972, a man on his way home from a Birmingham pub was attacked and knocked to the ground by three young men. The event – and the wider phenomenon of which it was allegedly part: mugging – was given much publicity in national British media in the ensuing months. As a result, Stuart Hall et al. argued, a new figure came to life, unifying a nation marked by widening class divisions;

> Young, black, bred in, or arising from the 'breakdown of social order' in the city; threatening the traditional peace of the streets, the security of movement by the ordinary citizens; motivated by naked gain, a reward he would come by, if possible, without a day's honest toil; his crime, /.../ impelled by an even more frightening need for 'gratuitous violence', an inevitable result of the weakening moral fibre in family and society, and the general collapse of respect for discipline and authority.
>
> (Hall et al. 1978: 160)

'Young, black, bred in', the criminal personified the active denial of hard work and responsibility: someone who inverted the values of family and tradition. By implication, one key actor responsible for the perceived injustice had been given a name: the mugger. Equally important, there was another story within this story. Beneath the heavily prejudiced notions of the dangerous classes, the ill-concealed racism in the media coverage, and other disturbing elements in the portrayal of the criminal, there was the desperate cry of its counterpart: the ordinary citizens. The ordinary citizens – tacitly white, British and hard-working – could not live; the life they expected could not be lived for a combination of tangible and less tangible reasons, associated with physical security and the breakdown of moral order. Even the most basic expectations of life were unfulfilled. Ordinary citizens were unable to walk the streets without risk of being attacked. There was moreover the imminent risk of a 'general collapse of respect for discipline and authority'. The fundamental order and morality of the world was being subverted and had to be restored – and along with it, the socio-moral worth of the individual, who depended on that order for recognition. This story has been retold many times since, and would become common property in the politics of criminal justice in many Western countries throughout the post 1968-era (Flamm 2005; Camp 2016; Murakawi 2014; Gottschalk 2006; Beckett 1997).

Crime was the ultimate proof of ordinary life becoming unliveable. It was never only about crime as concrete acts of transgression, however disastrous the consequences were at the personal level for those who were immediately affected, in terms of violence, addiction, or feelings of being aggrieved. As others have observed, public views on punishment tended to be embedded in a moral view of social order (Beckett 1997). Of course, not everybody supported harsher punishment. It was easy to find support for lenient sentencing in surveys, where the overarching moral concerns were supplemented by information on the circumstances of the specific act (Jerre 2013; Gottschalk 2006). Yet supplementary information on the realities of crime and sentencing was not always relevant. Those who believed that the moral order was endangered were also those who wanted harsher sentences, in any case. To significant sections of the populations in many Western countries, ideas on punishment were heavily influenced by concerns of moral decline and by the perception of living in a dangerous world (Tyler and Boeckmann 1997; King and Maruna 2009; Cheliotis 2013; Gerber and Jackson 2016). Crime became a symbol for the direction in which society seemed to be heading. Hence, members of the public would 'endorse punishment in a symbolic attempt to defend social order and moral cohesion' (Gerber and Jackson 2016: 131). Crime was taken to demonstrate that the moral principles of the world were being violated, by others and with disastrous consequences. It made life unliveable, along with other occurrences, which were likewise perceived to affect the world in the dimensions of order and morality, although not necessarily related in other ways. In a letter written in June 1968, a white father of five from North Carolina let his heart out. He has had it.

> I'm sick of crime everywhere. I'm sick of riots. I'm sick of "poor" people demonstrations ... I'm sick of the U.S. Supreme Court ... I'm sick of the lack of law enforcement .... I'm sick of Vietnam .... I'm sick of hippies, LSD, drugs, and all the promotion the news media give them .... But most of all, I'm sick of constantly being kicked in the teeth for staying home, minding my own business, working steadily, paying my bills and taxes, raising my children to be decent citizens, managing my financial affairs.
>
> (quoted from Flamm 2005: 12)

The letter-writer was sick of many things, ranging from Vietnam to demonstrations, from hippies to the Supreme Court, and the list could probably have been extended with other visible signs of disorder, or political change. Michael Flamm, who found the letter in an archive, interpreted it as testimony of the crises of law and order. At the end of 1960s, there was among many white Americans a pervasive sense that the basic fundaments of society were coming apart. It came to be articulated as a problem of order, where order was threatened by a combination of street crime, state-administered reforms, and political mobilization (Flamm 2005). Yet the perceived threat to moral order was merely one aspect of the letter. Implied in the brief analysis of the state of the nation, captured in the quote, was a testimony of a personal crisis of recognition. It was not only society that was coming apart at the seams, but also his identity as a white father of five, living in North Carolina. He did not recognize himself or his values in the papers he read, or in the television news; instead hippies and drug users got promoted. He was working hard, payed his bills and raised his children to be the same – for which he was 'constantly being kicked in the teeth'. He did what was expected of any responsible citizen, yet experienced no appreciation in return. Instead of gaining the usual enjoyment of the other for conventional investments – going to work, paying the bills, or raising children – there was the suspicion that others enjoy a good life, on his behalf, due to the erosion of existing institutions. He was losing his sense of direction in life, and articulated the personal despair as a breakdown of law and order. The two aspects came together in a paradoxical situation from which there was no escape. The personal crises could not be solved by being afforded recognition through existing institutions, since these institutions were unable to provide such recognition, while he, on the other hand, could do nothing but watch this happen, due to personal impotence.

In *Zarathustra*, Nietzsche described the 'angry spectator'. It was someone who was unhappy and impotent, 'impotent against that which has been – it is an angry spectator of everything past' (Nietzsche 2006: 2.20). Angry spectators were backward-looking and attached to historic wounds, preoccupied with the injustice. Fundamentally, however, the spectators were angry because they were torn between an entrenched desire for a certain way of life and the experience of being unable to fulfil that desire (Reginster 1997). The desired way of life was the one which conferred enjoyment of the other. It was the way of life that one had grown up to expect. But it was out of reach, and this produced bitterness, envy, *schadenfreude*, malice, hatred, and other symptoms of frustrated *thumos*. The perception of being cornered, and unable to lead the kind of life one grew up to expect, was central. It was a crisis of recognition, which was only acerbated by dwindling resources and opportunities, deep-seated economic and social changes. With respect to a Louisiana right-wing constituency in 2010s, Arlie Hochschild has described how it had become 'a struggle to feel seen and honored' (Hochschild 2016: 144; see also Cramer 2016; Lamont 2018). Many respectable citizens, it was felt in Louisiana right-wing circles, had to stand back, while others enjoyed recognition and other benefits, illicitly. Their experiences were embedded in shared, more or less implicit narratives, which endorsed the socio-economic hardship, while accounting for personal powerlessness and lack of recognition as effects of the activities of hostile others. The narratives narrowed down responsible groups and required redress. Ethnic and sexual minorities, drug users and criminals were seen to actively disrupt the world in the key dimensions of order and morality, with the conscious assistance of more established institutions, such as civil rights organizations, universities, federal government, or the liberal press (Hochschild 2016). Their way of life appeared impossible, everyday experiences of withheld recognition were reinforced, and pressure was mounting.

On Scheler's analysis, desire for vengeance was the initial response. Those responsible must be punished. The injustice experienced called for immediate redress, but that was impossible due to the impotence of the subject. What could the white North Carolinian letter writer do other than write letters, complain and vote for a right-wing candidate? Hence, the desire for vengeance was pushed back into the imaginary (Scheler 2017). The more the desire for revenge was pushed back into the imaginary, the more object-less it became, eventually transforming it into a durable way of relating to the world. Yet desire did not go away; on the contrary, it kept mounting, as new signs of everyday infractions of social esteem were encountered, reinforced and reinterpreted through existing political narratives. Over time, pressure was accumulated, building an almost insurmountable gap between desire and enjoyment. There seemed to be less and less that could bridge the gap between desire and enjoyment. Even the conventional rewards of work, family and propriety were becoming less capable of providing satisfaction. Just as the Slave in Hegel's dialectic was unable to provide recognition, because the recognition being offered had lost its meaning, existing institutions were devalued and had a reduced amount of esteem to offer. Ever more tension was building up, which could not find an outlet. There was no way out – yet pressure continued to mount on the subject, until it finally became unbearable. Hence the reference to 'psychological dynamite' which threatened to detonate. The tension was literally explosive.

The release of tension: the late-modern prison and death penalty

Revenge was the default option, but since the desire for revenge was repressed and unavailable, people turned instead to punishment. Punishment became an important instrument to defuse status concerns and temporarily restore social esteem to the 'angry spectator of everything past'. To Nietzsche, there was a marked difference; punishment was the weapon of the weak, for those who were unable to take revenge, because they were simply not strong enough (Nietzsche 1989: I § 10). Hope of retribution was consequently deferred to other actors. The criminal justice apparatus seemed capable of carrying out the revenge which the angry spectators would only dream of exacting themselves. Still it was *their* revenge, a revenge through proxy. The criminal justice system of the state could produce their revenge. In one sense, this constituted an adaptation to the modern condition. Before the nineteenth century, such an idea would have been inconceivable, or utopian, or confined to the domain of divine justice, as there was no state or system of criminal justice in which ordinary people could place their hope for general redress, as opposed to the punishment of specific crimes. With the passage to modernity, however, it became possible to imagine a state that could step in and act on behalf of groups of ordinary citizens. The emergence of a criminal justice apparatus, with modern police forces and a network of correctional facilities, in combination with the gradual spread of democratic ideas and electoral practices, may first of all have been bulwarks of the capitalist order. Inadvertently, the new state institutions also represented potential instruments of the audience. In the latter part of the nineteenth century, prisons located in the middle of cities and uniformed police officers patrolling the streets were highly visible manifestations of power, which made the state appear as a possible instrument for popular revenge. Paradigmatically, Durkheim (1997) launched the idea that punishment was exacted for the sake of the audience, channelling their vengeful passions, whereas Lenin (1965) would outline how the people should take control over the repressive apparatus of the bourgeoise state and use it for their own ends. In both cases, punishment came forth as representative of ordinary people.

Thus, instead of feeling impotent and forgotten and nurturing private fantasies of violence, the criminal justice system seemed to present an opening. The desire for revenge, which had been pushed back into the imaginary, was given an outlet, through the state: a legitimate outlet, moreover. In the current period, the observable rise of the 'penal state' (Garland 2013; McLennan 2001; Rubin and Phelps 2017) presented itself in the same way, as a vehicle for popular revenge on racialized groups, while being administered by the apparatuses of criminal justice. What has been argued with respect to the US situation in the 'age of colour-blindness', namely that the advances of the civil rights movement during the 1960s could not be confronted head on (Alexander 2010), may by extension apply to several other Western countries; ethnic minorities and non-citizens are grossly overrepresented in prisons everywhere. Vengeance had to come in a less than straightforward way. At the end of the twentieth century, it was not feasible to question the improvements in rights and status along the lines of gender, race, or sexuality in electoral politics. Civil liberties, sexual rights, equal opportunity and gender equality were embraced on the streets, in parliaments and in the courts. Instead, the revenge was exacted by the criminal justice system in a perfectly legitimate manner on individuals, not because of their newly acquired rights, but because they had violated the criminal law (Gottschalk 2006; Tonry 1995; Camp 2016).

The penal state promised rectification for the angry spectator: a release of the built-up tension, accompanied by the ever-present suspicion of being betrayed, even by the criminal justice itself. The release of accumulated tension and the lingering suspicion of betrayal can be traced in the response to convictions in high-profile cases, which fit perfectly with the stereotypical image of violent racialized men. On 10 August 2015, an Eritrean man grabbed a knife from a shelf in an IKEA store, just outside of Västerås, and stabbed two randomly chosen customers to death. The man had recently been denied asylum in Sweden, and was arrested on the spot, and tried during the autumn, as the refugee crisis dominated public discussion, following images of large numbers of people moving through Europe (Barker 2018). The trial was broadcasted live by public-service television. As the guilty verdict was announced, a series of new postings were added to an already 1,000-page-long thread on a large, publicly accessible website, which on a regular basis attracts all sorts of comments under the guise of colourful usernames. I have chosen postings associated with three different usernames (IMBILDEN, Kingstown and MorkaKrafter) which might be taken to illustrate the kind of satisfaction that the verdict provided to people under conditions of *ressentiment*. The postings were made within hours after the official announcement, made at 11.10 am, 30 October, and will be taken to exemplify how the communicated punishment was received by angry spectators. One may distinguish three different elements in the comments: (i) the temporary release of tension, (ii) the suspicion of the other's continued enjoyment despite the punishment, and (iii) the guilty verdict was a reminder which, contrary to appearances, reinforced the idea that existing institutions cannot be fully trusted.

First and foremost, there was the immediate release of tension. The accused man was not acquitted, as might be suspected, but instead sentenced in the severest possible way, in legal terms. The verdict was thus experienced as a welcome surprise.

> Have to say that I was positively surprised when the sentence fell. It turned out exactly as I had hoped. Life imprisonment, and after that: extradition.
> (IMBILDEN, posted at 8.40 pm; www.flashback.org/t2605798p898)

The release of tension should be real – the accumulated tension found an outlet in the announced verdict. Assuming the slowly accumulated tension, described by Scheler, the person under the anonymous username might escape the nagging bitterness, inferiority and hatred, and for a brief moment experience peace of mind. The satisfaction caused by the verdict may not last very long. Still, it was relief of distress, and as such, as temporary relief of distress, it was likely to reinforce the desire for more. The revenge was not enough. In fact, it might not be a revenge at all. The initial satisfaction could be accompanied by thoughts that the convicted man would enjoy the stay in prison.

> Commit murder and be allowed to stay in paradise Sweden. In prison, you will get TV, a bed, food, activities, medicine, health care, yes even education if you like. Swedish women will write letter to you if you are lucky, and you can get married and have sex.
> (Kingstown, posted at 7.32 pm; www.flashback.org/t2605798p897)

Despite being punished, the convicted man was suspected to enjoy life more fully than people in the audience. A foreign murderer would have everything, beginning with TV and food, and ending with marriage and sex. Between the lines, it was suggested that he would be allowed comforts which were denied some of the native Swedes who were honest and hard-working. Hence, they fear being let down by the very institution in which they placed their hopes for rectification. Finally, for some of the commentators there was a pervasive sense that those who were really responsible had escaped justice, this time as well.

> This entire story is like an allegory over the sick Swedish society. Some lunatic from Africa is allowed to come here and murder two entirely inno-cent Swedes, and the sanction is that he gets to stay and will be supplied with food and accommodation for indefinite time. I just wish that the disgusting political and journalistic elite, who are responsible for these murders .... one day will suffer themselves. I wish you all unfortune, misery and suffering.
>
> (MorkaKrafter, posted at 1.57 pm; https://www.flashback.org/
> t2605798p895)

The verdict offered little release of distress and instead served to reinforce tension. It was nothing but a reminder of the ongoing injustice. Within the context of a narrative, which was widely shared among sympathizers of right-wing populist parties at the time, the court proceedings represented a kind of a cover-up, or further proof of betrayal. As indicated by the response, it was less about the actual punishment than about the bigger picture; less about the pain and the censure imposed on the Eritrean man than about concerns for a by-gone world in the dimensions of order and morality. The sense that justice was being done was consequently illusionary, and the release of tension was postponed unto an uncertain future. Someday, the commentator hoped, the real perpetrators would be called to justice, yet without confidence that this wish would come true.

Angry spectators suffered from the radical tension between desire and satis-faction of social esteem, and doubted the robustness of the world in precisely those respects that might offer release of tension. The spectator's social status as well as the underlying stability of the moral order were called into question. As in previous historical periods, punishment was one way to satisfy status concerns. But satisfaction presumed a moral order with ontological clout. So, the world in the dimensions of order and morality had to be restored, or reshaped. For the spectator to be recognized by the enacted Other, the Other had first to be restored. Punishment seemed well positioned to do so. In a situ-ation when many established institutions – science, politics and journalism – were perceived to be unreliable, criminal justice appeared relatively unscathed and capable of establishing certainty and authority (Ericson 2007). The death penalty, above all, seemed exceptionally well suited in this respect. The basic script of the public execution was to cleanse 'that which is evil, restore order from chaos, and celebrate the moral and sacred authority of the law' (Smith 2008: 38). As such, it was embedded in the Hobbesian tale of the sovereign state, which enforced transgressions and enabled social existence by defying the state of nature. Capital punishment would remain tied to the early-modern script. But new elements were incorporated. In a US context, from the 1970s and onwards, capital punishment came to represent the front line in conservative politics; it stood for the return to an imagined world of responsible individuals, reliable institutions, and a well-ordered economy. Vestiges of illegitimate popular revenge were simultaneously transformed into criminal justice. The US courts made capital punishment more consonant with the rule of law, in an attempt to shrug off the mark of lynching and gain wider legitimacy, at the same time as it evolved into a cherished symbol, which communicated a range of political positions stretching far beyond issues of law and order (Garland 2010; see also Connolly 1999; Sarat 1999). To support capital punishment was to be part of the general backlash against civil rights, the welfare state and the counter-culture of the 1960s. It was a political statement, immediately rooted in a definite vision of the world in the dimensions of order and morality. The archaic penal script of the violent state as the bringer of order to chaos was thus reinvigorated by a modern, conservative vision of order restoration, and updated to reflect modern legal norms, to disassociate itself from the spectre of lynching and the spectacle of suffering. The script communicated absolute certainty and dedication – annihilation of moral evil, and definitive justice – while at the same relieving itself of the uncivilized and the unlawful. In the eyes of its supporters, capital punishment thus safeguarded the endangered moral order more effectively than other institutions.

The prison is the culturally dominant form of punishment in most parts of the Western world and currently far less associated with partisan politics. Following the stigma of the preceding 'Nothing works' period (Martinson 1974), the prison went from being outmoded to becoming a 'seemingly indispensable pillar of late modern social life' (Garland 2001: 199). The prison grew in size, embracing more and more people, mostly male, mostly racialized and mostly working class, throughout the Western world – consonant with the stereotypical image of the criminal as 'young, black, bred in' (Hall et al. 1978: 160) and partially satisfying the desire for recognition, by providing evidence of the omnipotence and the determination of the state, which was hoped to rectify anything through its institutions of criminal justice, among those who felt represented by it. In most Western countries, the prison was the ultimate punishment – in the absence of capital punishment – to demonstrate moral certainty and to uphold existing principles of status. It was a de-politicized revenge through proxy, which corresponded to a less activist stance among the spectatorship, compared to the death penalty. Themselves relatively shielded from criminal justice interventions, they could sit back and enjoy the overflow of prison iconography. The prison, as consumed through official statistics or through popular culture, may thus have provided relief of the accumulated tension, by enacting a world in which the audience – a core of affluent white people and beyond – felt protected and other people, mainly poor people of colour, were behind bars.

The satisfaction provided by imprisonment may not be reducible to the visible revenge on disadvantaged groups, who were thought to be unjustly favoured by other sections of the state apparatus. The current prison simultaneously enacts a different world, a world in which the revenge is organized around science, rehabilitation and risk management rather than around hypostatized moral categories. The danger which each inmate constituted should be defused during the prison stay, and upon release reinserted in society, all the time drawing on the original penal script of redemption. Prisoners in the nineteenth century were to pass through a stage of civil death, only to be reborn in the hands of designers, reformers and managers. By stripping the prisoner of rights, through solitary confinement, in a cell with only the Bible to read, the old identity should be erased, followed by a process through which the prisoner was requalified to become a model citizen in the community upon release (Smith 2009; Dayan 2011). This idea of redemption, or rehabilitation, set the prison apart from earlier penal practices, and remains entrenched in the basic fabric of the institution. While rehabilitation has to a large extent lost its religious connotation, it continues to inform current metanarratives of the prison. The institution was given a renewed moral-scientific rationale with the introduction of the cognitive behavioural programmes and the tools of risk assessment. At the turn of the century, *Cognitive Skills* was one of many similar cognitive-behavioural programmes for prisoners' rehabilitation. According to the manual, 'you can distinguish between successful and unsuccessful individuals through the fact that the former master a set of thinking and reasoning skills' (KVV 2000: 17). The teachers were instructed to convey the idea that the prisoners could learn to cope with extremely problematic social circumstances and become successful simply by using skills that they would acquire by participating in the programme. The parallel message was that prisoners would have to do most of the work themselves. The role of the prison service was to facilitate the transformation. Like neoliberal reform more generally, the emphasis was on individual responsibility, personal aspirations and a lack of external restrictions (Davies 2014; Rose 1999; Dardot and Laval 2013). Yet prospects for change were bleak. The large majority of prisoners were trapped at the margins of social life and would never turn into the good citizens intended by authors of the programme, not to speak about the prospects of ending up as winners in a rigidifying social stratification. The horizon of expectations was defined by employment opportunities in the low-wage sector, managing disruptive relationships, following the instructions of superiors and enduring abuse – all of which composed 'cognitive skills' in the scenarios in the training provided (Hörnqvist 2010). Compared to the golden age of social engineering, there was moreover the dwindling belief that change was at all possible. But officially, the prison clung to the promises of personal change and redemption, and explicitly denied the impasse of reinforced structural inequality. The disjunction between mandated agency and structural impasse was experienced by managers and inmates alike. Consequently, the prison assumed an 'as if'-character: many people in and around the institution – the prisoners, the staff, and the regulators – acted as if change was possible, although they no longer believed in it (Carlen 2008).

From its inception, the prison had been an enclosed space, unavailable to the general public, and few people knew about what happened behind the walls. Yet some of the things that happened inside the prison were part of other institutional encounters at the time, associated with unemployment, social insurance, health issues, disabilities and addiction (Castel 2003; Lødemel and Moreira 2014). Large groups of people, considered to be socially excluded, were approached in a moralistic fashion by state agencies or private subcontractors, which stressed their personal agency and closely monitored their behaviour. Alternatively, in a workplace setting, employees in all positions, workers and managers, were exposed to detailed regulation, close monitoring, performance measurement, audits and techniques of quality assurance (Power 1997; Moore and Robinson 2016). Hence, most people in the audience would, unbeknownst to the prisoners' treatment programmes, have had everyday experiences that were in some respects similar, confronted with inflated requirements and diminished prospects, followed by intensified supervision. They may not be locked up, yet their behaviour was closely monitored and they felt unable to change their situation, despite trying. The prison thus enacted the neoliberal structure-agency problem with which most people were already familiar. Under pre-modern conditions, the enactment of a shared dilemma might provide recognition to audiences, according to the analysis presented in previous chapters. Yet was it sufficient to dissolve the accumulated tension under the conditions of *ressentiment*? Maybe to some people in the audience. For angry spectators looking for rectification, on the other hand, anything that happened inside the prison which did not involve straight-forward imposition of pain would fail to satisfy. The mechanisms of *ressentiment* required suffering and degradation of the other.

Self-revaluation and world restoration

Given that pain was transformed into pleasure through the consumed punishment, how could something as base and culturally devalued as the imposition of pain on others be instrumental in transforming a group of humiliated and embittered observers of a crumbling order into elevated pillars of a restored order? Nietzsche pointed to the mechanism of revaluation: what was once bad became good. Revaluation was central in his treatment of *ressentiment* in the first essay of the *Genealogy of Morals*, which also contained the most elaborate discussion on the topic. The wider objective was to account for the origin of social morality, including notions of justice, good and evil, and of good and bad. The revaluation affected the standards according to which people and actions were judged to be good or bad (Kaufmann 1968; Reginster 1997; Solomon 1994; Râmbu 2016), and thus also came to define who were worthy of recognition.

In his treatment in the *Genealogy*, one specific actor – referred to as the priests – was attributed with the role of effecting the revaluation. In Nietzsche's conception of social space, the priests were part of the ruling class. Unlike the other part, the warriors, they were prone to *ressentiment*. The priests were weak, but strong enough to initiate the revaluation and create new values. On one interpretation, the priests relieved the angry spectators of guilt and pain, by sanctifying their decadent instincts and making them partake in a higher justice. The spectators' misfortunes were located in a third party, which was pinpointed by the priests as the cause of injustice and as the carrier of immoral qualities (Deleuze 1983). The role of the priests has been debated (Loeb 2018), as well as ignored (Ridley 2006), by Nietzschean scholars. Although peda-gogic, the idea of an external agent may be redundant. Essentially, revalu-ation was a matter of one group defining itself in relation to another group, bereaving it of moral value. The collective self-revaluation was inherent in the logics of *ressentiment*: a way to keep the world in moral order and assert social worth in a rigidly hierarchical environment, when the desire for status recog-nition was frustrated. The 'angry spectators' may not be able to change their situation or achieve the goals they had expected in life, despite the fact that they have worked hard and done everything right, as they saw it. Hence, they clung to what no one could take away from them: their own moral virtue and the bygone world assumed to have provided recognition. Yet the other was indispensable. Recognition of status was pursued and produced through the devaluation of others. It worked by negating all kinds of otherness, everything that was different from oneself, 'and *this* "no" is its creative deed' (Nietzsche 1989: I §10, emphasis in original). The perceived subordination was subtly transformed into a sense of superiority confirmed by the degradation of others. As the ultimate devaluation of the other, punishment was central. It was a self-revaluation through proxy, as the angry spectators depended on the state to exact the revenge. Punishment consequently provided the audience with a vehicle of moral self-transformation capable of bridging the widened gap between desire and enjoyment.

As often noted, the collective self-revaluation may involve an element of self-deception. Nietzsche as well as Scheler considered, on very different grounds, the resulting revaluation to be a normative distortion. Both of them made use of the metaphor of poison to express their stance. Nietzsche wrote that everything good about the other was misperceived 'through the poisonous eye of *ressentiment*' (Nietzsche 1989: I §11). To Scheler, *ressenti-ment* was a poison that affected the ability to detect what was in itself good and bad, regardless of the observer (Scheler 2017). On both accounts, the ability to reinterpret pain was central. At the core of Nietzsche's and Scheler's accounts of *ressentiment* was the idea that suffering and subordination in existing social structures were reinterpreted in moral terms. The way of life of the consumers of punishment, their concerns, tastes and aspirations were elevated, and reattached to the order and morality of the enacted world. Take, for instance, the 30-year-old electrician named Ben who commenced Michèle

Lamont's classic study on the *Dignity of Working Men*. He presented himself as a caring, responsible, hard-working man. As the backbone of society, he was suspicious of managers, who were minding their own careers, and contemptuous of the 'undeserving' parts of the US working class who could not provide for themselves. Ben also adopted a moral stance to punishment and thought that the death penalty should be used much more, a position that was underlined by his expressed willingness to physically abuse rapists and drug dealers who were detained in the local jail (Lamont 2000). Evidently, his wish to punish more, and harder, was one element in his self-representation as a caring, responsible, hard-working man. It was also a way of locating himself in a moral universe where he was placed far higher than his position on the social ladder. Ben rearticulated customary sociological divisions, the boundaries between social groups being separated by wealth and education and other assets, into a moral hierarchy, in which he emerged at the very top. His 'positional suffering' (Bourdieu 1999) was refined and given a higher meaning. Ben's readiness to communicate his views on the death penalty, displayed in the interview situation, also indicated one further characteristic of how punishment operates as a vehicle for revaluation. Just as one does not need to be physically present – in the courtroom or in the correctional facilities – to consume punishment, one does not have to be physically present at any specific site in order to show support. One can display support in social interactions in everyday life, with like-minded members of the community. One can moreover expect other people to be engaged and interested. Given that support for more severe punishment is to take part in the defence of a moral world (Beckett 1997; Garland 2010), to say things such as 'they should use the death penalty much more' is to take active part in a ritual, which is simultaneously a ritual of world restoration and a ritual of self-revaluation. By participating in the ritual, the angry spectators can re-enact themselves as elevated pillars of the world being restored. In the process, the experienced pain is transformed into pleasure, following the release of tension.

While *ressentiment* can find outlet in revenge, the revenge cannot be described as revenge. It must not present itself as such, as revenge, to a wider audience; 'what they are demanding is not called retribution', Nietzsche argued, 'but "the triumph of *justice*"' (Nietzsche 1989: I §14, emphasis in original). The desire for vengeance must be cloaked as justice. In one sense, this was an adjustment to the establishment of a state-administered system of criminal justice, and the modern concept of punishment, clearly separated from vengeance, over the course of the nineteenth century. The revenge had to be administered through the apparatuses of criminal justice; for spectators plagued by their perceived lack of influence, there was no real alternative. But it was more than merely the lack of alternative. In the context of *ressentiment*, legitimacy was crucial. As the revenge was authorized by the state, the violent rectification became legitimate, more or less by definition, in the Weberian sense of being manifestly legitimate in a community. Yet while the revenge may have been cloaked as justice, for practical or other reasons, it was also deeply moral. Without legitimacy, the proposed punishments could not be openly discussed and defended in the community. The moral force evaporated – and punishment degenerated to simple vengeance, or unlawful action, and one had to keep quiet about what happened, even if many people secretly celebrated it. The process of revaluation would be disrupted. If, on the other hand, the punishment could be explicitly endorsed, then one could take active part in the punitive ritual of world restoration, like Ben, the US electrician who supported the death penalty, and reap the satisfaction of moral superiority in the community of co-sympathizers. The revenge was thus shaped by social morality and by the procedural requirements that came with the *Rechtsstaat*. But it was not necessarily restrained. The basic condition of legitimacy did not necessarily restrain the violence, or the scope of the revenge. Instead, the charge was proportionate to the accumulated tension, and indicated the magnitude of the revenge. Justice was totalizing in character, not reducible to a singular event or minor reform, but rather a long-sought purge. The promise was 'that the world become full of the thunderstorms of our revenge, precisely that we would regard as justice' (Nietzsche 2006: 2.8). This was also the secret promise of criminal justice. The state was expected to put things right again, by means of all the violence it took to do so; hence the prospects of a world swept clean by the 'thunderstorms of our revenge'. It was never the individual act of punishment that provided release of distress, but rather the envisioned world, a world filled with thunderstorms of revenge. To the embittered and humiliated spectators, only a world purified in the dimensions of order and morality might offer relief of distress.

Read against the background of the Hegelian master-and-slave dialectic, *ressentiment* represents a continuation of the story of the dark side of recognition. As an expression of acute lack of status, or even obsession with status, *ressentiment* belongs to the *thumos*-spectra of desire. The desire for status recognition is, as discussed in Chapter 3, volatile, fundamentally ambiguous, torn between emotional responses to acts of disrespect and the overarching striving for social esteem in the community. It can be satisfied in several ways. Punishment may be wholly irrelevant for the satisfaction of desire. Under modern conditions, most people seek recognition of status through achievement-oriented institutions. Social status is to a large extent derived from formal merits and labour-market position (Weber 1972, Goldthorpe 1980; Sennett 2003) and translates into life chances, with respect to housing, health, and income, and is typically displayed through lifestyle and consumption (Bourdieu 1984). In other words: acutely felt status anxiety does not necessarily translate into a yearning for punishment. Instead, the punitive turn of *thumos*, discussed by Fukuyama (2012) and Sloterdijk (2010) as the defensive assertion of social morality, is implicated in the dynamics of desire, as one among several options. *Thumos* was in one sense blind, and there was no immanent logic according to which either direction – the bright or the dark side of recognition – was predetermined. The punitive turn of desire was rather an outcome, influenced by external conditions. On a Nietzschean ana-lysis, these were above all related to power asymmetries. The satisfaction of desire was always precarious, as well as jeopardized by lived inequality. There was a constant friction between acquired expectations and lived inequality. It was felt by all members of society, yet more by some than by others. The everyday workings of power threatened to thwart acquired expectations to be fully part of society, or rise above it. Following the analysis of the will, presented in the famous paragraph 19 in *Beyond Good and Evil*, this friction was the basic motor of social life. It could be channelled into the pursuit of conventional goals – a good education, prestigious home, gainful employ-ment, fine reputation, the expected life-style, or consumption – in the hope that these goals would be achieved and confer social esteem on the individual, in the eyes of others. Yet the lived inequality might just as well, depending on the circumstances, channel desire in a punitive direction, toward collective satisfaction through punishment. This was more likely, on this analysis, if conventional, achievement-oriented goals appeared blocked. Everyday experiences of injustice and humiliation, derived from the prevailing power structure, tended to deflect desire into a defensive and potentially violent affirmation of social esteem.

Ressentiment unfolded on the dark side of recognition. There is no immanent logic of desire according to which any particular direction is predetermined. The desire for social esteem is inherently ambiguous and may change direction due to the everyday workings of power. Yet there also appears to be a tipping point, after which people become obsessed with social status, oriented toward historical injustices and predisposed to one-sided assertion on a more durable basis. Following the punitive turn, desire will continue to seek satisfaction through the devaluation of others, and ultimately in the degradation of others. Instead of the postulated Hegelian development toward increased freedom, tolerance and equal rights, satisfaction is provided by reinforced intolerance, violence, calls for justice, the discovery of new groups to persecute, and new forms of deviance to punish. No matter how much suffering and condem-nation are being imposed on the other, lasting recognition of social esteem eludes spectators. They are angry, consumed by the idea of restoring social esteem, yet ultimately unsuccessful; despite the surge of revaluation, they will also be rewarded with renewed suspicion and bitterness. Staying within the context of *ressentiment*, there is no lasting relief to be found. Instead, sat-isfaction is trapped between the impotence of the angry spectator and the hopes for the powerful state, which could never efface the historical injustice, as Wendy Brown (1995) argued. In the *Genalogy*, the unbearable tension of *ressentiment* was eventually repressed, turned inwards and evolved into 'bad conscience', as a faculty of the soul (Nietzsche 1989). Alternatively, social morality could be transposed into higher values, associated with justice and morality. In that case, the obsession with individual status concerns would be deflected into idealized abstractions of the way of life of the community

(Paskewich 2014), and continue to direct punitive anger toward the other. None of the possible routes are mutually exclusive. At one moment, the angry spectators will be beset by guilt and shame, without any genuine hope of change; at another moment, they will see themselves as champions of higher values, supported by a violent state, and occupying a central position in the enacted moral universe.

The underlying pleasure formula was Platonic. On this model, pleasure was essentially relief from distress. There was hunger and the satisfaction of hunger (*Gorgias*); or the drive and the satisfaction of the drive (Freud 1915). *Ressentiment* covered both aspects: it accounted for the build-up of distress and the release of tension. Scheler's phenomenological approach showed how pressure was mounting without finding satisfaction under prevailing conditions, whereas the pleasures of *ressentiment* were described in terms of release of tension. The vengeful impulses disappeared for a little while and the individual was freed from the agony of envy and hate (Scheler 2017). An assumed state of status recognition constituted the horizon of expectations with respect to *ressentiment*, just as Plato had conceived of pleasure as the return to equilibrium. The angry spectators were backward-looking and hoped to efface the historical injustice and thus extinguish the pain, when revenge had restored the world and their rightful place in it. The transformation was thus consonant with the Platonic paradigm: on the one hand distress and on the other hand relief from distress. If anything, it involved a radicalization. The imagined revenge on all those who obstructed their way of life was especially charged with enjoyment, precisely because of the underlying pain and impotence. *Ressentiment* radicalized both the build-up of tension – Scheler used the expression 'psychological dynamite' – and its eventual release. Nietzsche referred to a coming thunderstorm of revenge that would sweep over the world. *Ressentiment* could oscillate between despairing individual complaints and consumption of punishment exacted by a state-administered criminal justice system. In the latter moment, when partaking in the powerful rituals of criminal justice, is there not anything more to modern pleasure than relief of distress? Under the conditions of *ressentiment*, the answer is – no, there is not. The satisfaction of punishment is relief of distress: the passing revaluation of the spectators through the revenge exacted by others, in their place. But as Nietzsche would argue in the *Will to Power*, there is much more to satisfaction than relief of status concerns; the one-sided assertion inherent in the 'thunderstorms of our revenge' could generate a sense of power, or a very different kind of pleasure. In several respects, the experience was the very opposite of *ressentiment*. This pleasure presupposed omnipotence rather than impotence: strength rather than weakness, and illegitimacy rather than legitimacy. It actualized the attainment of full satisfaction and transcendence, as opposed to a return to equilibrium, and corresponded to the Aristotelian paradigm: the excited absorption in activity. The next chapter deals with the other major form of pleasure, the obscene enjoyment of excessive punishment, under modern conditions.

References

Alexander, Michelle (2010) *The new Jim Crow: mass incarceration in the age of colorblindness*. New York: New Press.

Barker, Vanessa (2018) *Nordic nationalism and penal order: walling the welfare state*. Abingdon: Routledge.

Beckett, Katherine (1997) *Making crime pay: law and order in contemporary American politics*. New York: Oxford University Press.

Bourdieu, Pierre (1984) *Distinction: a social critique of the judgement of taste*. Harvard: Harvard University Press.

Bourdieu, Pierre (ed.) (1999) *The weight of the world: social suffering in contemporary society*. Oxford: Polity.

Brown, Wendy (1995) *States of injury: power and freedom in late modernity*. Princeton: Princeton University Press.

Camp, Jordan (2016) *Incarcerating the crisis: freedom struggles and the rise of the neoliberal state*. Oakland: University of California Press.

Carlen, Pat (2008) Imaginary penalities and risk-crazed governance. In P. Carlen (ed.), *Imaginary penalities*. Cullompton: Willan. pp 1–25.

Castel, Robert (2003) *From manual workers to wage laborers. Transformation of the social question*. New Brunswick: Transaction.

Cheliotis, Leo (2013) Neoliberal capitalism and middle-class punitiveness: bringing Erich Fromm's 'materialistic psychoanalysis' to penology. *Punishment & Society* 15(3): 247–273.

Connolly, William (1999) The will, capital punishment, and cultural war. In A. Sarat (ed.), *The killing state: capital punishment in law, politics, and culture*. New York: Oxford University Press. pp 187–205.

Cramer, Katherine (2016) *The politics of resentment: rural consciousness in Wisconsin and the rise of Scott Walker*. Chicago: University of Chicago Press.

Dardot, Pierre, and Laval, Christian (2013) *The new way of the world: on neoliberal society*. London: Verso.

Davies, William (2014) *The limits of neoliberalism: authority, sovereignty and the logic of competition*. London: Sage.

Dayan, Colin (2011) *The law is a white dog: how legal rituals make and unmake persons*. Princeton: Princeton University Press.

Deleuze, Gilles (1983) *Nietzsche and philosophy*. London: Athlone.

Dolgert, Stefan (2016) The praise of ressentiment: or, how I learned to stop worrying and love Donald Trump. *New Political Science* 38(3): 354–370.

Durkheim, Émile (1997) *The division of labor in society*. New York: Free Press.

Elgat, Guy (2017) *Nietzsche's psychology of ressentiment: revenge and justice in "On the Genealogy of Morals"*. New York: Routledge.

Ericson, Richard (2007) *Crime in an insecure world*. Cambridge: Polity.

Flamm, Michael (2005) *Law and order. Street crime, civil unrest, and the crisis of liberalism in the 1960s*. New York: Columbia University Press.

Freud, Sigmund (1915) Triebe und Triebschicksale. *Internationale Zeitschrift für Psychoanalyse* 3(2): 84–100.

Fukuyama, Francis (2012). *The end of history and the last man*. 20th anniversary edn. London: Penguin.

Garland, David (2001) *The culture of control: crime and social order in contemporary society*. Chicago: University of Chicago Press.

Garland, David (2010) *Peculiar institution: America's death penalty in an age of aboli-tion*. Cambridge, MA: Belknap.

Garland, David (2013) Penality and the penal state. *Criminology* 51(3): 475–517.

Gerber, Monica, and Jackson, Jonathan (2016) Authority and punishment: on the ideological basis of punitive attitudes towards criminals. *Psychiatry, Psychology and Law* 23(1): 113–134.

Gidron, Noam, and Hall, Peter (2017) The politics of social status: economic and cul-tural roots of the populist right *British Journal of Sociology* 68: S57-S84.

Goldthorpe, John (1980) *Social mobility and class structure in modern Britain*. Oxford: Clarendon.

Gottschalk, Marie (2006) *The prison and the gallows. The politics of mass incarceration in America*. Cambridge: Cambridge University Press.

Hall, Stuart, Critcher, Chas, Jefferson, Tony, Clarke, John, and Roberts, Brian (1978) *Policing the crisis: mugging, the state, and law and order*. London: Macmillan.

Harper, Aaron, and Schaaf, Eric (2018) Power, resentment, and self-preservation: Nietzsche's moral psychology as a critique of Trump. In A. Torres and M. Marc (eds.), *Trump and political philosophy: patriotism, cosmopolitanism, and civic virtue*. Cham: Springer International. pp 257–280.

Hochschild, Arlie Russell (2016) *Strangers in their own land: anger and mourning on the American right*. New York: The New Press.

Hörnqvist, Magnus (2010) *Risk, power, and the state: after Foucault*. Abingdon: Routledge.

Jerre, Kristina (2013) *The public's sense of justice in Sweden – a smorgasbord of opinions*. Diss. Stockholm: Stockholms Universitet.

Kaufmann, Walter (1968) *Nietzsche: philosopher, psychologist, antichrist*. Princeton: Princeton University Press.

Kierkegaard, Søren (1962) *The present age*. New York: Harper & Row.

King, Anna, and Maruna, Shadd (2009) Is a conservative just a liberal who has been mugged? Exploring the origins of punitive views. *Punishment and Society* 11(2): 147–169.

Kojève, Alexandre (1969) *Introduction to the reading of Hegel*. New York: Basic Books.

KVV (2000) *Reasoning and rehabilitation. Utdrag ur Handbok för undervisning i Cognitive Skills*. Norrköping: Kriminalvårdsverket/T3 Associates Training and Consulting Inc.

Lamont, Michèle (2000) *The dignity of working men: morality and the boundaries of race, class, and immigration*. New York: Russell Sage Foundation.

Lamont, Michèle (2018) Addressing recognition gaps: destigmatization and the reduc-tion of inequality. *American Sociological Review* 83(3): 419–444.

Lenin, Vladimir (1965) *The state and revolution: Marxist teaching on the state and the tasks of the proletariat in the revolution*. Peking: Foreign Language Press.

Lødemel, Ivar, and Moreira, Amilcar (2014) Introduction: waves of activation reform. In I. Lødemel and A. Moreira (eds.), *Activation or workfare? Governance and the neo-liberal convergence*. New York: Oxford University Press. pp 1–18.

Loeb, Paul (2018) The priestly slave revolt in morality. *Nietzsche-Studien* 47(1): 100–139.

McLennan, Rebecca (2001) The new penal state: globalization, history and American criminal justice. *Inter-Asia Cultural Studies* 2: 207–19.

Martinson, Robert (1974) What works? Questions and answers about prison reform. *The Public Interest* 35: 22–54.

Moore, Phoebe, and Robinson, Andrew (2016) The quantified self: what counts in the neoliberal workplace. *New Media & Society* 18(11): 2774–2792.

Murakawa, Naomi (2014) *The first civil right: how liberals built prison America*. Oxford: Oxford University Press.

Nietzsche, Friedrich (1989) *On the genealogy of morals*. New York: Vintage Books.

Nietzsche, Friedrich (1990) *Beyond good and evil: prelude to a philosophy of the future*. Harmondsworth: Penguin Books.

Nietzsche, Friedrich (2006) *Thus spoke Zarathustra: a book for all and none*. Cambridge: Cambridge University Press.

Nietzsche, Friedrich (2017) *The will to power*. London: Penguin Books.

Oudenampsen, Merijn (2018) The return of ressentiment. In Sjoerd van Tuinen (ed.), *The polemics of ressentiment: variations on Nietzsche*. London: Bloomsbury Academic. pp 167–185.

Paskewich, Christopher (2014) The roots of political community: thumos and tradition in ancient Greek thought. *Anamnesis*, http://anamnesisjournal.com/2014/09/roots-political-community-thumos-tradition-ancient-greek-thought, accessed 26 October 2019.

Power, Michael (1997) *The audit society: rituals of verification*. Oxford: Oxford University Press.

Râmbu, Nicolae (2016) *The axiology of Friedrich Nietzsche*. Frankfurt am Main: Peter Lang Edition.

Reginster, Bernard (1997) Nietzsche on ressentiment and valuation. *Philosophy and Phenomenological Research* 57(2): 281–305.

Ridley, Aaron (2006) Nietzsche and the re-evaluation of values. In C. Acampora (ed.), *Nietzsche's* On the Genealogy of Morals. *Critical essays*. Lanham: Rowman & Littlefield. pp 77–92.

Rose, Nikolas (1999) *Powers of freedom: reframing political thought*. Cambridge: Cambridge University Press.

Rubin, Ashley, and Phelps, Michelle (2017) Fracturing the penal state: state actors and the role of conflict in penal change. *Theoretical Criminology* 21(4): 422–440.

Sarat, Austin (1999) The cultural life of capital punishment. In Austin Sarat (ed.), *The killing state: capital punishment in law, politics, and culture*. New York: Oxford University Press. pp 226–256.

Scheler, Max (2017) *Das Ressentiment im Aufbau der Moralen*. Frankfurt an Main: Klostermann.

Sennett, Richard (2003) *Respect in a world of inequality*. New York: W. W. Norton.

Smith, Caleb (2009) *Prison and the American imagination*. Yale: Yale University Press

Smith, Philip (2008) *Punishment and culture*. Chicago: University of Chicago Press.

Sloterdijk, Peter (2010). *Rage and time: a psychopolitical investigation*. New York: Columbia University Press.

Solomon, Robert (1994) One hundred years of ressentiment: Nietzsche's Genealogy of Morals. In R. Schacht (ed.), *Nietzsche, genealogy, morality: essays on Nietzsche's On the Genealogy of Morals*. Berkeley: University of California Press. pp 95–126.

Taylor, Charles (1989) *Sources of the self: the making of the modern identity*. Cambridge: Cambridge University Press.

Taylor, Charles (1992) The politics of recognition. In A. Gutmann (ed.), *Multiculturalism and the politics of recognition*. Princeton: Princeton University Press. pp 25–74.

Tomelleri, Stefano (2017) Ressentiment and the turn to the victim: Nietzsche, Weber, Scheler. In J. Alison and W. Palaver (eds.), *The Palgrave handbook of mimetic theory and religion*. New York: Palgrave Macmillan.

Tonry, Michael (1995) *Malign neglect: race, crime, and punishment in America*. New York: Oxford University Press.

Tyler, Tom, and Boeckmann, Robert (1997) Three strikes and you are out, but why? The psychology of public support for punishing rule breakers. *Law and Society Review* 31(2): 237–265.

Weber, Max (1972) *Wirtschaft und Gesellschaft*. Tübingen: J. C. B. Mohr.

7 Obscene enjoyment

Between power and prohibition

In the *Genealogy of Morals*, Friedrich Nietzsche asserted that punishment could be festive: 'in punishment there is so much *festive!*' (Nietzsche 1989: II §6). The word 'festive' suggested the mood at a party where everyone was having a good time; the guests were really enjoying themselves, absorbed in conversation, dancing and drinking. The party was not ruined, if interspersed with punishment; quite to the contrary, the mood was heightened. It was no doubt Nietzsche's intention to conjure up associations to that effect. Published in 1887, the book was a testimony of the increasingly problematic nature of pleasure. The aphorisms, which are generally seen to be celebrating the pleasure of cruelty and deploring a bygone age of unrestrained assertion, can also be read as evidence that a certain kind of pleasure had come into conflict with modern sentiments and institutions. Instead of being an innocent sensation, which was the view of earlier philosophers, for instance Jeremy Bentham and Immanuel Kant, with the passage to modernity, in the context of punishment, pleasure was conceived of as a disruptive passion that should be suppressed in public. Hence, by saying that punishment was festive, Nietzsche called attention to a contradiction in modern life, which affected the mechanisms through which the pleasure of punishment was generated. At the same time, his claim must be taken literally: there *was* much festive in punishment. Punishment could provide intense excitation, also after the passage to modernity. It may be festive, but not in the sense of joining-in with everybody else, undisturbed by morality or shame, the passing of which Nietzsche seemed to lament in the *Genealogy*. Instead, what provided pleasure was the participation in something everyone knew was forbidden. The specifically festive character came from the breach of taboo. The spectator was complicit, together with other participants, and enjoyed it secretly. Psychoanalysis, which was being developed at the time by Sigmund Freud, captured the altered experience of pleasure. On his analysis, to enthusiastically take part in cruel punishments, along with other spectators, was festive precisely because of the violation of social conventions. Prohibition was constitutive of enjoyment. As Freud would say in *Totem and Taboo*: 'the festive feeling is produced by the liberty to do what is as a rule prohibited' (Freud 1955: 140).

Obscene enjoyment was the modern alternative, as unchecked expressions of excitement could no longer, or only under special circumstances, be acknowledged in public. The enjoyment was obscene – secretly embraced and disavowed in public. It was *ob skene* in the original Greek sense of being off-stage. In the classic tragedies, offensive scenes, especially scenes involving fatal violence, occurred off stage and were typically related by messengers (McKay 2010). Obscene enjoyment is assumed to differ from earlier forms of Aristotelian pleasure of punishment. The modern experience could not be understood as enjoyment in the Dionysic sense of immediate orgiastic loss of self (Eagleton 2005), in the carnivalesque sense of turning the world upside down (Hill 1972; Burke 2009), or in the unreserved embrace of sublime terror (Dennis 1996; Burke 1997). These frames no longer seemed applicable. The central line of division was the relationship to social prohibition. The element of prohibition was integral to the pleasure. Due to prohibition, the enjoyment was privately enjoyed and publicly disavowed. Still and in fact more than ever, pleasure had to be taken seriously, since it seemed to have lost none of its disruptive force. At a time when vengeance appeared to have been separated from punishment, and when pleasure had replaced anger as the main driver behind transgression, Nietzsche, and after him Freudian psychoanalysis, picked up what had been sidelined in the historic cleansing of punishment, from Plato to Hart: the personal, the disproportionate, all the passions, and the illegitimate – and turned *that* into an area of investigation. All the forbidden parts – obscene pleasure, anger, excess and the desire for vengeance – became the object matter for psychoanalytic approaches to law and punishment. In this sense, it was a return of the repressed. This chapter is entirely devoted to obscene enjoyment as a specifically modern pleasure of punishment. Each section is organized around authors who have stressed different aspects of the enjoyment; Lacan discussed the obscene enjoyment of being implicated in transgressive punishment; Žižek discussed the guilt-ridden enjoyment of guarding inglorious secrets, and Nietzsche the sense of power in partaking in unrestrained assertion, as spectator. I will elucidate the different aspects based on contemporary examples of transgressive punishments.

Obscene enjoyment of the other

In the *Genealogy*, Nietzsche had moved effortlessly from cruelty to punishment, without pausing to consider the law. The imposition of pain on others was central, while the relationship between the pain imposed and official law was secondary. In modern psychoanalysis, on the other hand, law and legitimacy were crucial. Lacan discussed the specific pleasure at play in overstepping the line to the domain of the forbidden and the irrational. The existing literature, which has explicitly addressed the pleasure of punishment, by using these exact terms in a modern context, is likewise centred on transgression. Its objective is to understand the pleasure of transgression – the enjoyment of being implicated, as witness or as perpetrator, in actions that violate rules and social norms. The focus on legal transgressions translated into the choice of empirical cases: torture, lynching and excessive forms of physical punishment. Spectators have been seen to draw pleasure from visual representations of degrading punishments, for instance from the Abu Ghraib torture pictures, or from lynching postcards (Adler 2015; Eisenman 2007; Debrix 2006; Sontag 2003). Judging by the standards of contemporary morality, the punishment was illegitimate, and the pleasure was likewise illegitimate – which the spectators moreover were intensely aware of. The pleasure was privatized and could not be openly acknowledged. It was thus referred to as 'hidden pleasure' (Adler 2015: 2). The influence of morality intensified the experience of pleasure, but was also seen to provoke conflicting reactions, including shame and disgust.

In Lacanian psychoanalysis, *jouissance* is the central concept to describe the pleasures involved. *Jouissance* can be translated as 'enjoyment', but the French original is often left untranslated to stress that it used as a technical term, to designate a special kind of enjoyment. Although the term is defined variously in Lacan's work (Miller 2000), it is typically used in the context of understanding the specific pleasures of transgression. Interestingly, it seems to have entered psychoanalysis by way of the master-and-slave dialectic, as a correlate to the Hegelian *Genuss* and its double meaning of enjoyment and consumption (Evans 1998). In one phase of the struggle for recognition, the fruits of the Slave's labour were consumed by the Master, which meant unrestrained enjoyment in this respect. The Master could extract anything from the Slave, except recognition. *Jouissance* indicated that one was in a position to extract enjoyment from the other's body, by force and without permission (Lacan 1999), just as the Slave had been at the Master's disposal. The element of transgression was constitutive of the experience. In *Seminar VII*, Jacques Lacan talked about 'the jouissance of transgression', excited by the fact that the subject knew that the action was prohibited (Lacan 1992: 195). I take it to describe the specifically modern experience of obscene enjoyment. The experience was distinguished by intense excitement, absorption in unrestrained assertion, awareness of prohibition, and mixed up with pain. At heart, it was a pleasure of the Aristotelian kind, characterized by enthusiasm or abandon, which accompany activities that are unimpeded. This may come across as counterintuitive, or far removed from the Aristotelian frame of reference. To Aristotle, pleasure was exemplified by the smooth construction of a house or, even better, by continuous contemplation (Taylor 2008). The experience depended on the uninterrupted flow of activity, which may but need not include excitement. If the activity was ordinary, such as building a house without mishaps, the element of excitement was measured. *Jouissance* typically accompany activities located at the other end of the spectra: activities which are prohibited and more likely to generate excitement. *Jouissance* stemmed from activities at the borderline of social morality, involving for instance sex and violence (Fink 1995) or, one might add, witnessing punishment. Witnessing transgressive punishment was to be absorbed in activity unrestrained by normative or legal conventions, while the spectator at the same time was acutely aware of the conventions. The secondary literature on *jouissance* unequivocally stressed the ensuing intensity of excitement. *Jouissance* has been defined as 'a mode of intensity, a type of arousal', which came from being involved in activities that were not altogether legitimate (Hook 2017: 611), or as intense pleasure mixed up with pain, which 'by its very nature is excessive' (Dean 2006: xvi). It is never pure enjoyment, but essentially a mix of pleasure and pain (Homer 2004; Fink 1995). Obscene enjoyment is entwined with physical pain, or with premonitions of disaster, in which the element of pain operates to intensify the experience. A future backlash, fatigue, the risk of exposure, shame or censure are constitutive of the experience.

While the experience was consistent with the Aristotelian conception of pleasure, the notion of *jouissance* effectively severed the link to individual well-being. On a classical analysis, enjoyment was thought to be something good, given certain basic qualifications. Present pleasures should not endanger future pleasures, according to Seneca's (2016) dictum. Lacan brought attention to the complex nature of pleasure, and questioned the tradition which assumed that pleasure was an index of the good. Ever since Plato, it was argued, 'all the philosophers have been led to discern not true pleasures from false, for such a distinction is impossible to make, but the true and false goods that pleasure points to' (Lacan 1992: 221). Whether 'good' referred to what was morally commendable or to what a good life was taken to involve, pleasure was by no means a reliable guide to the question about what was good, for individuals or for societies. The presumption in Lacanian psychoanalysis was the very opposite: enjoyment was suspicious and unreliable, or even 'a form of evil' (Lacan 1992: 189). Enjoyment represented an inversion of the Freudian pleasure principle, which guided individuals toward a moderate life built on the avoidance of pain (Schuster 2019). *Jouissance* stood for experiences of going too far, ignoring individual well-being, moral considerations, or disastrous outcomes. Beneath the bias toward excess was the constitutive role of prohibition and the dependence on the other. Enjoyment was deeply moral and amoral at the same time. The basic coordinates were inescapably set by the other, as an incarnation of social morality and hence indifferent to individual well-being. Precisely because it was fundamentally dependent on the other, enjoyment was potentially harmful to the subject. It could make people accommodate to estrangement, life-denying conventional tracks, or provide an incentive to enthusiastically embrace demise, death and destruction.

Like Hegel before him, Lacan located the ground for transgression in the dynamics of desire. The dynamic is inherently transgressive – in the prosaic sense that it is dictated by dissatisfaction and lack, and prompts action which goes beyond the present state. Most of the time the transgressive dynamic is channelled in conventional tracks. The desire for social esteem is above all a constant and powerful incentive to pursue conventional courses of action in any society. It is the urge to belong and escape the fear of being dismissed. But it does not stop there: the desire was from the outset linked to excess and transcendence. The winged *thumos*-horse in Plato's parable on the chariot was presented in a discussion of transcendence, in which 'god-sent madness' was valued over 'man-made sanity' (*Phaedrus* 244d). Unless checked by reason and external conditions, the desire to belong evolved into the wish to distinguish oneself, within the same group, or to assert the group in relation to other groups, to gain a fuller satisfaction. Lacanian psychoanalysis would stress the latter aspect of desire: the striving toward transcendence. Full satisfaction was strictly speaking unattainable. Satisfaction necessarily involved a stroke of disappointment (Braunstein 2003). Yet desire was inherently boundless, always 'striving for something else or something more' (Copjec 1994: 55). The injunction *encore!* – more, more! – would govern the consumption of anything (Lacan 1999), the consumption of punishment being no exception. Punishment provided partial satisfaction while promising complete satisfaction, or a more satisfying satisfaction, which eluded the audience and intensified a craving for more of the same. The same dynamic could be seen to apply to all kinds of punishment, legal or extra-legal. Yet there may be an additional quality to enjoyment derived from transgressive punishment, which reinforced the movement toward something more, or something else. Beyond the necessarily partial character of the enjoyment, it was also sustained by the element of transgression, the excitement generated by the breach of taboo, when the consumed punishment violated basic legal principles. The pain and suffering being imposed on others may be a necessary requisite. Yet due to the centrality of prohibition, obscene enjoyment was in a sense self-sufficient.

Starting with Lacan's series of lectures in 1959–1960, enjoyment was increasingly associated with transgression of moral rules and with intense excitement that endangered the subject (de Kesel 2009). The underlying concern was to understand how people commit acts in the knowledge of the disastrous consequences to themselves, or to others. One could be aware about all dangers, or be convinced that nothing good would come out of it, and still continue the course of action. In *Kant avec Sade*, Lacan discussed one of Kant's examples on human motivation. The setting was altogether imaginary. Imagine someone standing outside a house, sexually excited. The object of desire was in the house, and the person was free to enter and have sex. Kant offered no further details. The prospect of sexual intercourse was not spelled out, but the implications were clear enough. Nothing stood in the way; it was a just small gap between desire and satisfaction. The door was open and the sex presumably consensual. Now, Kant introduced the death penalty as deterrence. Assume that gallows were erected on the other side of the house. The person was still free to go inside and have sex, but she or he would be hanged on the spot, upon leaving the house. Imagine that you were in this situation: would you still satisfy your desire despite facing a certain death? To Kant, the answer was self-evident, as it did not involve the moral law. The person was not obliged to do anything. It was simply a calculation of pleasure and pain. Hence, considering the dire consequences, the person would restrain whatever passions were in motion and refrain from rushing into the house (Kant 1914). But Lacan was not so sure; the prospects of a certain death could sustain rather than contain the movement of desire.

> It is possible that a partisan of passion, who would be blind enough to combine it with questions of honor, could make trouble for Kant by forcing him to recognize that no occasion precipitates certain people more surely toward their goal than one that involves defiance or even contempt for the gallows.
>
> (Lacan 2006: 782)

Under certain conditions, the punishment would not present itself as pain and censure to be avoided at all cost, but in a different light. If mixed up with notions of social esteem, and if the expectations of others were taken into consideration, the gallows could turn into a challenge. The prospect of the gallows could incite the person to enter the house and have sex – and then be executed. If that were to happen, what made the option involving a certain death irresistible was not sexual excitation, or the fact that the night might have involved everything that person could possibly dream of in terms of sexual pleasure. Nor could the embrace of a certain death be attributed to an innate force, such as the Freudian death drive. Had it been simply a matter of choosing to be executed or not – there was no house, no sex and nothing to win – the person would probably just have walked away. Instead, if the option turned out to be irresistible, it was rather because of a mix of social esteem and prohibition. In the quote above, Lacan interposed that the desire for social esteem was activated. In an earlier comment on the same thought experiment, he added another detail: that the desire was illicit. Kant had said nothing about that, merely that the person would be executed. On this basis, Lacan could insist that there was something wrong with how Kant had formulated the problem; 'the night spent with the lady is paradoxically presented to us as a pleasure that is weighed against a punishment to be undergone' (Lacan 1992: 189). This is a false paradox, since prohibition, pain and unrestrained assertion were constitutive of *jouissance*, and not opposed to it. In this case, the illicit character of the desire, the displayed defiance of death and the certainty of the punishment were part of the enjoyment of the one single night of sex.

Kant's example was part of an argument on the moral law. In this context, the 'have sex, then be hanged' example illustrated the lack of obligation; the person could easily abstain and thereby avoid execution. It was juxtaposed to another example, which proved Kant's point that under different circumstances one would have to choose a certain death, if required by the moral law. In the second example, an individual was once again threatened with execution, this time by a wilful sovereign. There was only one way to avoid the impending execution: to bear false witness against someone else, who was an honourable person and had done nothing wrong (Kant 1914). In this case, the moral law was implicated, and the person would have to overcome any personal preferences and prepare to be executed. Truth must be told and the sovereign had to be defied, as it was a matter of moral obligation. The two examples were originally designed to contrast a sheer pleasure calculus with the force of moral duty. However, picking up on Lacan's discussion, Slavoj Žižek argued that Kant's two examples may not be that different. Just as 'tell the truth, then be hanged' activated the moral law and became a duty, so could 'have sex, then be hanged' become an obligation which had to be performed regardless of the consequences. Rather than being tempered by the prospect of the gallows, desire was further reinforced and took on the character of duty; 'true "passion" is uncannily close to the fulfilling of one's duty in spite of the external threat' (Žižek 1991: 239, emphasis removed). By entering the house and defying an imminent death, the person would be carried by the sense of fulfilling a moral duty. It was not a duty in any straightforward way, as envisaged by Kant, issued by a universal moral law. Instead it was a 'weird and twisted ethical duty' (Žižek 2006a: 79), shaped by social morality, and reassured only through the eyes of the other.

Lacanian approaches in the disciplines of cultural studies and psycho-analysis have tended to dominate the analysis of the pleasure of punishment as *jouissance* (de Sutter 2015; Aristedemou 2014). The dominance was a nat-ural consequence of the overwhelming silence on pleasure in social science. As pleasure was effectively historicized in the influential approaches of Durkheim, Elias and Foucault, psychoanalysis enacted a conceptual 'return of the repressed' and picked up what had been sidelined in the historic cleansing of punishment. Yet the return was partial and came with a qualification: it strictly concerned the illicit pleasure of transgressive punishment. The quali-fication was significant. Legitimate punishment was a non-issue – unless it violated its own principles and became transgressive. The day-to-day practices of imprisonment were not considered, or implicitly dismissed as unexciting, as they were governed by the regular law (Žižek 1991). The concept of punish-ment, as something distinct from the arbitrary combination of violence and pain, had little place in this body of work. The imposed violence could, but need not, be understood as punishment by onlookers. What mattered was the element of transgression. It was the illegitimacy of the interventions that were seen to generate pleasure: the intense excitement of being absorbed in trans-gression, mixed up with pain and the awareness of prohibition.

Nightly punishment – forging a community of spectators

Slavoj Žižek elaborated on the Lacanian analysis of obscene enjoyment. In particular two further characteristics, which shaped the audience's experience, were brought to attention. First of all, the basic morality of transgression was emphasized. The punishment relied on notions of a higher justice, which was embedded in social morality and embraced by the community, although never stated explicitly. It was not stated explicitly, because the punishment could not stand public insight, or legal investigation. Yet people sensed its underlying morality, in the full knowledge that it was a blatant legal violation. Punishments were meted out according to a nightly law, which operated parallel to the regular law and mandated transgression. It could turn into a manifest contradiction but normally the interplay between the two laws would produce obscene enjoyment. Secondly, Žižek discussed the subterraneous impact on community cohesion. The obscene enjoyment generated by transgressive punishment would turn into a lasting bond, which tied the individuals together as a community. Everybody knew but no one spoke about what happened, or how they felt about it. While being secretly shared within the community, it could not be openly acknowledged. Collective disavowal became a guilt-ridden requirement for full membership.

In *The Metastases of Enjoyment*, and scattered across Žižek's work, one can find references to an 'obscene "nightly" law', which operated parallel to the existing legislation (Žižek 1994: 54; see also Žižek 1991; 1997). In some senses, it was like any other kind of law. The nightly law was first of all experienced as a law by people who were familiar with it. It issued commands, incentives to act, which were perceived as unconditional, law-like injunctions. The nightly law further resembled the regular law by being grounded in specific notions of justice. Although unwritten, it contained a string of conceptions which authorized and dictated punishment. But there, the similarity ended. While the regular law conferred qualities that were considered indispensable for ordered state administration and for keeping passion at bay, in the name of reason, impartiality and legitimacy (Hegel 1952; Hart 1959; Nozick 1981), in psychoanalysis, on the other hand, the law incorporated much more than the criminal code and assumed many of the characteristics which, since antiquity, had been associated with vengeance, such as passion, excess, and sacred duty. The nightly law would support the very opposite of rational punishment: illegitimate, passionate and excessive punishment. It accompanied the regular law as a shadow, encompassing the 'obscene unwritten rules', which 'sustain Power as long as they remain in the shadows' (Žižek 1997: 93).

The redoubling was seen to be inherent in the institution of law. The nightly law always accompanied the regular law as a shadow and mandated transgressions that could not withstand public light. Its law-like injunctions had a sacred character, and represented a higher and necessarily unacknowledged justice, as opposed to punishment issued according to the regular law, which was restrained by notions of universality, of binding rules and respect for the rights of individuals. The nightly law could authorize transgressions, if the regular law was perceived to stand in the way, or if it was perceived to be insufficient, according to the principles of the nightly law. In such cases, the punishment would be condoned or even mandated, while at the same time being strictly prohibited according to the regular law. The experience must, although Žižek never discussed the matter, be seen as decidedly modern. In early-modern Europe, it made little sense to speak of a nightly law, since the rational surface and the obscene underside of the law coincided at the scaffold. When cruel punishment was an intentional display of explicitly stated principles of power, there was nothing to expose, and no prohibited enjoyment. Everything was carried out in broad daylight, and there was less space for a nightly law. But the establishment of the *Rechtsstaat* restrained certain kinds of punishment, which were not according to the law, at the same time as public expressions of enjoyment were rendered inappropriate at the end of the nineteenth century, all of which created the conditions for the nightly law, and hence obscene enjoyment, to emerge.

The law was literally nightly, and could not be exposed to the light of day. Bypassing rather than defying the enacted law, it thrived on secrecy and shed public scrutiny. As long as the nightly law remained tacit and underexposed, the authorized punishments involved no contradiction. The relationship between the two laws has been described as one of subtext and stated letter. Intuitively, members of the group understand that 'there is more to law than its official face', and that they know 'that the official rules do not apply to them' (Dean 2006: 35). In response to the exposure of the Abu Ghraib photographs in 2004, the official response from the US Army was that no such orders had been issued. It was claimed that soldiers on the ground were not instructed to torture and to degrade prisoners. That may well be true, but it did not mean that the torture was a strictly private initiative of a group of wayward soldiers. As Žižek remarked, usually there are 'no formal orders, nothing is written, there is just unofficial pressure, hints and directives are delivered in private'. The torture was not officially authorized. Instead, the Abu Ghraib prisoners were simply exposed to the 'obscene underside' of the publicly endorsed values of personal dignity, rule of law, and democracy (Žižek 2006a: 370). The nightly law was the obscene, impassioned underside, and the regular law was the rational surface, the prohibitions of which reinforced the enjoyment of seeing soldiers fighting for freedom and democracy in the Abu Ghraib prison. The illegality of torture did not enter into contradiction with military regulations, nor did it contradict self-conceptions of decency, but rather confirmed the sacred character of the fight. In a similar vein, it has been suggested that a large part of the audience deny and denigrate news reports on police brutality, or disclosure of prison violence, while secretly enjoying scenes of police brutality or prison violence as a deserved, additional revenge (Connolly 1995). The obscene enjoyment may be collectively shared and collectively disavowed, at one and the same time. Similar observations apply to hazing, lynching, domestic violence, ethnic cleansing and other illegal practices that were understood by the audience as punishment. To be implicated – as punisher, or as witness – generated enjoyment, as long as it remained unacknowledged (Žižek 1997; 2006b; 2015). If spelled out, everything – the practices, the silent endorsement, the obscene enjoyment – would be contradicted by the law, or by the self-understanding of the audience as law-abiding.

The two kinds of law can be separated in theory but co-exist in any legal context, one shadowing the other. Žižek's most illuminating example is the 1992 movie *A Few Good Men*. It was a Hollywood movie about two US Marine soldiers, who are on court martial for murdering a fellow soldier by the name of Santiago. The script was inspired by an incident that took place a few years earlier on the Guantanamo Bay naval base, and long before it was turned into an infamous detention camp for alleged terrorists. On that occasion, one soldier had been blindfolded and beaten up – but not murdered – by a group of fellow soldiers, following rumours of a report being filed on military misconduct. In the movie, Santiago, the murdered soldier, had broken the ethical code of the Marines Corps in a similar fashion. He had informed on one of the soldiers in his unit, who had fired into Cuban territory. Fenceline shooting was strictly prohibited in official military regulations, and it was obvious that the murder constituted a punishment for snitching. That was also the approach of the defence lawyer, in the attempt to shift the blame away from the two soldiers on trial. The murder was, the defence argued, an extrajudicial execution based on the ethical code of the Marines and authorized by a higher-ranking officer, who was also the base commander. Everybody in the unit knew what had happened, and why it happened. It was in accordance with a higher law, in this case referred to as Code Red, which mandated the illegal punishment of a fellow soldier. But in the courtroom setting, none of witnesses wants to admit that the murder was a Code Red order. Nobody pretends to know, and nobody will say that the punishment was deserved. Witnesses even denied that there was such a thing as Code Red (Žižek 1994; see also Žižek 1997).

Normally, the two kinds of law coexist but are never brought into relationship with one another. The contradiction remains dormant, and provides a source of obscene enjoyment. In this respect, *A Few Good Men* is exceptional, since at the end of the movie, the nightly law was pulled out of the shadows and stated openly in the courtroom. The contradiction became unavoidable. The base commander was caught in a lie during cross-examination, and was, moreover, insulted on behalf of his profession by the questions being asked. His final line of defence was to say that the killing of Santiago was deeply deplorable but had to be understood in the wider scheme of things. He invoked the world in the dimensions of order and morality, in which the US military kept everybody, including the lawyer, safe.

> I have a greater responsibility than you can possibly fathom. You weep for Santiago and you curse the marines. You have that luxury. You have the luxury of not knowing what I know: That Santiago's death, while tragic, probably saved lives. And my existence, while grotesque and incomprehensible to you, saves lives.
>
> (Sorkin 1991)

Civilians and other people in the courtroom could not appreciate this version of tragic choice. Abide by the rules and the nation may perish, sacrifice one soldier and the nation will survive. As Agamemnon felt compelled to sacrifice Iphigenia, his daughter, the base commander was forced to sacrifice Santiago.

The dilemma was unavoidable and he had to choose – in the light of that dilemma – between saving the nation and Santiago's life. Yet the defence lawyer insists; 'did you order the code red?' – to which the reply is, first, 'I did the job you sent me to do'. When asked a second time, he makes the confession: 'you're goddamn right I did' (Sorkin 1991). Bewildered, the base commander is arrested on the spot. Suddenly, he was not above the law. The nightly law had entered into contradiction with the ordinary legal system. Spelled out in the courtroom, it had little leverage, and the regular law took precedence.

A Few Good Men showed the basic morality of excessive punishment, and moreover illustrated Žižek's second point about the subterranean impact on community cohesion. The obscene enjoyment produced by the tension between illegality and Code Red strengthened the community. Members of the group were bound together by guilt-ridden solidarity. In the context of *A Few Good Men*, it was not the report on the fenceline shooting that was punished by death, but rather what the report indicated: that the soldier did not fully identify with the group and maintained a distance to the Marine Corps' spirit and moral ontology. That was the inner meaning of Santiago's crime. He had to be punished as he violated the principles upon which the group was built. To break the silence after the murder would have involved a renewed violation of the nightly law, not dissimilar to the one which mandated the original punishment. To fail to comply in the cover-up would be to distance oneself from the group and everything it represented. The entire military base was involved in the cover-up, and no one would speak out in the criminal proceedings, testifying to the strength of its moral bond. At the same time, there was an awareness of prohibition and of the disproportionate character of the punishment – a death penalty for snitching, covertly executed, was inconsistent with official self-representations, and charged compliance with guilt and shame. The primordial lie – nothing happened! – would thus found the community anew by forging bonds of 'solidarity-in-guilt' (Žižek 1994: 58). The transgressive punishment, which confirmed the sacred order of their world, also became the inglorious secrets which brought the community members together. Participation in collective practices of transgression and disavowal became a requirement for membership in the group (Aristodemou 2014). No member of the group could escape the legacy of the injustices committed for the group. Through the joint transgression of existing legal constraints, the whole community manifested its moral cohesion; internal social contradictions were replaced by bonds of obscene enjoyment (Finkelde 2018).

The idea of transgression as the source of social order was deeply rooted in psychoanalysis. While Freud located the foundation in a distant past, in the proverbial killing of the father, Lacan thought of social order as rooted in continuously ongoing practices of transgression and disavowal (Hook 2017; Glynos 2001). Excessive punishment may be disruptive in the lives of individuals, but a powerful stabilizing force in human history, as it binds people together. The bond was made up of obscene enjoyment. There was no need to take actual part in the punishment to have the enjoyment. The cover-up involved a continuous flow of activity, which generated absorbed arousal consistent with Aristotelian pleasure, unless interrupted by a criminal investigation, or otherwise actively challenged. The pleasure was by no means pure, it was not the forgetfulness of being completely absorbed in activity. It was mixed with pain, shame and guilt as a result of being complicit in excesses that could not be openly justified. In return, the individual would be fully recognized by the group, which shared the same secret and the sense that they were all in this together. By partaking in the collective disavowal, members of the audience proved their worth, in the eyes of one another. It was the basic recognition of social worth: to be accepted as fully part of the group. Once again, thus, obscene enjoyment comes uncannily close to fulfilling a moral duty. It may also come close to relief of status unease. As the excessive punishment passes into collective memory, there will be a point in time when the initially felt intense excitement has subsided. It would be a phase during which the obscene enjoyment of the inglorious secrets would change and turn into a recognition of being a worthy member of the community. What had happened would not change, or be forgotten; nor would the need to anxiously guard the secret change. But participation in the practices of disavowal would involve satisfaction of desire in the realm of ordinary status, decency and social conventions, as opposed to the obscene excitement at the time of the transgression and in the immediate aftermath. The obscene would transform into the ordinary, and the nature of satisfaction would change accordingly, into Platonic pleasure.

Žižek's discussion of the nightly law and 'solidarity-in-guilt' rested on the idea that certain things – the transgressive punishment, the accompanying enjoyment and the nightly law itself – were necessarily unacknowledged. They could not be openly admitted or explicitly justified, as the ending of *A Few Good Men* demonstrated. When the nightly law was spelled out, the regular law prevailed. Yet a different ending is by no means inconceivable, an ending in which the base commander walked away from the court without being arrested, despite confessing to the murder. Transgressions are necessarily unacknowledged only in relation to a specific time and place. Genocide, torture and extra-judicial killings are disavowed, and turn into solidarity-in-guilt, under certain conditions, depending on the prevailing relationships of power and on the strength of social conventions. In other times, the excitement will be openly acknowledged, shared with others in the group, and even celebrated as a sign of status. To understand the openly acknowledged yet still obscene enjoyment of the audience, we must supplement psychoanalysis and return to Nietzsche.

The forward thrust of unrestrained assertion

To some extent, all punishment contains an element of collective assertion of status. Besides the defensive move, in defending one's way of life, visible in the Code Red murder of Santiago, or in the *ressentiment*-driven support for capital punishment, there is, in addition, the forward thrust: the unrepentant assertion of social status, in relation to other groups. Under certain conditions, there are no second thoughts within the audience, no need for cover-up. Besides the awareness of the prohibition, there is just the excitement of pulling it through. This is another aspect of the modern experience. The enjoyment of unrestrained self-assertion and the accompanying sense of invincibility were elaborated by Friedrich Nietzsche. In the *Will to Power*, he criticized the Platonic notion of pleasure as satisfaction of lack and argued for a conception of pleasure that corresponded to the Aristotelian paradigm of unimpeded activity.

> The desire for more is of the essence of pleasure: it is the experience of power increasing, of the difference in power entering consciousness.
> (Nietzsche 2017: 695)

This can be seen as a re-statement of the Lacanian dynamics of desire. The Nietzschean will is inherently transgressive and entails a similar kind of excitement as *jouissance*, an intense absorption in activity, which is oblivious to other concerns, including potential pain (Moyaert 2010; Reginster 2006). In the context of transgressive punishment, the enjoyment was obscene, as it was inevitably shaped by the awareness that basic legal conventions and the integrity of the other were violated. But as opposed to Lacanian approaches, prohibition was secondary for the generation of enjoyment. Instead, pleasure was explicated by reference to the experience of power. Although power and prohibition operated in conjunction, the main aspect to Nietzsche was the consciously experienced excitement of prevailing against resistances and hardship, in a social context marked by competition and inequality: 'the difference in power entering consciousness'.

During a rally at the Indiana State Fairgrounds in Indianapolis on the evening of 20 April 2016, the topic of waterboarding was brought up by Donald Trump. He was at the time campaigning to become the Republican party's presidential candidate. Before a congregated audience of 4,000 people, Trump commented on an earlier debate with competitors for the nomination.

> It was a question, 'what do you think about waterboarding?' ... and he [Ted Cruz] gave a nothing answer; a weak, pathetic answer. Like we always give. They asked me: 'What do you think about waterboarding, Mr Trump?' I said, I love it. [loud cheers from the audience: 'Yeah!'] I love it – I think it's great. And I said, 'the only thing is, we should make it much tougher than waterboarding'. And if you don't think it works folks, you're wrong. [audible sounds of approval from the audience]
> www.youtube.com/watch?v=Yx1DQY5a8So (transcribed from a video-recording made by MSNBC, originally uploaded 21 April 2016, retrieved 21 October 2019)

The short video-clip from the event, which was made public by the news channel MSNBC, captured the speaker and did not show the audience in view. Yet judging from the simultaneously recorded sound, parts of the audience appear to enthusiastically embrace the prospect of excessive cruelty. At the decisive moment, one can only hear sounds of approval. As Trump exclaimed 'I love it!', the response from the Republican crowd was immediate. People cheered and yelled in return. So, he went on to promise aggravated techniques of interrogation; 'we should make it much tougher than waterboarding'. Simply waterboarding was not fully satisfactory, and more was required.

To publicly confess one's love of torture may seem perverse. But in context, the remarks were not perverse. The issue – why not torture? – had been raised anew as part of the War on Terror. Waterboarding meant that a captive was restrained on a board, lying on his back and leaning slightly backwards, with a cloth covering the mouth and the nose. Water was then poured over the cloth to produce an immediate sensation of drowning. It was one of the techniques that had been most discussed by US advocates of torture (Luban 2014). Hence, the presidential candidate did not express a love of torture for its own sake, or for his own personal pleasure. Instead, torture signalled his determination to stand up for the group. The excessive punishment defended the way of life of the audience against external threats. It was presented as a response to the violations of political Islamists in the Middle East. As many times as Trump repeated that he loved waterboarding in the recorded video-clip, he interposed statements about another terror, emanating from a group of people who were callously beheading Westerners, or drowning people in cages.

> They can chop off heads, they can drown people in steel cages, right, they can put people in steel cages, by 25 and 50 people, and drop 'em in the water, and pull 'em up an hour later. And we can't waterboard... How stupid are we?
>
> www.youtube.com/watch?v=Yx1DQY5a8So (transcribed from a video-recording made by MSNBC, originally uploaded 21 April 2016, retrieved 21 October 2019)

The question 'how stupid are we?' was posed rhetorically. Torture was seen to be necessary in the face of an external enemy who was unsurpassed in ruthlessness and not restrained by legal conventions. But judging from the enthusiastic embrace of the need, torture was not anything that regrettably had to be done. It was a necessity happily endorsed. Clearly, it was a matter of the '*jouissance* of transgression'; the sudden outburst of excitement is inexplicable without reference to prohibition. To publicly display enthusiasm at the prospect of torture was a breach of convention. Shouting 'yeahhh!' was triggered by the transgression inherent in 'I love waterboarding'. The spectators knew that torture was wrong – prohibited by laws, by internal regulations, and human rights conventions. They moreover knew that it was highly inappropriate to say that one loves torture with the TV cameras on, as opposed to admitting it amongst a close circle of friends. Hence, if the largely Republican audience enjoyed the utterances by the presidential candidate, prohibition was one important source of the enjoyment. But the enjoyment was not necessarily unacknow-ledged, and nor was the proposed waterboarding. It was all affirmed, on stage and in the arena. The enjoyment was no longer obscene in the original Greek sense of being off-stage. Instead of being publicly disavowed – 'nothing happened!' – torture was publicly embraced, in the full knowledge that it was forbidden. The enjoyment was obscene only thanks to the continued strength of the taboo. Immediately following the declaration of love of waterboarding, captured in the video-recording, came a stated awareness of the prohibition. 'But you know', Trump reminded them, 'there are laws, we have laws that we have to abide by'. Prohibition did not, however, operate to support a defen-sive solidarity-in-guilt. Instead, the audience felt empowered, on the offensive, and could close ranks with their leader *in spe*, who had proven himself as a leader by saying what was generally considered unutterable. The audience, for a long time better acquainted with the principles of the nightly law that could not stand public disclosure, no longer had to deny what was already being done in their name.

The self-conscious breach of taboo was thus one source of enjoyment. The political context suggested that power could be an additional source of enjoy-ment. The presidential candidate promised to make the nation 'great again', in this way, by asserting the spectators' social worth through punishment. This was the additional source of enjoyment: the assertion of status over against others. The spectators' enjoyment also came from the unrestrained assertion of relationships of power contained in the defiant 'I love it' and in the subtext of 'we have laws that we have to abide by', namely: we'll do it anyway. On a Nietzschean reading, the enthusiasm of the Trump audience was not due to relief of distress, or the prospect of an imagined revenge, associated with *ressentiment*, nor was it the kick of doing the forbidden, associated with the '*jouissance* of transgression'. Rather, it was the basic sense of power, associated with the assertion of status, there and then, in the arena, together with every-body else. The sudden outburst – triggered by 'I love it!' and 'it works folks' – represented the basic thrust forward, to be part of a collective which asserted its status, proving itself over against other social forces, and transgressing all kinds of boundaries, including legal constraints and moral conventions. The sense of power corresponded to an Aristotelian understanding of pleasure as the additional element of activity. It was the excitement of overcoming resist-ance. Pleasure stemmed from being able to act and prevail despite restraints – literally all kinds of restraints – and continue the activity without having to adjust. Whatever was in the way of the constant desire to assert oneself, as argued by Bernard Reginster (2006; 2018), was overcome, and that in itself generated pleasure. On this reading, it was the self-assertion over against others, rather than the interplay between the regular and the nightly law, that accounted for the enjoyment. The law constituted one kind of resistance, yet there was nothing special about it. To overcome normative considerations, or fear of future sanctions, might generate intense excitement, but so could many other things, including toppling tyrants, or beating fascists. Resistance was a wider concept, covering all potential hurdles which had to be overcome, including conscious opposition, everyday inequality, or lack or resources, to generate pleasure as a conscious experience of power.

Nietzsche's view on pleasure was a corollary of his notion of the will. Commenting on the apparent simplicity of Schopenhauer's notion on what prompts people to act, Nietzsche argued that willing was 'above all something *complicated*' (Nietzsche 1990: §19, emphasis in original; see also Leiter 2009; Clark and Dudrick 2009). Rather than being a faculty of human consciousness, or a single drive, the will was made up of a multitude of emotional responses, expectations and concerns, accompanied by sensations of success or failure. The expectations and the concerns were jeopardized in the encounter with the lived inequality and the everyday workings of power. People were not always able to attain, what they expected for themselves and cared about, because of the distribution of resources or because of interventions to maintain or challenge privilege. So, they had to do something to satisfy desire. The all-pervasive friction between self-assertion and limited options was action-prompting, and propelled people to act, again and again, to overcome obstacles placed in their way by circumstances. Pleasure was thus dependent on successful management of resistance, and inextricably tied to the social context. The achievement of conventional goals which conferred social esteem no doubt generated pleasure. But pleasure was experienced most intensely when the assertion of status was unimpeded, and went beyond imposed limitations. Consequently, when the audience was mobilized around a violence that transgressed legal safeguards, the sense of power was unsurpassed; 'to practise cruelty is to enjoy the highest gratification of the feeling of power' (Nietzsche 1997: §18). By practising or being witness to cruelty, people will experience intense excitement and a heightened sense of power, or even a brief moment of omnipotence.

As observed by the early-modern theorists of the sublime, the experience of terror from a safe position can produce the most intense sensations of awe and excitement. In their case, it was an impersonal terror, which was capable of causing significant pain and destruction, exemplified by volcanos, monsters, or famine (Dennis 1996): eruptions of violence which may be experienced by the spectators as stunning and powerful, but not as expressions of their own power. The modern experience of obscene enjoyment, on the other hand, assumes that the terror being consumed is one's own terror, as opposed to being a force of nature. The terror experienced from the safe position of the spectator's seat is felt to be consciously exerted by the group to which one belongs. This generates obscene enjoyment partly because terror is by definition prohibited, and partly because of the accompanying sense of power. The latter aspect, the experienced boost of power, can be interpreted in terms of identification with the aggressor, or, alternatively, as collective assertion over against the other. Along one line of interpretation, excessive cruelty can dissolve the boundaries between those who exact and those who witness the punishment. The experience of our own terror 'allows us to blend a joy in our own cartoon-like unkillability with the contrary pleasures of being decentred and dissolved' (Eagleton 2005: 44f). In that moment, the audience will identify with the agents of punishment, who appear as omnipotent guardians of the moral world of the entire group. As such, the excessive acts are invitations to everyone who belongs to that world to partake not only in the defence of its order but also in the celebration of its greatness – and the accompanying feeling of invincibility. A slightly different reading, acknowledging the role of resistance in the Nietzschean conception of pleasure (Reginster 2006; 2018), stresses that the terror of the other is crucial for the enjoyment of one's own terror. The audience at the Indianapolis rally were presented with the threat of an external enemy who was 'chopping off heads' and beyond that could subvert their own way of life, assisted by the naivety of influential groups who believed in the rule of law. The challenge to their rightful place in the world was powerful, dangerous and treacherous, all of which were features that meant that the overcoming of the challenge, through waterboarding and other demonstrations of one's own terror, promised an all the greater sensation of pleasure, since, on Nietzsche's analysis, pleasure was proportional to the resistance put up by the other. Hence, without necessarily experiencing any unmediated identity with the aggressor, the audience would reap the enjoyment of collectively asserting their status over against others.

Obscene enjoyment and *ressentiment* were rooted in the same desire. Yet the two modern pleasures of punishment were different from one another. Like the previous forms of Platonic pleasure, *ressentiment* offered temporary relief of distress of status concerns. At the same time, *ressentiment* raised the stakes and involved the restoration of both moral order and social esteem. Driven by the acute sense of impotence and injustice, angry spectators saw in the newly established system of criminal justice a powerful vehicle for 'the thunderstorms of our revenge' (Nietzsche 2006: 2.8), which could produce the experience of being rectified and acknowledge them as the backbone of society, in the key dimensions of order and morality. The state-administered punishment could be conceived as wholesale vengeance yet remained circumscribed in certain respects. It was essentially legitimate, and tied to existing legal bodies. In all these respects, the pleasure provided by excessive forms of punishment was the very opposite. Obscene enjoyment presupposed a position of strength rather than impotence, the illegitimacy of the entire undertaking, the illicit character of pleasure and the transgressive nature of punishment. The seemingly unrestrained assertion actualized the attainment of full satisfaction and transcendence, as opposed to the release of a tension accumulated by the basic squeeze between options and expectations. Sometimes, however, there was a fine line. The temporary relief of distress concerning one's basic social worth, which the imagined revenge could offer an anxious and angry audience, may turn into the affirmation of themselves as cornerstones in a social order where they reign supreme: a moral universe where they join forces with the state to put things right again, by means of the violence it takes to do so. In the transition, feelings of impotence may pass into a sense of omnipotence, and relief of status concerns may pass into the obscene excitement of transgression. Further down the road a transition can take place in the other direction, from intense excitation in the immediate aftermath of the exacted punishment to mundane relief of distress: the recognition of being a worthy member of the community, as participation in the processes of disavowal becomes routine. From being triumphant, punishment transforms into a requirement for decency and acceptance as fully a part of the group. Žižek's (1994) notion of solidarity-in-guilt comes uncannily close to the relief produced by the fulfilment of moral duty.

Obscene enjoyment and *ressentiment* were part of a larger story, encapsulated in the Hegelian master-and-slave dialectic. A kernel of recognition was central to both kinds of pleasure. In the context of *ressentiment*, it was all about regaining recognition, through legitimate punishment. Yet there was an element of recognition also in the consumption of one's own terror. Witnessing punishment being exacted in spite of legal safeguards, or in disregard of the excessive pain imposed, can offer instant recognition, which unites the two sides of *thumos*: being accepted as part of the group and asserting oneself over against others. Social morality and existing relationships of power supplied the basic coordinates in both cases. What came across as one-sided assertion, omnipotence and insularity may turn out to be heavily dependent on the other – in the shape of the big Other, or in the fine-tuned sensitivity of what presented social esteem in the eyes of others. Punishment operated in the middle of this dynamic with the capacity to provide recognition. Inserted in between desire and enjoyment, punishment could offer relief of the spectators' status concerns, or, alternatively, it could produce obscene enjoyment of taking part in collective self-assertion. Yet as discussed throughout the book, desire is deeply ambiguous. The desire to be fully included or to distinguish oneself over against others does not necessarily translate into a yearning for punishment, but can just as well turn into the achievement of conventional goals, or whatever happened to confer social esteem on an individual, as well as the collective endeavour of social justice, likewise driven by notions of morality and justice, albeit in a very different direction: toward extended rights, new standards of respect, and levelling of power asymmetries. The dynamic is inherently transgressive, pushing beyond existing conditions. But the direction of transcendence, whether the desire will develop into punitivity, into individual achievement, or into social justice, is not inherent in the dynamics of desire. The basic ambiguity of the desire for social esteem is at the same time a space for indeterminacy. Whether the progressive side or the regressive side of recognition takes precedence will be determined by external conditions, conscious actions and interventions. The direction of desire is ultimately a political question.

References

Adler, Amy (2015) The pleasures of punishment: complicity, spectatorship, and Abu Ghraib. In A. Sarat and C. Ogletree (eds.), *Punishment in popular culture*. New York: New York University Press. pp 236–256.

Aristodemou, Maria (2014) *Law, psychoanalysis, society: taking the unconscious seriously*. Abingdon: Routledge.

Braunstein, Nèstor (2003) Desire and jouissance in the teachings of Lacan. In J.-M. Rabaté (ed.), *The Cambridge companion to Lacan*. Cambridge: Cambridge University Press. pp 102–115.

Burke, Edmund (1997) *The writings and speeches of Edmund Burke. Vol. I. The early writings*. Oxford: Clarendon.

Burke, Peter (2009) *Popular culture in early modern Europe*. Farnham: Ashgate.

Clark, Maudemarie, and Dudrick, David (2009) Nietzsche on the will: an analysis of BGE 19. In K. Gemes and S. May (eds.), *Nietzsche on freedom and autonomy*. Oxford: Oxford University Press. pp 246–268.

Connolly, William (1995) *The ethos of pluralization*. Minneapolis: University of Minnesota Press.

Copjec, Joan (1994) *Read my desire: Lacan against the historicists*. Cambridge, MA: MIT Press.

Dean, Jodi (2006) *Žižek's politics*. New York: Routledge.

Debrix, François (2006) The sublime spectatorship of war: the erasure of the event in America's politics of terror and aesthetics of violence. *Millennium* 34(3): 767–791.

de Kesel, Marc (2009) *Eros and ethics. Reading Jacques Lacan's seminar vii*. New York: State University of New York Press.

Dennis, John (1996) The grounds of criticism in poetry. In A. Ashfield and P. de Bolla (eds.), *The sublime: a reader in British eighteenth-century aesthetic theory*. Cambridge: Cambridge University Press. pp 35–39.

de Sutter, Laurent (ed.) (2015) *Žižek and law*. Abingdon: Routledge.

Eagleton, Terry (2005) *Holy terror*. Oxford: Oxford University Press.

Eisenman, Stephen (2007) *The Abu Ghraib effect*. London: Reaktion.

Evans, Dylan (1998) From Kantian ethics to mystical experience: an exploration of jouissance. In D. Nobus (ed.), *Key concepts of Lacanian psychoanalysis*. London: Rebus Press. pp 1–28.

Fink, Bruce (1995) *The Lacanian subject: between language and jouissance*. Princeton: Princeton University Press.

Finkelde, Dominik (2018) The 'secret code' of honour – on political enjoyment and the excrescence of fantasy. *Culture, Theory and Critique* 59(3): 232–261.

Freud, Sigmund (1955) *Totem and taboo and other works. The standard edition of the complete psychological works of Sigmund Freud. Vol. 13 (1913–1914)*. London: Hogarth.

Glynos, Jason (2001) The grip of ideology: a Lacanian approach to the theory of ideology. *Journal of Political Ideologies* 6(2): 191–214.

Hart, H. L. A. (1959) Prolegomenon to the Principles of Punishment. *Proceedings of the Aristotelian Society* 60: 1–26.

Hill, Christopher (1972) *The world turned upside down: radical ideas during the English revolution*. London: Maurice Temple Smith.

Hegel, Georg Wilhelm Friedrich (1952) *The philosophy of right*. Oxford: Oxford University Press.

Homer, Sean (2004) *Jacques Lacan*. London: Routledge.

Hook, Derek (2017) What is "enjoyment as a political factor"? *Political Psychology* 38(4): 605–620.

Kant, Immanuel (1914) *Kritik der praktischen Vernunft. Immanuel Kants Werke. Band V*. Berlin: Cassirer.

Lacan, Jacques (1992) *The seminar of Jacques Lacan. Book VII. The ethics of psychoanalysis: 1959–1960*. New York: W. W. Norton.

Lacan, Jacques (1999) *The seminar of Jacques Lacan. Book XX. On feminine sexuality, the limits of love and knowledge: encore 1972–1973*. New York: W. W. Norton.

Lacan, Jacques (2006) *Ecrits: The first complete edition in English*. New York: W. W. Norton.

Leiter, Brian (2009) Nietzsche's theory of the will. In K. Gemes and S. May (eds.), *Nietzsche on freedom and autonomy*. Oxford: Oxford University Press. pp 107–126.

Luban, David (2014) *Torture, power, and law*. Cambridge: Cambridge University Press.

McKay, Carolyn (2010) Murder ob/scene: the seen, unseen and ob/scene in murder trials. *Law Text Culture* 14(1): 79–93.

Miller, Jacques-Alain (2000) Paradigms of jouissance. *Lacanian Ink* 17: 8–47.

Moyaert, Paul (2010) What is frightening about sexual pleasure? Introducing Lacan's jouissance into Freudian psychoanalysis via Plato and Aristotle. In E. Dorfman and J. de Vleminck (eds.), *Sexuality and psychoanalysis: philosophical criticisms*. Leuven: Leuven University Press. pp 21–33.

Nietzsche, Friedrich (1989) *On the genealogy of morals*. New York: Vintage Books.

Nietzsche, Friedrich (1990) *Beyond good and evil: prelude to a philosophy of the future*. Harmondsworth: Penguin Books.

Nietzsche, Friedrich (1997) *Daybreak. Thoughts on the prejudices of morality*. Cambridge: Cambridge University Press.

Nietzsche, Friedrich (2006) *Thus spoke Zarathustra: a book for all and none*. Cambridge: Cambridge University Press.

Nietzsche, Friedrich (2017) *The will to power*. London: Penguin Books.

Nozick, Robert (1981) *Philosophical explanations*. Cambridge, MA: Harvard University Press.

Plato (2005) *Phaedrus*. Trans. by C. Rowe. Harmondsworth: Penguin.

Reginster, Bernard (2006) *The affirmation of life*. Cambridge, MA: Harvard University Press.

Reginster, Bernard (2018) The will to power. In P. Katsafanas (ed.), *The Nietzschean mind*. Adingdon: Routledge. pp 105–120.

Schuster, Aaron (2019) Beyond satire. The political comedy of the present and the paradoxes of authority. In W, Mazzarella et al. *Sovereignty, Inc.: three inquiries in politics and enjoyment*. Chicago: University of Chicago Press. pp 161–250.

Seneca (2016) *Seneca's letters from a Stoic*. New York: Dover Publications.

Sontag, Susan (2003) *Regarding the pain of others*. New York: Farrar, Straus and Giroux.

Sorkin, Aaron (1991) *A Few Good Men*, revised third draft. www.imsdb.com/scripts/A-Few-Good-Men.html, accessed 4 October 2019.

Taylor, C. C. W. (2008) Pleasure: Aristotle's response to Plato. In *Pleasure, mind, and soul: selected papers in ancient philosophy*. Oxford: Oxford University Press. pp 240–264.

Žižek, Slavoj (1991) *For they know not what they do: enjoyment as a political factor*. London: Verso.

Žižek, Slavoj (1994) *The metastases of enjoyment.* London: Verso.
Žižek, Slavoj (1997) *The plague of fantasies.* London: Verso.
Žižek, Slavoj (2006a) *How to read Lacan.* London: Granta.
Žižek, Slavoj (2006b) *The parallax view.* Cambridge, MA: MIT Press.
Žižek, Slavoj (2015) Postscript: the rule of law between obscenity and the right to distress. In L. de Sutter (ed.), *Žižek and law.* Abingdon: Routledge. pp 220–247.

Index

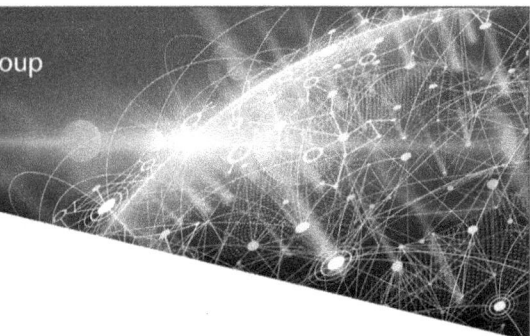

For Product Safety Concerns and Information please contact our EU
representative GPSR@taylorandfrancis.com
Taylor & Francis Verlag GmbH, Kaufingerstraße 24, 80331 München, Germany